Looking at the Landscape

*Other Chester Society for Landscape History
titles from the same publisher*

Sharon M. Varey and Graeme J. White (Editors)
***Landscape History Discoveries
in the North West*** (2012)

Sharon M. Varey and Graeme J. White (Editors)
***Landscapes Past and Present:
Cheshire and Beyond*** (2016)

Looking at the Landscape: Glimpses into the History of Cheshire and Beyond

Papers researched and written by members of
Chester Society for Landscape History
to celebrate the 35th anniversary
of the Society in 2021

Edited by
Sharon M. Varey
and **Graeme J. White**

University of Chester Press

First published 2022
by University of Chester Press
Parkgate Road
Chester CH1 4BJ

Printed and bound in the UK by the
LIS Print Unit
University of Chester
Cover designed by the LIS Graphics Team
University of Chester

Editorial Material
© University of Chester, 2022
Images
© the respective photographers/
copyright holders, 2022

All Rights Reserved
No part of this publication may be reproduced, stored in a retrieval system or transmitted in any form or by any means without the prior permission of the copyright owner, other than as permitted by UK copyright legislation or under the terms and conditions of a recognised copyright licensing scheme

A catalogue record of this book is available
from the British Library

ISBN 978-1-910481-11-0

CONTENTS

List of Colour Plates — vii

Abbreviations — ix

Notes on Contributors — xi

Preface — xiii

Looking at the Landscape: An Introduction: — 1
Sharon M. Varey and Graeme J. White

1. The Christian Landscape of Early Medieval Chester and Wirral: — 9
   Thomas Pickles

2. Contrasting Settlements Along the Dee Valley Frontier: Defence, Crossing, Refuge: — 31
   Graeme J. White

3. Cringlemire – Taming a Lakeland Landscape: — 63
   Maggie Taylor

4. Early Nineteenth-Century Growth in Three North Shropshire Market Towns and the Influence of the Ellesmere Canal: — 84
   Robert Ginder

5. 'Estimating the Effects of the Railway on Chester is not Easy': — 116
   Chris Pilsbury

6.	Carnegie Libraries in Cheshire: **Vanessa Greatorex**	137
7.	The Effect of Planning Laws on Settlement Development in Twentieth and Early Twenty-First Century South-West Cheshire: **Polly Bird**	165

Index of Places	201
Index of Subjects	207

LIST OF COLOUR PLATES

Plate 1: St John's church, Threapwood, an early nineteenth-century 'civilising' addition to the dispersed settlement (2022).
Photograph: Graeme White. — 55

Plate 2: Cringlemire (2018).
Photograph: Mike Taylor. — 56

Plate 3: Early nineteenth-century listed buildings in Whitchurch and Ellesmere (2022).
Photographs: Robert Ginder. — 57

Plate 4: An early illustration of Chester Station from *Bradshaw's Guide*
(Creative Commons ref. CC BY-SA 4.0). — 58

Plate 5: The Queen Hotel – a fine example of a railway hotel (2022).
Photograph: Chris Pilsbury. — 59

Plate 6: Neston Carnegie Library in 2014. The oval window in the gable is now largely obscured by trees.
Photograph: Vanessa Greatorex. — 60

Plate 7: A 1909 perspective drawing of Stockport Central Carnegie Library by Roger Oldham of Bradshaw Gass & Hope. Hope Archives, scanned by Lingard, Public Domain. — 61

Plate 8: Malpas town centre (2022) showing how the clustering of older buildings in the centre of the town distracts from the presence of modern buildings hidden from view downhill.
Photograph: Graeme White.   62

ABBREVIATIONS

B&CR: Birkenhead and Chester Railway
CALS: Cheshire Archives and Local Studies
CCC: Chester City Council
Ches. Hist.: *Cheshire History*, followed by volume number and date
CWaC: Cheshire West and Chester Council
CWCLP: Cheshire West and Chester Local Plan
C&HR: Chester and Holyhead Railway
CRADP: Chester Rural Area District Plan
CRSJC: Chester Railway Station Joint Committee
CSLH: Chester Society for Landscape History
DB: Domesday Book
edn: edition
fo(s): folio(s)
GWR: Great Western Railway
JCAS: *Journal of the Chester Archaeological Society*
L&NWR: London and North Western Railway
NGR: National Grid Reference
NWMR: North Wales Mineral Railway
n./ns: note(s)
OE: Old English
ON: Old Norse
OS: Ordnance Survey
rev.: revised
RDC: Rural District Council
RDP: Rural District Plan
RSLC: Record Society of Lancashire and Cheshire
s.a.: (Latin: *sub anno*) under the year
Ser.: Series
[*sic*]: (Latin: thus) indicates that an unexpected word or spelling appears as in the original and is not a mistake
SO&CJR: Shrewsbury, Oswestry & Chester Junction Railway
Soc.: Society

TDHS: Transactions of the Denbighshire Historical Society
THSLC: Transactions of the Historic Society of Lancashire and Cheshire
TNA: The National Archives UK
VCH: Victoria County History, followed by county (abbreviated) and volume number, e.g. *VCH Ches.*, V i, *VCH Shrops.*, IV

NOTES ON CONTRIBUTORS

Polly Bird is a retired author and bookbinder. She has an MA in Landscape, Heritage and Society and her PhD examined land-ownership and settlement change in south-west Cheshire from 1750 to 2000. She has had 18 non-fiction books published and also contributed articles to local history journals.

Robert Ginder is a retired aeronautical engineer and a former Fellow of the Institution of Mechanical Engineers. He conducted government-funded research on the design of gas turbine compressors, authoring many technical reports and publications. He has contributed to several local history projects based in Cheshire, Shropshire and Staffordshire, and has a particular interest in towns, trade and transport during the period of the Industrial Revolution.

Vanessa Greatorex is a medievalist, landscape historian and conservation volunteer who is addicted to reading, hence her interest in libraries. Her four degrees include the MA in Landscape, Heritage and Society and a PhD focusing on medieval Chester. Her editorial clientele spans six continents and her publications include local history books, historical fiction and well over 100 articles, mostly on history-related topics.

Thomas Pickles is Senior Lecturer in Medieval History at the University of Chester, current Chair of the Chester Archaeological Society, and General Editor for the Brepols book series *Studies in the Early Middle Ages*. He has published widely on the early medieval Church in Britain, including most recently *Kingship, Society, and the Church in Anglo-Saxon Yorkshire* (2018).

Looking at the Landscape

Chris Pilsbury is a retired teacher and a graduate of the MA in Landscape, Heritage and Society. He is particularly fascinated by the history of railways, their impact on society in general, and the development of the urban landscape in particular. He was a founder member of the Flint and Deeside Railway Preservation Society, subsequently the Llangollen Railway Society.

Maggie Taylor has worked in industry and higher education. Since 2018, she has been a Heritage Adviser to Thelwall's Conservation and Community Heritage Project working with volunteers, schools and community groups to capture and share the township's history.

Sharon Varey is Associate Editor of the county history journal, *Cheshire History*. A former graduate of the MA in Landscape, Heritage and Society, her PhD focused upon landscape change in north Shropshire. As well as co-editing the other two CSLH volumes with Graeme White, she has written landscape history articles relating to Cheshire and north Shropshire, along with a short series of landscape inspired booklets.

Graeme White is Emeritus Professor of Local History at the University of Chester and has been President of CSLH since its foundation in 1986. Among his recent books are *The Medieval English Landscape* (2012), *The Magna Carta of Cheshire* (2015) and *On Chester On: A History of Chester College and the University of Chester* (2014, 2021). He is also Editor of *Cheshire History*.

PREFACE

This book is the outcome of a Research Day held in October 2021 to celebrate the 35th anniversary of Chester Society for Landscape History (CSLH). An event held by the members, for the members, it is testimony to the Society that the talks delivered at the conference, and the papers which are presented in this volume, have all been contributed by CSLH members. Who could have imagined, back in 1986, that so many members of the Society would actively contribute to local landscape history research? As Richard Muir pointed out at the turn of the century: 'the powerhouse of landscape history lies with the unsung fieldworkers, professional and amateur, the research students and the local enthusiasts'.[1] CSLH is such a powerhouse for this is the third volume of selected papers containing members' research, published by the University of Chester.[2]

CSLH has had to say a sad farewell in recent years to a few long-standing members, some of whom were instrumental in the founding of the Society. Sadly, 2021 was no exception for it saw the passing of three such individuals: John Whittle, Mike Kennerley and Joan Bradley who all had close ties to the Society. John Whittle contributed an article on Walk Mill in Foulk Stapleford in our first volume, *Landscape History Discoveries in the North West* (2012) and edited *Waverton: A History of its People and Places* (2002). Mike Kennerley was instrumental in researching and compiling material for the Society's first booklet entitled *The Lost Gardens of Hoole* (2008). Joan Bradley, not an author but nonetheless a stalwart and knowledgeable supporter of CSLH, was particularly known for her good company on Society field trips and social occasions.

In producing a volume of this nature, the editors would like to express their thanks to a number of individuals who have helped bring this third volume to fruition: not least, Dr Sarah Griffiths, the Managing Editor of University of Chester Press, who is herself a member of CSLH. The editors would particularly like to thank her for all her advice, help and encouragement with this publication.

Looking at the Landscape

The assistance of the University Graphics Team and Print Unit has also been much appreciated. Special thanks are due to Mike Headon who, along with the editors, contributed to the organisation of the Research Day and the proposal for this volume. *Looking at the Landscape* would not have made it into print if it had not been for the research and commitment of our contributors. We would like to thank them all for putting up with our suggestions and editorial interventions. On behalf of our contributors, we would also like to extend our thanks to the many others who have helped, supported and encouraged our authors along the way. We hope you enjoy reading the results of their endeavours as much as we have.

Sharon M. Varey and Graeme J. White
May 2022

Endnotes
[1] R. Muir, *The NEW Reading the Landscape: Fieldwork in Landscape History* (Exeter, 2000), xiii.
[2] Previous volumes in the series are: S.M. Varey and G.J. White, eds, *Landscape History Discoveries in the North West* (Chester, 2012) and S.M. Varey and G.J. White, eds, *Landscapes Past and Present: Cheshire and Beyond* (Chester, 2016).

LOOKING AT THE LANDSCAPE: AN INTRODUCTION

Sharon M. Varey and Graeme J. White

Every landscape has its own unique story to tell. There may be similarities, there may be patterns, but no two agrarian, coastal, woodland, industrial or urban landscapes will develop in exactly the same way.

The study of landscape history is about making sense of the various landscapes that surround us. It embraces many disciplines including history, archaeology, botany and geology and many branches within each discipline. Within the scope of history, for example, one may draw upon the social, economic, political or cultural dimensions of the subject, informed by the written or spoken word. Similarly, within archaeology: field walking, excavation, aerial photography and remote surveying may all play a part. The overall aim is to understand how and why a particular landscape in any area looks the way it does. To do this, many factors need to be taken into account.

In order to understand a landscape, we need to ask questions about what we see – the what, how, when and why. Why does a particular feature or landscape look the way it does? What factors have affected it? When did this happen? Who was involved? As Mick Aston – a previous speaker to CSLH – pointed out, proper landscape research needs to ask questions and wherever possible answer them.[1] Sometimes the answers are relatively simple, sometimes the factors involved are complex and, all too often, answers result in further questions. And so, the 'more one delves, the more one finds there is to learn'.[2]

The title of this volume, *Looking at the Landscape*, emphasises the importance of visual skills in our assessment, training our eyes to see elements from the past and continuing to ask ourselves questions of all that we see. No less important is actually *walking* the landscape under study and carrying out fieldwork – visiting buildings, settlements, lines of communication and other features to gain first-hand knowledge of sites on the ground. In this sense, CSLH members follow the Hoskins and Aston tradition of learning and working in the field, using first-hand observation, armed with an OS map.

Key words and themes spring to mind when considering landscape evolution: *continuity, adaptation* and *change* through time. To these we should add: *intent, design, development* and *impact*. What was the intention or reason behind siting a house, railway or castle in a particular place? Who was responsible for the design or layout of a building, settlement or field system? How did it evolve? How did it develop through time? When did this happen? Why did it change and develop in the way that it did? What was its impact on the landscape? Did it influence other features, either directly or indirectly? Was this impact felt purely locally or was it part of a development regionally or even nationally? Questions abound once one starts to consider these simple words and themes. But, just as important, is our search for answers.

To a greater or lesser extent, every contributor to this book has considered these key words and themes as they have sought to explain features in our landscape and find answers to specific research questions. In a volume of this nature, one encompasses and celebrates variety. Topics range in time from landscapes of the tenth century to those of the twenty-first. Some of our contributors consider a broad sweep of terrain, others focus on specific buildings, settlements or the impact of transport systems within the landscape.

An individual building within its setting is the focus of **Maggie Taylor**'s paper on Cringlemire: a nineteenth-century house overlooking Lake Windermere in the Lake District. Intent, design and development are discussed in considerable detail: the Nicholsons' intention to buy a plot of land to build a pleasure home; the implications of the physical landscape and environment in relation to the design and the development of the project. Subtitled

An Introduction

'Taming a Lakeland Landscape', this paper reveals that this was no ordinary house-build. In the construction of Cringlemire, intent affected design and development. Adaptations and *taming* were indeed necessary to ensure the successful completion of the project.

One might question why a house in the Lake District finds its way into a publication largely centred upon Cheshire. The answer is simple. The connection is James Nicholson, a Warrington solicitor. Nicholson was the owner of Thelwall Hall near Warrington. As a Cheshire businessman, Nicholson was not alone in owning rural estates in more than one county. The nineteenth and early twentieth centuries witnessed many industrial employers buying land and estates in more tranquil rural settings. A case in point is the founder of Port Sunlight (Wirral), William Hesketh Lever, who bought a site at Rivington near Chorley (Lancashire) in 1899 and from 1906 engaged Thomas Mawson – who also worked on the grounds at Cringlemire – to lay out the terraced gardens to accompany the house he had built there.

Vanessa Greatorex similarly considers individual buildings in her study of Cheshire's Carnegie Libraries. Although nearly 400 Carnegie Libraries were built nationwide, Greatorex brings a heightened awareness of the structures that can be found on our doorstep in Cheshire: analysing location, common architectural features, initiatives and processes which have left a distinctive legacy in particular towns. Importantly, she discusses the buildings' changing function and use today. We are all aware of former mills, factories and barns that have been converted into spacious modern housing or office space. But, what does the future hold for these large early twentieth-century public buildings in our ever changing urban landscape?

Moving from a focus on individual buildings, **Graeme White** considers three contrasting settlements on the western 'frontier' of Cheshire – its border with Wales. For this paper, we are transported back in time to the medieval and early modern periods when the border with Wales was far more than a simple boundary demarcated on a map. Each settlement is different, the pattern and layout of each being influenced by the character of the border with Wales at different points in time. The settlements which come under the spotlight are Aldford, a castle-town where the emphasis was on defence; Holt, a former Roman industrial centre, where the crossing of the River Dee between England and Wales was of prime concern during the medieval period; and Threapwood, an area of disputed wasteland which became a place of refuge between two countries. This is yet another paper which reveals that intent affects design and development.

One interesting aside to White's paper is that the 'border' between England and Wales has had much greater prominence in our everyday lives recently, during the pandemic. National restrictions differed depending on whether you lived in England or in Wales. Our heightened awareness of this issue today can help us appreciate a time when the border really was set within a 'frontier zone'.

Moving forward in time, **Polly Bird** considers how planning laws have affected settlement development in south-west Cheshire. An important recurring theme in landscape history is the ownership of land and its management. The individual landowner and the pattern of landownership has been one of the most important factors in shaping our landscape. Often seen as the 'agent of change',[3] the role of the landowner was gradually replaced, to a great extent, by local and national government during the course of the twentieth century. Increasingly, since the Second World War, planning policy has affected the landscape, leading Trevor Rowley to comment that the role of local and national government is 'central' to understanding landscape development and change in the modern era.[4] In this paper, Bird shows how planning laws, whilst initiating a degree of change, have in this instance largely maintained the settlement pattern determined by the major landowners of the eighteenth century.

An Introduction

Tom Pickles similarly considers a broad sweep of terrain in his study of the early Christian landscape of Chester and the Wirral peninsula. In discussing a period with a sparse documentary archive, Pickles draws upon archaeological, textual, architectural and – notably – linguistic evidence to consider the impact of Viking activity on the English church. Having provisionally reconstructed the pre-tenth-century distribution of Christian religious communities within his chosen area, he argues persuasively that subsequent Scandinavian settlement should be seen primarily not as disruptive but as providing continuity and, indeed, enrichment to the landscape of Christian observance. Chester and Wirral became places for interaction between peoples of different tongues, including Old Norse, one consequence being the forging of Anglo-Scandinavian Christian identities which have left their mark on the area to this day. As Hoskins himself put it in an oft-quoted observation, 'Everything in the landscape is older than we think'.[5] In showing that the Scandinavian impact on the ecclesiastical landscape of the area both maintained previous patterns and helped to carry them forward to our own time, Pickles reinforces the validity of this statement.

Yet while some landscapes exhibit remarkable, perhaps surprising, continuity, transport developments in the late eighteenth and nineteenth centuries did bring about significant changes destined to have a profound impact upon the appearance of Britain. The canal network not only linked industrialising towns but was important for transporting bulk cargoes such as agricultural products across the country to help feed a growing population. Often, canal construction worked in harmony with the landscape – following the contours for example – but fantastic feats of engineering, such as the Pontcysyllte aqueduct originally built for the Ellesmere Canal, were achieved because of mankind's desire to transport goods across the country more efficiently.

Robert Ginder analyses the impact of the Ellesmere Canal upon the development of three predominantly agricultural market towns of north Shropshire. Using the information gleaned from trade directories, he shows how agricultural and retail trades blossomed in the early decades of the nineteenth century as a direct result of the construction of the canal. Its impact was such that it gave Ellesmere 'a new, modest prosperity'.[6] This was reflected in early nineteenth-century construction of town houses and civic buildings in Ellesmere, Wem and Whitchurch. In north Shropshire, the importance of the Ellesmere Canal was relatively short-lived. However, surviving traces of canal infrastructure and associated buildings still reveal its former importance to both industrial and rural areas as a means of transportation.

From an engineering point of view, the railways continued what the canals began. They manipulated the landscape on a grand scale, leaving behind ever more spectacular bridges, cuttings, viaducts and tunnels as they linked communities and regions. The railways not only made a direct physical impression on the landscape. Their greatest impact was the way they changed most people's lives and in so doing indirectly changed much of the landscape. One only has to think of the growth of the tourist resort, made possible by the arrival of the railways at many coastal destinations.

Chris Pilsbury discusses the impact of the railway on Chester. His starting point is an assertion made in the *Victoria County History* that 'estimating the effects of the railway on Chester is not easy'.[7] Pilsbury looks at the impact of the railway on the city landscape: how the railway did not damage but respected the historic city, yet the financial benefits were visible in the construction of grand hotels and public buildings. When discussing the impact of the railway on Chester, Pilsbury points out that one also has to consider the development of Chester's suburbs, industrial Saltney and residential Hoole, both situated close to, but outside, the earlier city.

A feature of all the papers in the book is their concern to place Cheshire in a wider context, in keeping with the title: 'Cheshire and Beyond'. An association between Thelwall and the Lake District has already been stressed. The two papers covering the medieval period

An Introduction

highlight relationships with Scandinavia and Wales respectively. The studies of Carnegie Libraries and of settlements in the south-west of the county set these developments against a background of nationwide initiatives and legislation. The two papers that discuss the impact of specific transportation links naturally allude to communication beyond the county boundaries: one focused on a canal which linked Cheshire with Shropshire, the other a railway network which by 1840 could bring visitors to Chester from London, Birmingham, Liverpool and Manchester. These cross-county connections remind us that Cheshire is very well placed for the study of landscape history, surrounded by markedly different landscapes to north, west, south and east.

The editors hope these papers will inspire others to explore their local landscapes, ask questions about what they see, take up the challenge to find out more and, in so doing, answer some of the many questions about the development of the British landscape. The large variety of topics covered in this volume shows the wide scope of research currently being undertaken by CSLH members. One hopes that many readers will feel inspired to visit some of the places mentioned, to see for themselves the sites that have inspired others and possibly ask their own questions when looking at the landscape.

Endnotes

[1] M. Aston, *Interpreting the Landscape: Landscape Archaeology in Local Studies* (London, 1985), 18–19.

[2] D. Hooke, *England's Landscape: The West Midlands* (London, 2006), 22.

[3] G. Astil, 'Fields', in G. Astil and A. Grant, eds, *The Countryside of Medieval England* (Oxford, 1992), 84.

[4] T. Rowley, *The English Landscape in the Twentieth Century* (London, 2006), 8.

[5] W.G. Hoskins, *The Making of the English Landscape*, rev. edn by C.C. Taylor (London, 1988), 12, with Taylor himself quoting this in his own General Introduction (8). Cf., for example, J. Wylie, *Landscape* (London, 2007), 32; J.S. Carroll, *Landscape in Children's Literature* (London, 2011), 4; and E. McEvoy, 'Gothic and the Heritage Movement in the Twentieth and Twenty-First Centuries' in C. Spooner and D. Townsend, eds, *The Cambridge History of the Gothic, III, Gothic in the Twentieth and Twenty-First Centuries* (Cambridge, 2021), 137–58, at 150.

[6] J. Newman and N. Pevsner, *The Buildings of England: Shropshire* (rev. edn, London and New Haven, 2006), 262.

[7] *VCH Ches.*, V i, 172.

1

THE CHRISTIAN LANDSCAPE OF EARLY MEDIEVAL CHESTER AND WIRRAL

Thomas Pickles

Opening his chapter on 'The Tenth-Century Reformation', Sir Frank Stenton made general remarks on the effects of Viking raiders, conquerors and settlers on the English Church. He bookended his opening paragraph with two bold statements:

> There can be no question that the Danish invasions of the ninth century shattered the organization of the English church, destroyed monastic life in eastern England, and elsewhere caused distress and anxiety which made the pursuit of learning almost impossible.

> Throughout England the Danish raids meant, if not the destruction, at least the grievous impoverishment of civilization.[1]

He subsequently observed that 'There is no evidence that the Danes who settled in England were fiercely antagonistic to Christianity', and that 'Little is known about the process by which the conversion of the Danelaw was actually brought about.'[2] He was inclined to think that 'the fact that no traditions of the work have survived suggests that it owed less to the labours of missionaries than to the example of the Christian social order of Wessex and English Mercia', and that 'It was the lack of any provision for a regular supply of clergy which most seriously imperilled Christianity in Danish England in King Alfred's time.'[3]

Since Stenton was writing, in the 1940s, a wealth of local and regional interdisciplinary studies has transformed our understanding of ecclesiastical organisation amongst the Old English-speaking peoples. Working with textual, archaeological, architectural, sculptural and onomastic evidence, scholars have identified networks of seventh-, eighth- and ninth-century religious communities which re-emerged as twelfth- and thirteenth-century mother churches; alongside these religious communities, local churches were established in greater numbers from the tenth century onwards.[4] Studies of some regions of northern and eastern England with evidence for Viking conquest and settlement have revealed structural continuity – the survival of religious communities which were also later mother churches as foci for preaching, conversion and commemoration – and a comparable level of investment in local churches.[5] This paper will add to that picture by reconstructing the early Christian landscape of Chester and Wirral and reconsidering its development in the context of Viking activity.

The surviving evidence for Chester and Wirral presents an attractive laboratory for exploring the impacts of Viking activity, and the historiographical status quo justifies the exercise. During the tenth century members of a dynasty of Viking kings, known as the descendants of Ivarr, competed to control York and Dublin, and dominate trade routes between the Irish Sea and the North Sea, including via Chester.[6] From the Roman period onwards, Chester and Wirral had connected histories – though the Dee was navigable to Chester, which was itself a significant port, Meols and Hilbre were Irish Sea transhipment points, and the Roman road running from Chester up Wirral facilitated movement overland.[7] A large army of 'Danes' from amongst the East Angles and Northumbrians temporarily occupied Chester in 893.[8] At the beginning of the tenth century, the later *Fragmentary Annals of Ireland* claim that a Norse leader, Ingimundr, sailed from Ireland to Britain, sought out Æthelflæd, lady of the Mercians, was settled on land near Chester, coveted the wealth of the city and its lands, gathered Viking allies to attack it, but was defeated.[9] Flesh is placed on these bones by material and linguistic culture. Alan Thacker and David Mason expertly assembled the strands of evidence suggesting that Viking traders operated in tenth-century Chester: the Castle Esplanade silver hoard, deriving from their mixed bullion, hack-silver and coinage economy; the Hiberno-Norse ringed pins and oval brooch; the Old Norse names amongst the moneyers; the organisation of Handbridge in Scandinavian carucates; and the dedication of churches to SS Bridget and Olaf.[10] More recently, Paul Everson and David Stocker have argued that the Hiberno-Norse crosses at St John's Church are the material reflex of a group of Viking traders associated with a strand on the River Dee below the church.[11] Even clearer evidence survives from tenth-century Wirral. Thanks to David Griffiths we recognise the key contribution of Viking traders around the Irish Sea zone to the beach site at Meols.[12] Particularly because of the efforts of Stephen Harding we accept that the corpus of Old Norse place-names and field-names represents a concentrated settlement of Old Norse speakers in northern Wirral.[13] Putting all this together, David Griffiths set out a model for the organisation of a number of Irish Sea communities, including Wirral, based on Norwegian courtyard sites comprising buildings in sub-circular formation at meeting places designated as 'things', accompanied by nausts (boathouses) and large mound burials.[14]

Considered in this context, the development of the Christian landscape in Chester and Wirral deserves further attention (Figure 1, overleaf). Within Chester, Alan Thacker constructed persuasive arguments for two early religious communities, an intramural community on the site of St Werburgh's (now the Cathedral), and an extramural community on the site of St John's.[15] Beyond Chester, Nick Higham reconstructed the landscape of early religious communities and mother churches across Cheshire, including Wirral.[16] Their arguments provide a starting point for thinking again about ecclesiastical development in Chester and Wirral. First, they were produced prior to Richard Bailey's volume of the *Corpus of Anglo-Saxon Stone Sculpture* for Cheshire, which brought to light new evidence that needs to be incorporated. Second, subsequent studies of our surviving Old English and Old Norse ecclesiastical place-names permit reinterpretation of some evidence.

Looking at the Landscape

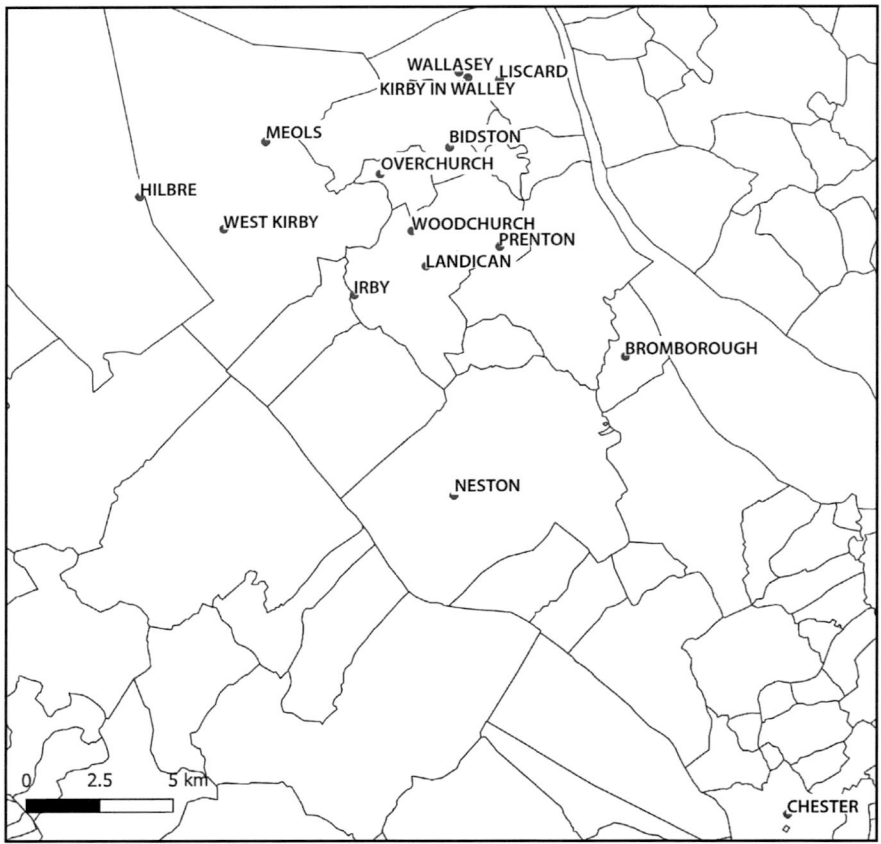

Figure 1: Map of Chester and Wirral – Principal Sites Referred to in the Text. Contains OS Data Crown Copyright and Database Right 2021. An Ordnance Survey/EDINA Supplied Service.

The Christian Landscape Before Viking Activity

The Christian landscape of Chester and Wirral before the tenth century is not well served by evidence, but Old Norse-speaking settlers probably encountered some established religious communities and cult centres.

The Christian Landscape of Early Medieval Chester and Wirral

There were two religious communities in Chester, on the sites of the Cathedral and St John's church, perhaps from as early as the seventh century, probably in the tenth century, and certainly in the eleventh century.[17] The Cathedral is located within the north-eastern quarter of the former Roman fortress. The monks of St Werburgh's, who occupied the site, believed that the Community was originally dedicated to St Peter.[18] The foundation of religious communities in Roman ruins, dedicated to St Peter, was a regular phenomenon in the later seventh and early eighth centuries, arising from the connection between the Roman mission of Pope Gregory the Great and the conversion of the Anglo-Saxons to Christianity. The restoration of Chester in the time of Æthelflæd, ruler of the Mercians, was probably the moment when it acquired an association with the Mercian princess, St Werburgh.[19] Two fragments of stone sculpture may be connected with this moment. One is a fragment from the corner of a recumbent slab (Figure 2). The other is an incomplete grave-marker (Figure 3, overleaf). The broader context of stone slabs and markers, along with the high quality of the carving, suggests commemoration of Christian elites, and the decoration connects them to Christian manuscripts, ivories, metalwork, and stone monuments from regions under West Saxon and Mercian control.[20] St John's is located outside the walls of the former Roman fortress, adjacent to

Figure 2: Chester (Unknown Provenance) 1A. Copyright *Corpus of Anglo-Saxon Stone Sculpture*. Photograph: K.P. Jukes and D.J. Craig.

Figure 3: Chester (Unknown Provenance) 2A. Copyright *Corpus of Anglo-Saxon Stone Sculpture*. Photograph: K.P. Jukes and D.J. Craig.

Figure 4: Chester (St John) 2a-bA. Copyright *Corpus of Anglo-Saxon Stone Sculpture*. Photograph: K.P. Jukes and D.J. Craig.

the amphitheatre. The clergy of St John's believed that Æthelred, king of the Mercians, had founded it in the later seventh century.[21] Excavations have shown that the amphitheatre *vomitoria* (entrance and exit passages) were blocked, perhaps in the post-Roman period, possibly to create a fortification, and have uncovered a multi-phase sequence including mid-Saxon occupation.[22] The corpus of tenth-century Hiberno-Norse crosses from the site of St John's and from nearby locations suggests an important tenth-century church (Figure 4).[23] Edgar, king of the English, following his coronation at Bath, visited Chester in 973 to receive the submission of neighbouring kings; a twelfth-century tradition suggests that he was rowed up the Dee to the monastery of St John's.[24] When the Domesday inquest was completed, 1086 x 1088, there were two flourishing religious communities, St Werburgh's and St John's.[25] Between them they shared priority over the burial rights in Chester, suggesting ancient origins. So this makes it possible that we have intramural and extramural communities founded as early as the seventh century, and very likely that these communities existed when Vikings were active in Chester and Wirral.

At the northern end of Wirral it seems probable that there were religious communities at Woodchurch and Overchurch, and a religious community or hermitage and cult site on Hilbre Island (Figure 1). At the tip of Wirral the onomastic evidence suggests a British or Irish enclave. Wallasey derives from the Old English genitive plural *wala* + *ēg*, meaning something like 'island of the foreigners or Britons'.[26] Liscard seems to derive from Brittonic or Old Irish, meaning 'hall at the rock'.[27] Landican perhaps derives from Brittonic *Lann* + personal name *Tecan*, a form which was sometimes elsewhere employed for a religious community, referencing an early saint and his or her enclosure.[28] Landican became known to Old English speakers as Woodchurch, *wudu* + *cirice*, which changed under the influence of Old Norse speakers to *wudu-kirkja*.[29] Within Woodchurch parish is Prenton, recorded in early forms as Old English *prēosta-tūn*, 'estate of the priests'.[30] An analysis of the whole corpus of *prēosta-tūnas* has argued that they were formed when the lands of early religious communities were expropriated in the eighth, ninth or tenth centuries, leaving only a small endowment for clergy.[31] Together this suggests the possibility of a British religious community, whose church was recognised by Old English and Old Norse speakers, and whose lands were expropriated in the eighth, ninth or tenth century, to leave clergy with a small endowment.

Overchurch is central to the tip of Wirral. Part of an early ninth-century slab or shrine cover, originally from Overchurch, was moved to Upton and rebuilt into Upton church, then rediscovered in 1887 (Figure 5, overleaf). Along one face it carries a runic inscription: *Folc arærdon bec[cun]* | *[gi]biddath fore Æthelmun[d]*, 'The people raised up a monument; pray for Æthelmund'. As David Parsons observed, this is part of a broader corpus of Anglo-Saxon Christian commemorative inscriptions, overwhelmingly associated with religious communities; as he suggested, we might

Figure 5: Overchurch 1A. Copyright *Corpus of Anglo-Saxon Stone Sculpture*. Photograph: K.P. Jukes and D.J. Craig.

therefore interpret *folc* as 'laity' or 'congregation', and deduce that 'Æthelmund was a priest whose memorial was sponsored by his lay congregation'. The form of the inscription and the zoomorphic interlace on the other face seem to look north and east to the kingdom of the Northumbrians and south to the Mercians, perhaps reflecting the fact that Wirral was a liminal zone on the edge of both peoples and polities.[32]

Hilbre is a tidal island of a type well-known for early Christian religious communities.[33] The place-name Hilbre descends from the Old English female personal name *Hildeburg* + ēg, 'island'.[34] The corpus of names of this type is dominated by Old English masculine names, and this is one of only two known instances where a female name occurs.[35] To explain this we might look to parallels where places with religious communities were named by combining the name of a prominent early member with Old English elements including *burh, ceaster, ciric* and *stow*; the western distribution of some of these suggests that the Brittonic-speakers' practice of combining *llan/lan* with a saint's name could have influenced Old English speakers, which is striking in light of the proximity of Brittonic and Old

English speakers on Wirral and of Landican (above) to Hilbre.[36] Hildeburg, then, could have been one of the large number of local Anglo-Saxon saints for whom evidence only emerges in the post-Conquest period, and whose identities are often obscure.[37] Excavations on the island have uncovered a probable pre-Conquest building, a tenth- or eleventh-century cross-head (Figure 6) and an eleventh-century slab.[38] This evidence and this suggestion are independent of the later legendary associations with a Saint Hildeburgh, which have been shown to carry no weight.[39]

Figure 6: Hilbre Island 1A. Copyright *Corpus of Anglo-Saxon Stone Sculpture*. Photograph: K.P. Jukes and D.J. Craig.

The Christian Landscape of Wirral During and After Viking Settlement

Indications that one or more religious communities survived Viking settlement are provided by the Old Norse place-name *kirkja-bý(r)*, 'farm/estate with, of or at the church', at Kirby in Walley and West Kirby. Brief attention to the full corpus of *-bý(r)* names and the sub-category of *kirkja-bý(r)* names is necessary to understand their significance.

Following the persuasive arguments of Lesley Abrams and David Parsons, place-names incorporating the Old Norse element *-bý(r)* probably bear witness to a widespread and comparatively early settlement of Old Norse speakers of relatively low status. First, they are overwhelmingly associated with other Old Norse elements and in a significant number of instances their earliest forms preserve Old Norse grammatical inflexions: this suggests that they were coined and kept alive by Old Norse speakers, not by Old English speakers who had borrowed Old Norse elements. Second, they incorporate a wide variety, rather than a limited stock, of Old Norse personal names: they probably result from a large number of settlers associated with the land in local contexts, not a narrow elite of landlords. Third, the Old Norse personal names are in long forms, whereas shortened forms were fashionable in the eleventh century: they may belong to the tenth century. Fourth, the names are associated with subsidiary settlements on lower quality land: they look like lower status holdings. Fifth, the names occur alongside Old Norse field-names: the settlers were working and naming the fields.[40]

The *kirkja-bý(r)* names form an exceptional sub-category, as Gillian Fellows-Jensen recognised, and there are good reasons for thinking they point to surviving religious communities by identifying some of their endowments. Interestingly, though names in *kirkja-bý(r)* refer to a church, no recorded religious communities were designated *kirkja-bý(r)*: it did not apparently mean religious community. Places with names in *kirkja-bý(r)* occur in some landscapes where there were many other places with churches in the tenth century, and only a proportion of the places called *kirkja-bý(r)* certainly had churches when the names were being coined: it did not apparently mean 'a *farm* with a church' either. Unlike other *-bý(r)* names, names in *kirkja-bý(r)* do not refer to an Old Norse proprietor or an environmental feature, and they often belong to places where there is evidence for an earlier settlement, on good quality land, from which parishes were named: it did not apparently refer to a subsidiary place in the hands of an Old Norse-speaking settler of lower status. Most significantly, there is a common pattern whereby a known or suspected religious community is flanked by places called *kirkja-bý(r)*. Worth noting is the fact that these names were sometimes applied to several places in relatively close proximity, failing to distinguish between them, which required further Old English or Old Norse qualifiers to distinguish them in non-local contexts. Taking all these characteristics into account, it seems likely that *kirkja-bý(r)* was coined for places which were outlying holdings of religious communities and remained in their hands, meaning 'farm of the church/Church', in contradistinction to those farms in the hands of Old Norse settlers, and that they survived in the hands of the religious community long enough for the names to become customary and worth retaining despite the shortcomings of their generic form. Occasionally, religious communities founded smaller subsidiary communities on outlying lands, which may account for odd instances where a place called *kirkja-bý(r)* was designated a *monasterium* in the twelfth century, though it was never the location of a reformed monastery.[41]

Turning back to Wirral, Kirby in Walley and West Kirby represent one particular instance of these trends (Figure 1). Above it has been suggested that Woodchurch and Overchurch had pre-tenth-century religious communities; the evidence for Woodchurch reveals that Old Norse speakers recognised and referred to the church, causing Old English *ciric* to become Old Norse *kirkja* for a time. Woodchurch was perhaps provided with a stone monument in the eleventh century.[42] Yet neither Woodchurch nor Overchurch became a *kirkja-bý(r)*; instead, this place-name was applied to places from which immediately adjacent parishes were named – Kirby in Walley and West Kirby. If we consider Wirral as a whole, there is tenth-century sculpture suggesting the existence of other churches at Neston, Hilbre, Bidston and Bromborough,[43] but these places retained Old English names, and the tendency was for Old Norse speakers to name places with reference to an Old Norse personal name, an ethnic group, or an environmental feature.[44] Either Woodchurch or Overchurch, or both, could have been surviving religious communities with endowments at Kirby in Walley and West Kirby, designated 'the farm of the church/Church' by Old Norse settlers, and either or both could have retained those lands long enough to explain why these names became customary and worth retaining, despite requiring qualifiers to distinguish them in non-local contexts. After the Norman Conquest, West Kirby and

Hilbre were granted first to St Évroul in Normandy, and then to St Werburgh's in Chester, and West Kirby was referred to as a *monasterium*, though the known cell of St Werburgh's was on Hilbre; this may reflect the fact that whichever religious community held West Kirby had established a small subsidiary community on the lands there associated with a hermitage or cult site on Hilbre.[45]

The Formation of Anglo-Scandinavian Christian Identities

A reflex of the interactions between existing religious communities and Old Norse-speaking settlers may be found in the corpus of stone sculpture in Chester and on Wirral. The Redcliff quarry is thought to have been the stone-source for a tenth-century workshop supplying sculpture for St John's Church and for sites across Wirral. From St John's and from neighbouring areas a number of stone cross-heads survive, carved on sandstone which could derive from Redcliff. The form of these cross-heads is distinctive, with the four arms of the cross joined by a circle, and they are known as wheel-heads or circle-heads. Irish high crosses are the likely source (Figure 4). Their distribution and some decorative elements suggest a tenth-century date, and an association with Ireland and Scandinavia.[46] Concentrations of such monuments sometimes occur at the sites of known or suspected early religious communities alongside others with similar associations, such as crosses incorporating scenes identifiable from later sources for Old Norse mythology and recumbent grave-markers known as 'hogbacks', and alongside monuments with images reflecting clerical expertise.[47] At St John's there is one small fragment carved with an unknown, but probably Christian, figural scene, presumably requiring clerical expertise.[48] In sum, the activities of Hiberno-Norse traders may lie behind their distribution and particular concentrations may reflect the role of communities of clergy at significant nodes in the trading network in providing Christian memorials to them. Hence, as noted above, Paul Everson and David Stocker have argued that St John's, the workshop, and the concentration of monuments there was connected to a strand on the Dee below the church and the activities of Hiberno-Norse traders. Further related monuments survive across Wirral at Neston, West Kirby, Hilbre and Bromborough.[49]

Considered in more detail, this corpus of monuments on Wirral may reveal that interactions between clergy and Old Norse-speaking settlers resulted in the forging of new Anglo-Scandinavian Christian identities. A fragment from a cross-shaft at Neston carries an image of a priest praying (with his arms uplifted in what is known as the *orans* position), in his full mass vestments, with a clear articulation of his alb (tunic), chasuble (liturgical vest), a chalice, and a maniple (band draped over the arm) (Figure 7, overleaf).[50] Either from St Werburgh's, St John's, or from the putative communities at Overchurch and Woodchurch, or from Neston itself, someone with clerical knowledge and expertise, as well as access to visual representations of clergy, must lie behind this image, whatever its intended meanings. Two further fragments reinforce this impression. One is from the top of a cross-shaft, where the shaft joined the cross-head: on one main side it carries an image of two figures fighting, which might be a secular scene, but has plausibly been identified as a representation of David and Goliath, an episode sometimes interpreted typologically as a prefiguration of Christ's victory over Satan (Figure 8, overleaf).[51] The other is from the lower part of a cross-shaft: on one main side it depicts a hunt scene incorporating a human figure with spear and a hound attacking a hart, which may be a secular image, or might represent Christ or the Christian soul pursued by devils, with the lower part of two unidentifiable figures, male and female, above; on the remaining side it shows two confronted horsemen with crossed spears (Figure 9, overleaf).[52] Indeed, though it cannot be ruled out that they are merely images relating to secular pursuits and status, Richard Bailey notes that 'Most of the surviving scenes on Neston 2 and 3 are ones which would be entirely familiar in early medieval psalter illustrations or commentaries.' He acknowledges that they could ultimately derive from a wide range of earlier Irish or

Figure 7 (top left): Neston 1A. Copyright *Corpus of Anglo-Saxon Stone Sculpture*. Photograph: K.P. Jukes and D.J. Craig.

Figure 8 (top right): Neston 2C. Copyright *Corpus of Anglo-Saxon Stone Sculpture*. Photograph: K.P. Jukes and D.J. Craig.

Figure 9 (bottom left): Neston 3A. Copyright *Corpus of Anglo-Saxon Stone Sculpture*. Photograph: K.P. Jukes and D.J. Craig.

Pictish models, but that 'female figures with knotted pigtails are a characteristic element in female portraiture in Viking Age art'.[53] Equally, other places at nodes in the trading network where there are concentrations of tenth-century Hiberno-Norse monuments include images requiring clerical expertise alongside scenes like these with obvious, or potential, Christian meanings.[54]

Figure 10: West Kirby 4A. Copyright *Corpus of Anglo-Saxon Stone Sculpture.* Photograph: K.P. Jukes.

With this in mind, it is striking that the corpus of recumbent grave-markers known as 'hogbacks' has two unusual outliers on Wirral at West Kirby and Bidston, and that both have far-flung analogues at places which were nodes in that trading network with just such concentrations of monuments. At West Kirby,

Figure 11: Bidston 1A. Copyright *Corpus of Anglo-Saxon Stone Sculpture.* Photograph: K.P. Jukes.

alongside the wheel-headed crosses, survives a 'hogback' carved on non-local stone imported from North Wales across the Dee (Figure 10); its long, narrow and tall form, its combination of 'wheel-and-bar' decoration and an interlace plait, and its roof tiling have comparators in a Cumbrian stop-plait school, in a huge concentration of monuments, some reflecting clerical expertise and others carrying Old Norse mythology, at Lythe in North Yorkshire, and amongst the monuments at the royal centre at Govan on the Clyde.[55] At Bidston, an unusually small 'hogback' is of a distinctive 'extended-niche type' with probable origins at Brompton in North Yorkshire, where there is another profusion of cross-shafts, some with images reflecting clerical expertise, and 'hogbacks', and with connections to animals carved on monuments at York and at Barmston in East Yorkshire (Figure 11, previous page).[56] Unsurprisingly, then, when this monument was first published Richard Bailey argued that it was the memorial of a Meols trader operating the Dublin–Chester–York route, whose allegiance to Yorkshire roots was being expressed.[57]

Conclusions
In line with scholarship on other regions, an interdisciplinary analysis of the Christian landscape of early medieval Chester and Wirral suggests that Viking activity did not shatter existing ecclesiastical structures and that local clergy probably played an important part in the conversion and Christianisation of Old Norse-speaking settlers. In conclusion it seems worth speculating on how and why this was so, and what were the effects?

A starting point is to consider the circumstances in which such clergy continued to exist. Across the regions subjected to Viking conquest and settlement, as Julia Barrow has most recently and comprehensively emphasised, episcopal sees experienced significant disruption.[58] This raises the question of how new clergy were trained and ordained. In thinking about the supply of clergy, it is worth, with Fiona Edmonds, dwelling on the long-term evidence for connections around and across the Irish Sea, which produced visible movements of ecclesiastics and transmissions of ecclesiastical culture in the seventh and eighth centuries, and might also have done so in the tenth century.[59] In this light we should ask whether such movements lie behind the transmission of Irish forms and images requiring clerical expertise on to stone sculpture from Lancashire, Cumbria and Yorkshire. Like John Blair, we should be attentive to the exceptional survival of evidence from Ely, which offers a passing glimpse of a community of hereditary clergy at Horningsea in Cambridgeshire.[60]

A next step is to acknowledge, as historians and archaeologists have long been arguing, that if we are to use the term Viking for

The Christian Landscape of Early Medieval Chester and Wirral

the activities of Old Norse-speaking raiders, traders, conquerors and settlers, we must recognise that it denotes, not an identity or ethnicity, but an occupation. Doing so opens up more room for the fact that Vikings included men and women, and members of various peoples co-opted from across the very wide Viking 'diaspora'. Some Vikings, therefore, were probably from Christian peoples. When Christian rulers turned Viking poachers into gamekeepers, by settling them in coastal territories, or established peace with, or exerted overlordship, over them, it was common for Viking leaders to undergo baptism, sometimes with the Christian ruler as godparent, and occasionally to intermarry with members of that ruler's family.[61] No such details survive in the later accounts of Ingimundr, but it would have been quite usual in his situation to convert. Old Norse-speaking settlers then worked in local landscapes alongside members of Christian peoples. Recall that amongst the moneyers in tenth-century Chester were people with British, English, Irish, Norse, and perhaps Frankish names.[62] Remember that the linguistic traces of a Brittonic or Irish enclave centred on Wallasey survived Old Norse settlement and notice that amongst the Old Norse names coined on Wirral was Irby, *Íra-bý(r)*, 'the farm/estate of the Irish'.[63]

A final stage is to put this evidence into play with the significance of Chester and Wirral to tenth-century kings. A picture of Wirral as a place where a Christian Mercian ruler settled an Hiberno-Norse leader and his followers, and where Brittonic-, Old Irish-, and Old English-speaking Christians, as well as Christian clergy, worked with Old Norse-speaking settlers, presents an attractive context for two major events located at Chester and on Wirral. King Æthelstan defeated an alliance of leaders and their armies drawn from amongst the Irish, Scots, Hiberno-Norse and Strathclyde Britons at *Brunanburh* in 937, cementing his status as overlord of Britain.[64] Out of the various suggestions for the location of *Brunanburh*, the strongest case is for Bromborough on Wirral.[65] If this is correct, the battle occurred somewhere close to the boundary of the Old Norse settlement on Wirral, near to one of the churches reflecting the connections between St John's, Chester and Wirral. King Edgar, as we have seen, travelled to Chester with his fleet to assert his own overlordship over Britain, where six or eight British, Irish and Scottish kings pledged allegiance to him; the twelfth-century tradition is that they did so by rowing him up the River Dee to St John's, where the clergy may have been commemorating Viking Irish Sea traders as Christians. Chester and Wirral thus appear as theatres for negotiating relationships between Brittonic-, Old Irish- and Old English-speaking Christians and Old Norse speakers at both a local and a transnational scale.

Endnotes
[1] F.M. Stenton, *Anglo-Saxon England* (2nd edn, Oxford, 1947), 427.
[2] Stenton, *Anglo-Saxon England*, 427–28.
[3] Stenton, *Anglo-Saxon England*, 428.
[4] J. Blair, ed., *Minsters and Parish Churches: The Local Church in Transition, 950–1200* (Oxford, 1988); P. Sims-Williams, *Religion and Literature in Western England, 600–800* (Cambridge, 1990), esp. 360–95; J. Blair, *Early Medieval Surrey: Landholding, Church and Settlement* (Stroud, 1991); J. Blair, *Anglo-Saxon Oxfordshire* (Stroud, 1994), 56–77, 111–16; T. Hall, *Minster Churches in the Dorset Landscape*, British Archaeological Reports, British Series 304 (Oxford, 2000); J. Blair, *The Church in Anglo-Saxon Society* (Oxford, 2005), esp. 149–66, 295–323, 368–425; J. Pitt, 'Mynsters and Parishes: Some Evidence and Some Conclusions from Wiltshire', in A. Langlands and R. Lavelle, eds, *The Lands of the English Kin: Studies in Wessex and Anglo-Saxon England in Honour of Professor Barbara Yorke* (Leiden, 2020), 407–26.
[5] R. Morris, *Churches in the Landscape* (London, 1989), 93–167; D.M. Hadley, *The Northern Danelaw: Its Social Structure c.800–1000* (London, 2000), 216–97; D.M. Hadley, *The Vikings in England: Settlement, Society and Culture* (Manchester, 2006), 192–236; T. Pickles, *Kingship, Society and the Church in Anglo-Saxon Yorkshire* (Oxford, 2018), 128–62, 224–77.
[6] C. Downham, *Viking Kings of Britain and Ireland: The Dynasty of Ivarr to A.D. 1014* (Edinburgh, 2007).
[7] The papers in P. Carrington, ed., *'Where Deva Spreads her Wizard Stream': Trade and the Port of Chester: Papers from a Seminar Held at Chester, November 1995* (Chester, 1996) provide an excellent overview.

[8] *The Anglo-Saxon Chronicle: A Revised Translation*, ed. and trans. D. Whitelock (London, 1961), 56.

[9] *Annales Cambriae: The A text From British Library, Harley MS 3859, ff. 190r–193r*, transcr. H.W. Gough-Cooper (1st edn, November 2015), published online by the Welsh Chronicles Research Group: <<http://croniclau.bangor.ac.uk>> accessed 6/12/21, 22, a464.1; *Fragmentary Annals of Ireland*, trans. J. Newlon Radner and electronic ed. B. Färber, M. Fomin and E. Purcell for Corpus of Electronic Texts: <<https://celt.ucc.ie/published/T100017.html>> accessed 6/12/21, FA 429.

[10] A.T. Thacker, 'Early medieval Chester 400–1230', in *VCH Ches.*, V i, *British History Online*: <<http://www.british-history.ac.uk/vch/ches/vol5/pt1/pp16-33>> accessed 6/12/21; D. Mason, *Chester AD 400–1066, From Roman Fortress to English Town* (Stroud, 2007), 89–139. 'Carucate', notionally the amount of land a plough team could cover in a year, sometimes appears in Domesday Book as a unit of taxation instead of 'hide'.

[11] P. Everson and D. Stocker, 'Transactions on the Dee: The 'Exceptional' Collection of Early Sculpture from St John's, Chester', in J. Hawkes and E. Cambridge, eds, *Crossing Boundaries: Interdisciplinary Approaches to the Art, Material Culture, Language and Literature of the Early Medieval World: Essays Presented to Professor Emeritus Richard N. Bailey, OBE, on the Occasion of his Eightieth Birthday* (Oxford, 2017), 160–78.

[12] D. Griffiths, 'Early Medieval Material: AD 400–450 to 1050–1100' and 'The Early Medieval Period', in D. Griffiths, R.A. Philpott and G. Egan, *Meols: The Archaeology of the North Wirral Coast*, Oxford University School of Archaeology: Monograph 68 (Oxford, 2007), 58–77, 399–406.

[13] P.R. Cavill, S. Harding and J. Jesch, eds, *Wirral and Its Viking Heritage* (Nottingham, 2000); S. Harding, *Viking Mersey: Scandinavian Wirral, West Lancashire and Chester* (Birkenhead, 2002); S. Harding, *Ingimund's Saga: Viking Wirral* (Chester, 2016).

[14] D. Griffiths, 'Settlement and Acculturation in the Irish Sea Region', in J. Hines, A. Lane and M. Redknap, eds, *Land, Sea and Home: Proceedings of a Conference on Viking-Period Settlement, at Cardiff, July 2001*, Society for Medieval Archaeology Monograph 20 (Leeds, 2004), 125–38.

[15] A.T. Thacker, 'Chester and Gloucester: Early Ecclesiastical Organization in Two Mercian Burhs', *Northern History*, XVIII (1982), 199–211.

[16] N.J. Higham, *The Origins of Cheshire* (Manchester, 1993), 128–40.

[17] Thacker, 'Chester and Gloucester', 199–211; Mason, *Chester AD 400–1066*, 33, 63, 86–87, 122–23.
[18] Henry Bradshaw, *Life of St Werburge of Chester*, ed. E. Hawkins, *The Holy Lyfe and History of Saynt Werburge of Henry Bradshaw* (Chetham Soc. 1st ser. XV, Manchester, 1848), 152.
[19] *Anglo-Saxon Chronicle*, ed. Whitelock, 61; 'Mercian Register', *s.a.* 907.
[20] R.N. Bailey, ed., *Corpus of Anglo-Saxon Stone Sculpture, Volume IX, Cheshire and Lancashire* (Oxford, 2010), 70–73, Chester (Unknown Provenance), nos 1–2.
[21] *Annales Cestrienses*, ed. R.C. Christie (RSLC, XIV, 1887), 11.
[22] T. Wilmott and D. Garner, *The Roman Amphitheatre of Chester, Volume 1: The Prehistoric and Roman Archaeology* (Oxford, 2018), 434–35.
[23] Bailey, *Corpus … Cheshire*, 62–69, Chester (St John), nos 1–9 and Chester (City Walls), no. 1.
[24] The earliest reference to this event is: *Anglo-Saxon Chronicle*, ed. Whitelock, 77, D(E) *s.a.* 972. The tradition about St John's is in *The Chronicle of John of Worcester*, ed. and trans. R.R. Darlington, P. McGurk and J. Bray (Oxford, 1995), II, 422–24. For an exhaustive discussion of the sources: D.E. Thornton, 'Edgar and the Eight Kings AD 973: *textus et dramatis personae*', *Early Medieval Europe*, X(1) (March, 2001), 49–79.
[25] *DB Cheshire*, fos 263 a, b.
[26] J. McN. Dodgson, *The Place-Names of Cheshire: Part IV* (Cambridge, 1972), 323–24.
[27] Dodgson, *Place-Names of Cheshire: Part IV*, 324–26; R. Coates, 'Liscard and Irish Names in Northern Wirral', *Journal of the English Place Name Society*, XXX (1997/98), 23–26.
[28] Dodgson, *Place-Names of Cheshire: Part IV*, 266–67.
[29] Dodgson, *Place-Names of Cheshire: Part IV*, 274.
[30] Dodgson, *Place-Names of Cheshire: Part IV*, 272. The earliest forms are *Prestune* (1086 x 1088) and *Prestona* (1096–1101 in 1280). Later forms are *Premptona, Prenton, Printon*, prompting Dodgson to suggest these early forms were an error and propose the OE personal name *Præn* + *tūn*. However, together the combined context of Llan-Tecan and *Wood-ciric/kirkja* argue in favour of accepting the early *prēosta-tūn* forms.
[31] T. Pickles, '*Biscopes-tūn, Muneca-tūn* and *Prēosta-tūn*: Dating, Significance and Distribution', in E. Quinton, ed., *The Church in English Place-Names*, English Place-Name Society Extra Series 4 (Nottingham, 2009), 39–108.

[32] Bailey, *Corpus ... Cheshire*, 91–94, Overchurch 1, quotation at 94.
[33] J.D. Craggs, ed., *Hilbre: The Cheshire Island, Its History and Natural History* (Liverpool, 1982), is the essential guide to the island, its history, and its flora and fauna.
[34] Dodgson, *Place-Names of Cheshire, Part IV*, 302–4.
[35] M. Gelling and A. Cole, *The Landscape of Place-Names* (Stamford, 2000), 37–44.
[36] Blair, *Church in Anglo-Saxon Society*, 80–81 and n. 8, 216–17 and ns 143, 145, including analysis and examples.
[37] J. Blair, 'A Saint for Every Minster? Local Cults in Anglo-Saxon England', and 'A Handlist of Anglo-Saxon Saints', in A. Thacker and R. Sharpe, eds, *Local Saints and Local Churches in the Early Medieval West* (Oxford, 2002), 455–565.
[38] R.A. Philpott, 'Excavations on Hilbre Island, 2006/7 and 2016/17: A Possible Early Medieval Building', *JCAS*, LXXXVIII (2018), 127–29; Bailey, *Corpus ... Cheshire*, 81–82, Hilbre Island 1–2.
[39] S. Craggs, 'Hilbre Island in Medieval Times: A Few Legends Revisited', *Ches. Hist.*, XLIV (2004–5), 14–28, esp. 15–20.
[40] L. Abrams and D.N. Parsons, 'Place-Names and the History of Scandinavian Settlement in England', in Hines, Lane and Redknap, *Land, Sea and Home*, 379–431.
[41] G. Fellows-Jensen, 'The Vikings' Relationship with Christianity in the British Isles: The Evidence of Place-Names Containing the Old Norse Element *Kirkja*', in J.E. Knirk, ed., *Proceedings of the Tenth Viking Congress, 1985* (Oslo, 1987), 295–308; Pickles, *Kingship, Society and the Church*, 244–53.
[42] Bailey, *Corpus ... Cheshire*, 132–33, Upton 1, and 146–47, Woodchurch 1.
[43] Bailey, *Corpus ... Cheshire*, 49–51, 53–57, 81–82, 85–90.
[44] For instance, Dodgson, *Place-Names of Cheshire: Part IV*, 279–80, Thurstaston, *þorsteinn-tūn*, 'Thorsteinn's farm'; 287–88, Frankby, *Frankebýr*, 'Frenchman's farm' or *Franki-býr*, 'Franki's farm'; 264–65, Irby, *Íra-býr*, 'farm of the Irishmen'; 271–72, Pensby, *Penn-býr*, 'farm at a hill called Penn'; 319, Lingham, *lang-holmr*, 'long marsh'.
[45] *The Chartulary or Register of the Abbey of St Werburgh, Chester*, ed. J. Tait (Manchester, 1920), II, 289–91.
[46] Bailey, *Corpus...Cheshire*, 31–33.
[47] Pickles, *Kingship, Society and the Church*, 235–43, 253–69.
[48] Bailey, *Corpus ... Cheshire*, 68, Chester (St John) 8.

[49] Bailey, *Corpus ... Cheshire*, 53–54, Bromborough 3; 81, Hilbre Island 1; 86–88, Neston 2 and 3; 133–35, West Kirby 1, 2 and 3.
[50] Bailey, *Corpus ... Cheshire*, 85–86, Neston 1.
[51] Bailey, *Corpus ... Cheshire*, 86–87, Neston 2.
[52] Bailey, *Corpus ... Cheshire*, 87–89, Neston 3.
[53] Bailey, *Corpus ... Cheshire*, 88–89. Corpus numbers Neston 2 and 3 are illustrated in Figures 8 and 9.
[54] Pickles, *Kingship, Society and the Church*, 253–69.
[55] Bailey, *Corpus ... Cheshire*, 135–36, West Kirby 4.
[56] Bailey, *Corpus ... Cheshire*, 49–51, Bidston 1.
[57] R.N. Bailey and J. Whalley, 'A Miniature Viking-Age Hogback from the Wirral', *Antiquaries Journal*, LXXXVI (2006), 345–56.
[58] J. Barrow, 'Survival and Mutation: Ecclesiastical Institutions in the Danelaw in the Ninth and Tenth Centuries', in D. Hadley and J. Richards, eds, *Cultures in Contact: Scandinavian Settlement in England in the Ninth and Tenth Century* (Turnhout, 2000), 155–76.
[59] F. Edmonds, *Gaelic Influence in the Northumbrian Kingdom: The Golden Age and the Viking Age* (Woodbridge, 2019).
[60] Blair, *Church in Anglo-Saxon Society*, 294.
[61] S. Coupland, 'From Poachers to Gamekeepers: Scandinavian Warlords and Carolingian Kings', *Early Medieval Europe,* VII (1998), 85–114.
[62] Mason, *Chester AD 400–1066*, 135.
[63] Dodgson, *Place-Names of Cheshire: Part IV,* 264–65, Irby, Íra-býr, 'farm of the Irishmen'.
[64] *Anglo-Saxon Chronicle*, ed. Whitelock, 69–70, s.a. 937.
[65] P. Cavill, 'The Place-Name Debate', in M. Livingston, ed., *The Battle of Brunanburh: A Casebook* (Exeter, 2011), 327–50, remains the most persuasive analysis.

2

CONTRASTING SETTLEMENTS ALONG THE DEE VALLEY FRONTIER: DEFENCE, CROSSING, REFUGE

Graeme J. White

The people of medieval Cheshire were all too conscious of its position as a border county between England and Wales. Under the year 1256, the *Annales Cestrienses*, the annals of Chester Abbey, wrote of the future Edward I visiting the county to receive the homage and fealty of the nobility of Wales and Cheshire, after which 'he left Chester and returned to England'.[1] And, as a frontier shire, it was underpopulated and under-resourced, with the lowest recorded rural population, lowest number of plough teams and lowest total valuation of rural landholdings of any fully covered English county in Domesday Book.[2] The character of the medieval shire is reflected, for example, in a landscape in which, although some of the basic elements of the 'champion' countryside of the Midlands – planned nucleated settlements and planned strip systems – were certainly present, the sparse population meant that they were generally on a small scale, sitting alongside dispersed farms and hamlets with associated enclosed fields.[3]

The sharply defined wooded upland known as the Lyme, which gives us place-names such as Lyme Park and Newcastle-under-Lyme and is now thought to derive from the Latin *limen* (threshold) or *limes* (boundary)[4] – was seen as a barrier between Cheshire and the rest of England. In about 1195, the Chester monk Lucian wrote in his treatise *De Laude Cestrie* that the earl of Chester enjoyed special privileges because his county was separated from the rest of England by 'the wood of Lime'. The same idea surfaced 20 years later in clause 10 of the Cheshire Magna Carta, exempting Cheshire's barons from having to fight for the earl beyond the Lyme and

Looking at the Landscape

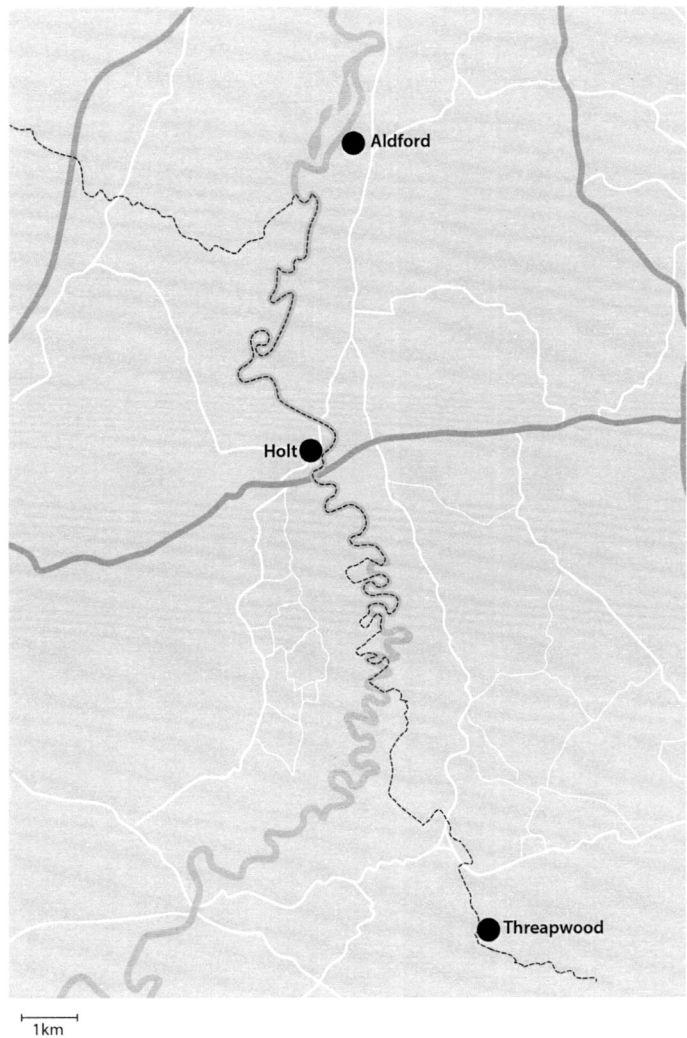

Figure 1: Map of the three frontier settlements, showing the meandering course of the River Dee, the modern Anglo-Welsh border (thin dotted line) and routeways.

placing the major responsibility for garrisoning Chester castle on the earl's 'knights from England' rather than on those from within the county.[5] At an uncertain date, but probably in the 1220s – when the earl was at odds with Henry III's government – he forbade the 'men of Lyme' from making clearances in the woods because it would reduce their effectiveness as a defensive barrier against the rest of the kingdom.[6]

Clearly, there was a lively separatist tradition in Cheshire, which outlived – indeed, was enhanced in response to – the takeover by the crown when the line of Anglo-Norman earls died out in 1237. Discrete Cheshire institutions survived until the sixteenth century (and in some respects until 1830),[7] while the county's distinctiveness was celebrated in literature at least until the seventeenth.[8] But here it is the western frontier of this border county that is our focus, and in particular three settlements along that frontier, all close to the River Dee. Those settlements are Aldford, Holt and Threapwood. The differences in the morphology of each of these settlements reflect the character of the frontier at the time they either originated or took their present form, and the contrasting roles they played on that frontier (Figure 1, opposite).

As a community, **Aldford** (NGR SJ4159) existed in some form before the Norman Conquest but seems to have developed between the late eleventh and mid-thirteenth centuries as a castle-town set within a volatile frontier, guarding a north–south route which serviced a series of borderland settlements. The emphasis here was on Defence. **Holt** (NGR SJ4154) is a small planned town, again with a castle, but established later, in the immediate aftermath of the Edwardian conquest of North Wales in the late 1270s and early 1280s. Holt did not command a route *along* the border but *across* it, with its late thirteenth-century castle overlooking a new bridge across the Dee between England and Wales, and thus between Cheshire and the March. This represents the frontier as a Crossing. The origins of **Threapwood** (NGR SJ4445) probably lie in the mid-sixteenth century, after the national border had been fixed under

Looking at the Landscape

Henry VIII. It took on the role as a place of Refuge between two counties and countries. Threapwood developed as an irregular squatter settlement, the other two were planned. These contrasting characteristics are still apparent today.

A key point to stress is that although all three settlements lie very close to the modern border with Wales – and did so when Cheshire still enjoyed its integrity prior to reorganisation in 1974 – this border has fluctuated from time to time. Domesday Cheshire extended into modern Flintshire and part of Denbighshire and it was only in the 1160s that, as a result of Welsh resurgence, a western and south-western border broadly similar to today's was established, with the kingdom of Powys overseeing Maelor Saesneg east of the Dee and the kingdom of Gwynedd pushing east of the River Clwyd to control at least part of the area west of the Dee estuary. There was further fighting in the reigns of John and Henry III, with the Dee-Clwyd area effectively a disputed frontier zone and the border itself ill-defined, before Edward I's campaigns of 1277 and 1282–83 led to the establishment of boundaries recognisable as those of today. These were formalised by the Statute of Rhuddlan of 1284. Flintshire was created as a county to be run on English lines, often linked to the administration of Cheshire, with Maelor Saesneg – adjacent to the land on which Threapwood would develop – becoming 'Flintshire Detached'.

Other border territories were granted by Edward I to loyal barons, including his military companion John de Warenne, earl of Surrey. He was given what became known as the lordships of Bromfield and Yale, just across the River Dee south-west of Aldford. The 1284 boundary was finalised by the Acts of Union with Wales in 1536 and 1543, when Denbighshire was created as a new county in place of the lordships once held by Warenne and others. As far as our three settlements are concerned, Aldford in its present form dates to a period before the boundaries with Gwynedd and Powys were finally settled: it was part of a vulnerable, indeterminate frontier area, and there were other places defending Cheshire with similar motte-and-bailey castles further west, as at Pulford and Dodleston. As for Holt and Threapwood, they are consciously positioned on a national boundary settled in 1284 and confirmed in 1536.

Let us turn to the morphology of the three settlements in turn.

Aldford

Aldford is not mentioned in Domesday Book but is generally thought to be covered by one of the two entries for neighbouring Farndon. It appears as a holding of Bigot de Loges from Hugh earl of Chester, with seven villeins, three bordars and two fishermen and a valuation which – unusually for Cheshire which suffered greatly from William the Conqueror's 'Harrying of the North' – had increased from £2 in 1066 to £6 two decades later.[9] The other entry for Farndon, usually taken to represent the present settlement of that name, describes a holding of the bishop of Chester with a recorded population of over 20, at least two of whom were priests.[10] It has been well argued that, while Farndon was almost certainly the site of a pre-Conquest minster, the part which now constitutes Aldford, which was held by Edwin earl of Mercia before 1066, may have been a corresponding high-status secular site. It was possibly the place referred to by the *Anglo-Saxon Chronicle* (C and D) when it says that King Edward the Elder died at Farndon in 924.[11] Aldford lay close to a former Roman road which had once linked the military bases at Chester and Wroxeter. This road ran south from Chester through present-day Handbridge and Eccleston, crossing the River Dee from west bank to east by a ford near the site of the nineteenth-century Iron Bridge, which lies about a third of a mile or a half-kilometre north of Aldford's motte-and-bailey castle. The castle, though presumably a post-Conquest feature, lies adjacent to the Roman road, with Margary claiming that the eastern perimeter of the bailey follows the line of the agger.[12] All this suggests that it may have been built when the road was still in use, with the purpose of guarding the ford. For its part, the parish church is also found immediately to the south of the castle (Figure 2, overleaf).

Looking at the Landscape

Figure 2: The street pattern of Aldford, from OS 1st edn 6 inches to 1 mile, Cheshire, sheet no XLVI, surveyed 1869–74: reproduced by permission of CALS and the owner/depositor to whom copyright is reserved. The castle site lies east of Woodhouse Farm, just north of the church. The triangular green is in the centre of the map, with its apex south of the graveyard. What is now the B5130 runs south from the top of the map, over the bridge then south again past the smithy and school along the eastern side of the settlement. (Not to scale.)

Contrasting Settlements Along the Dee Valley Frontier

Although the church is a rebuild of 1866,[13] its proximity to the castle implies continuity from a pre-Conquest arrangement of thegnly or noble residence – the 'high-status' forerunner of the castle – and accompanying place of worship, an arrangement encountered all over England, frequently so in the Marches.[14]

However, when the place-name is first recorded in the mid- to late twelfth century, the ford is referred to as 'old': *Aldeford*.[15] For example, the record of a perambulation of disputed land at nearby Gorstilowe, undertaken on the orders of Henry II when he had temporary custody of the estates of Hugh II earl of Chester between 1173 and 1177, mentions 'inferior pars nemoris de Aldeford' – the lower part of the wood of Aldford – as one of the indicative features. This does not of course prove that the ford, though 'old', was necessarily obsolete, but it raises the prospect that, not long after the construction of the castle, the Roman route was replaced by a road which, leaving Chester at a three-way junction at Boughton, kept east of the river along the course still followed today by the B5130 south towards Churton. Indeed, this is the route described about 1195 by the Chester monk Lucian. He drew spiritual messages from the major intersection, advising the traveller heading east to follow the straight path towards 'Villam Christi' (Christleton) and avoid the roads to left and right; the latter (the present B5130) was the one which led to 'Veterem Vadum', the old ford.[16]

The likelihood is that both a castle and a settlement existed at Aldford by the twelfth century at latest, but that the castle had been built alongside the old Roman road. The Domesday settlement may also have been in the immediate vicinity. However, by the 1190s that road had been superseded by today's route from Chester to Aldford, now known as the B5130. The layout of the settlement we see today, with its planned street pattern, triangular green and roads surrounding it in the form of a rough square, clearly respects this later (modern) road which forms the eastern side of the square. It appears therefore to post-date the establishment of the later road, rather than being based around the Roman one (Figure 2, opposite).

Looking at the Landscape

Fuller evidence comes from the following century. Whereas the motte-and-bailey design implies a late eleventh to mid-twelfth century origin for Aldford castle, the first clear documentary reference to it is not until 1276: a Close Roll mentions Richard of Orreby's service for the manor of Gawsworth, namely the supply of one footman with haubergeon (shirt of chain mail) at Peter of Ardern's castle of *Aldeford* in time of war.[17] This ties in with the fruits of archaeological investigation, including geophysical survey and excavation, which suggests that, far from being abandoned as most motte-and-baileys had been by then, Aldford castle was strengthened sometime in the thirteenth century, with a stone tower being added to the motte and work being carried out on the bailey banks.[18] Meanwhile, in 1254, Henry III granted to Walkelin of Arderne a weekly Tuesday market and a three-day annual fair in mid-September at Aldford. The first record of a rector here dates to about 1300.[19] These late scraps of evidence need not deter us from attributing a much earlier, pre-Conquest, origin to some form of settlement here, but the reinforcement of the castle and the development of a market and fair point to a quickening of activity during the course of the thirteenth century. It is the arrival of the market and fair – which may possibly have preceded the formal grant – which offers the most likely context for the laying out of the present street pattern. English Heritage's Historic Towns Survey of 2003 surmised that the annual fair was held on the triangular green and the weekly market took place either here or in the churchyard (Figures 3 and 4, opposite).[20]

By the late middle ages, the castle had evidently fallen into disuse. By 1738, the date of an estate map of Aldford, the green had largely been parcelled into small enclosures, some with buildings within them, and there had been expansion of the settlement eastwards between the green and the Chester to Churton road (B5130), although extensive areas of open field remained in the form of arable strips further south.[21] But these later developments do not disguise the fact that in the mid-thirteenth century this was

Figure 3: The apex of Aldford's triangular green, with churchyard to right and streets defining the green to left and at far end (2017). Photograph: Graeme White.

Figure 4: Aldford's triangular green in 2017, from its eastern side. Photograph: Graeme White.

a market centre attached to a castle, apparently planned around a triangular green which offered protection to livestock in the heart of the settlement. At that time, before the Edwardian conquest of North Wales, it lay within a potentially hostile frontier zone. Henry III campaigned against Gwynedd in the 1240s, pushing the extent of English control as far as the Clwyd, only for Gwynedd under Llywelyn ap Gruffudd to recover land east of the Clwyd in the following decade: a plausible context for the (undated) strengthening of the castle and just at the time of the formal grant of market and fair.

So Aldford reflects the paramount need for defensibility within a vulnerable frontier: sheltering beneath a castle still in use in the mid- to late thirteenth century, guarding its animals inside an enclosed green, providing a trading centre along a road which ran north–south linking Chester with other border communities such as those at Farndon and Shocklach. In its planning around a protected green, it has parallels with several settlements in the northernmost counties of England, an area exposed to Scottish raiding. Embleton (Northumberland), Gamblesby (Cumbria) and Trimdon (co. Durham) are cases in point.[22] A particularly relevant example is Castle Bolton (North Yorkshire), where the castle with associated narrow enclosed green and planned settlement (almost certainly replacing an earlier one) appear to have originated in the late fourteenth century (Figure 5, opposite).[23] Despite the different geopolitical contexts in which these places were set, similar challenges prompted similar solutions.

Holt

Notwithstanding the importance of Holt as an industrial centre in Roman times, its medieval history is usually said to begin in 1282, when, as part of his successful campaign to conquer North Wales, Edward I granted what became known as Bromfield and Yale on the west side of the River Dee to one of his military companions, John de Warenne earl of Surrey. Although on the Welsh side of what became the national boundary, the settlement obviously carries an Old English name, meaning 'wood', having also initially been known as the town (and castle) of the Lion.[24] John de Warenne was succeeded by his grandson and namesake in 1306. Between them, they built a riverside castle, certainly in existence by 1308,[25] and had it designed in a distinctive and innovatory pentagonal style, scarcely recognisable from the fragment which remains. The Warennes also provided a church (dedicated like Farndon's on the opposite side of the river to the seventh-century missionary bishop of Lichfield, St Chad), and laid out a planned town. A borough charter granted by the elder John de Warenne in 1285 is referred to in a sixteenth-century royal confirmation.[26] In 1338 his grandson began the building of a stone bridge across the Dee, which replaced

Figure 5: The street pattern of Castle Bolton (North Yorkshire), from OS 1st edn 6 inches to 1 mile, Yorkshire, sheet no LXVII (1856, surveyed 1854), with castle to left and narrow enclosed green centre, reproduced by permission of North Yorkshire County Record Office. (Not to scale.)

a ferry and carried a fortified tower gateway part-way across; the tower, still existing in 1734, had disappeared by 1854, but much of the bridge itself is now thought to be the original fourteenth-century structure despite earlier opinion that it dates to the late fifteenth or early sixteenth century.[27]

Looking at the Landscape

The population of the settlement when it was surveyed in 1315 was about 650, of whom 152 were described as 'burgesses'; settlers had come not only from Cheshire but from southern and eastern England. These figures show the town to be larger at that time than important royal foundations such as Conwy and Caernarfon, although like virtually every other English or Welsh town its numbers declined thereafter in line with the general downturn in population.[28] After the direct Warenne line died out in 1347 the complex came to the fitzAlan earls of Arundel, although it was under Richard II's control within his short-lived 'Principality of Chester' between 1397 and 1399, following Arundel's execution as one of the 'Appellants' opposing the king. In this brief period, Holt castle became Richard II's personal treasury, where he kept his own considerable stock of funds beyond the reach of the exchequer. After restoration to the fitzAlans by Henry IV, castle and town subsequently passed to Sir William Stanley in 1484, only for the castle to be forfeited to the crown on Stanley's execution for treason in 1495. It survived in a somewhat neglected state until the civil war, falling to the parliamentarians in 1647 and being used thereafter as a quarry, notably by Thomas Grosvenor who between 1675 and 1683 shipped much of the stone along the Dee to build his Eaton Hall.[29]

So this was a settlement commanding a crossing of what was in theory a pacified border between England and Wales, when trade was to be encouraged between the two. In November 1282, shortly after the grant of the territory around Holt to John de Warenne, the king had been advised 'to tell Earl Warenne to keep watch at [Bromfield], for much supplies enter the land without anyone's knowledge':[30] a comment which implies that concealed trade – smuggling – was already well established in the locality and that steps needed to be taken to control it. Accordingly, the construction of a castle to guard the river crossing was a logical measure, as was the laying out of an accompanying market town where trade could be supervised. The town was duly planned on a grid pattern, with market places outside the castle to which traders and other travellers were directed by the layout of streets. Although there is no reference to the formal grant of a market, in 1391 one was being held 'on Tuesdays, Sundays and on other days yearly'; by 1411 this was down to a Friday market only and even this waned in the sixteenth century, but fairs were still being held here in 1587 on 11 June and 17 October.[31] There was both a broad space immediately north of the castle and a rectangular one opposite the church where these markets and fairs could have been held, and they doubtless occupied the broad main streets of the grid as well (Figure 6, overleaf). As for the tower part-way across the bridge, this would have served to control access and as a toll-booth. On the side facing England there was a carved lion passant, and in 1627 a jury declared that 'The County of Chester doth repair the Bridge to the Lyon'. A similar lion was once to be seen over the castle entrance and they are almost certainly associated with the alternative lion-related names for Holt.[32]

Keith Lilley has analysed the towns in North Wales associated with the Edwardian conquest and has drawn a comparison between the grid system of streets at Holt and that at Flint, about 20 miles (32 kilometres) to the north-west, although Flint was a royal foundation on the coast rather than a baronial one inland.[33]

> The similarities in their layout lie in the common use of parallel streets and narrow longitudinal street-blocks. Both plans also lack latitudinal streets, except for those cross streets positioned mid-way and at either end of the town. Like Flint, Holt's plan also extends from the castle gates and takes an overall 'playing-card' shape.

Flint was a product of the first Edwardian incursion of 1277, Holt of the second in 1282, but Lilley goes on to suggest that the same designer may have been responsible for both. Yet, as he acknowledges, there are also significant differences – the positioning of the churches and, above all, the absence of any surrounding defences at Holt (either earthworks or stone), which contrasts not only with Flint but with the other Edwardian planned towns in North Wales, including the

Looking at the Landscape

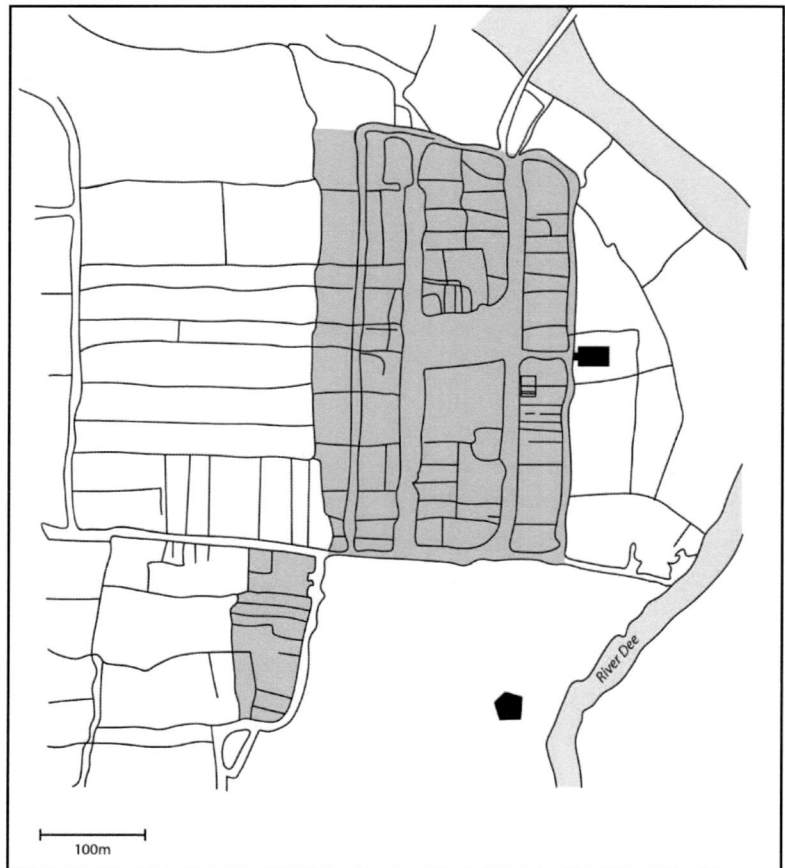

Figure 6: The street pattern of Holt, based with permission on Figure 10.3, The new towns of 1282–84: Holt, Caernarfon, Conwy, Harlech and Criccieth, in K. Lilley, 'The Landscapes of Edward's New Towns: Their Planning and Design' in D. Williams and J. Kenyon, eds., *The Impact of the Edwardian Castles on Wales* (Oxford, 2009), 99–113, with modifications. The castle is shown in black at the bottom, the church in black on the right and the bridge over the river in the top right corner. A large rectangular market place is shown west of the church and there is also an opening out of the streets at the junction immediately north of the castle.

baronial foundation at Denbigh. There was evidently an intention to construct a perimeter wall, since a survey of 1391 records that 'in the time of war each burgess or his [heirs] or assigns shall find for the burgage one garrison man at their own cost for guarding and warding the lord's castle there until the said town be enclosed with a wall of lime and stone'.[34] But this was a century after the establishment of the town, and in the event no enclosing fortification was ever built. At the very least, it seems fair to say that a town wall was not a priority, either for the Warennes or for the later lords of Holt, and – given the importance of this feature elsewhere – this is surely significant. At Holt, the castle guarding the river crossing seems to have been regarded as sufficient defence.

Lilley may well be right in suggesting that the plan of Flint influenced that of Holt, but the latter was a town laid out with an 'open grid', not an enclosed one. Holt was primarily a trading settlement at a river crossing, designed to attract visitors rather than repel them, while controlling their access. The road across the Dee between south-west Cheshire and Bromfield, initially via the ferry, and later via the bridge, was consciously routed through the town, from one end to the other, past church and castle, and into the market places (Figure 7, overleaf). The deliberate diversion of roads so that they passed through market places is a phenomenon which has been noted elsewhere, as at Dunster and Montacute (Somerset) and Thame (Oxfordshire),[35] and a particularly apposite comparison with Holt, again involving a river bridge, may be drawn with St Ives (Huntingdonshire, now Cambridgeshire). This was laid out by Ramsey Abbey for an annual Easter fair granted in 1110 by Henry I: destined, indeed, to be one of the greatest fairs in England in the twelfth and thirteenth centuries, specialising in cloth. At one end of the town was the earlier settlement of Slepe, where the parish church stood close to a road leading from the abbey some 11 miles (18 kilometres) to the north. The crossing of the River Ouse at this point (presumably by a ford) was deliberately superseded by a new wooden bridge built about a quarter of a mile (0.4 kilometres) from

Figure 7: The medieval bridge across the River Dee between Farndon and Holt, viewed from the English side. Over the river, the road turns left and passes St Chad's church, Holt, the tower of which is shown in the distance (2017). Photograph: Graeme White.

the church, first recorded in 1107 and replaced by the present stone one about 1414. The town was developed between church and bridge and those traversing the river were now obliged to pass through to an exceptionally broad street, the *Strata*, the focus of the fair and of other trading activities (Figure 8, opposite).[36] This was a settlement, like Holt, designed to attract visitors and to take advantage of its river crossing.

Threapwood

Threapwood is generally agreed to mean 'disputed wood', from the Old English *threop*, meaning a dispute. The name first occurs, according to the *Place-Names of Cheshire*, in a Patent Roll of 1548, then again in ministerial accounts of 1550.[37] The National Archives has the record of a Chancery court case dating to 1553–55 in which

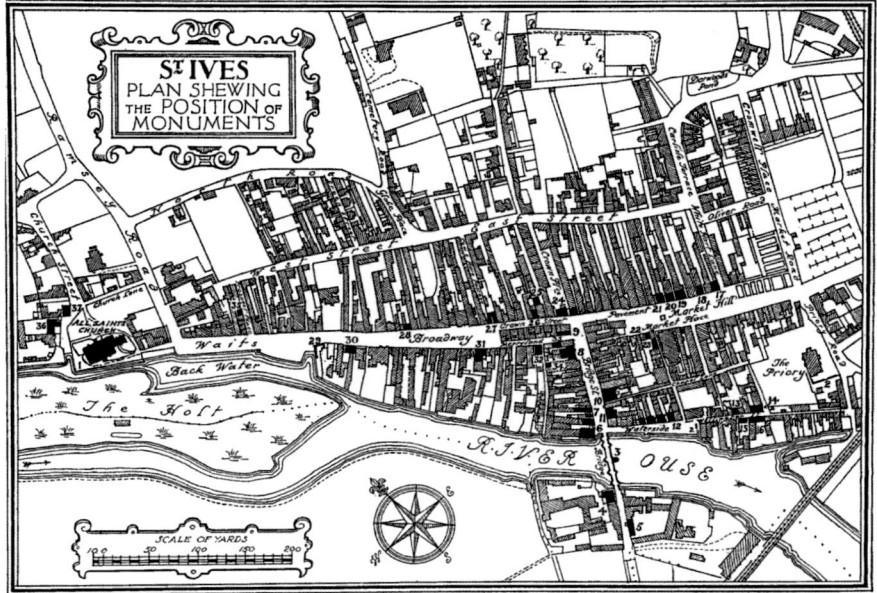

Figure 8: The street pattern of St Ives (Hunts.), reproduced with permission from the Historic England archive (*Royal Commission on Historical Monuments for Huntingdonshire*, HMSO, 1926, 212–20).

John Lloyd claimed a messuage and land in Worthenbury and Threapwood against Elizabeth Verch, David ap Res and others, which may hint at the beginnings of enclosure and settlement.[38]

This sudden referencing of Threapwood around the middle of the sixteenth century is telling. It suggests that its most likely origins are as a settlement in common wasteland on the boundaries of Flintshire Detached (Maelor Saesneg) and Cheshire, after the national boundary had been confirmed in 1536. It became effectively a 'no-man's land' for squatters. The place is best described 200 years later in a letter from the MP for Chester, Philip Henry Warburton, to the Lord Chancellor dated 4 August 1753, in which he described it as common, partially 'covered with seven and twenty cottages and small enclosures', but 'reputed to be in no County, Parish, Town or Hamlet':

> As neither the Sheriff of Chester or Flint were ever known to exercise the office in this place, so no offence, criminal or capital, committed in this place can be tried in either of those Counties or anywhere else ... The same inconvenience with regard to the jurisdiction of Justices of the Peace and as there is no County in which any ejectment can be brought, where can the right, if there be any, to the cottages and enclosures exist but in the present occupants? [so rendering it impossible to proceed to an organised enclosure of the common] ... It is, my Lord, as an obstruction to public Justice and that some effective way may be found out to have the Laws put in execution in this Place.

The Lord Chancellor replied that 'such a place must be the seat of much Disorder and Irregularity and the asylum of many disorderly persons to the interruption of Justice'. A generation later, the naturalist, traveller and antiquarian Thomas Pennant wrote that Threapwood was 'from time immemorial a place of refuge for the frail fair, who make here a transient abode clandestinely to be freed from the consequences of illicit love. Numbers of houses are scattered over the common for their reception.'[39]

So Threapwood served as an unregulated refuge, especially for 'disorderly persons'. Until Queen Anne's reign (1702–14), as another part of Warburton's letter makes clear, it was used by men escaping press-gangs, but this loophole was closed by legislation to allow Threapwood to be counted as part of Cheshire for that purpose. As Pennant suggests, it also became a place where unmarried women went to have their babies – especially, it would seem, after the Settlement Act of 1662 – before or after they were removed from parishes elsewhere. Threapwood's reputation for lawlessness and immorality persisted into the nineteenth century: 254 children born out of wedlock have been counted in baptism registers between 1817 and 1874.[40] However, St John's church was erected in 1815 (Plate 1), a Congregational chapel opened in 1850 and a National school was built in 1843. All eventually had a beneficial impact.[41] An inspector's report on Threapwood school four years after it had opened said that 'the character of the labourers before the establishment of the school was not only ignorant but immoral and in every way uncivilised', before adding that 'Education appears, as usual, to have produced a salutary effect'.[42] As for the church, Threapwood became an ecclesiastical parish in 1817, transferring to the diocese of St Asaph in the 1850s before returning to England in 1920 under the Welsh Church Act of 1914.[43]

Threapwood's rather confused frontier status is apparent from the fact that for most of the nineteenth century, 228 acres lay in Flintshire Detached (Maelor Saesneg) and 150 acres in Cheshire, with the boundary of that time still apparent today from 'Frontier House', a prominent building bearing the date 1892. However, there was a boundary change in 1896, since when the bulk of the township (248 acres) has been in Cheshire.[44]

The landscape today still evokes the character of a squatter settlement, with small wooded enclosures, an irregular road pattern, and no overall plan (Figure 9, overleaf), although the Village Design Statement of 2013, drawn up by local residents to inform future planning decisions, was at pains to accentuate the positive, stressing how much the place had changed. Now it had become 'a unique rural settlement of dispersed individual dwellings, co-existing in harmony with a natural environment that provides a feeling of space and personal privacy'.[45] Essentially, Threapwood is a peculiarity, a dispersed settlement which grew up in defiance of authority without reference to any focal point: a particular type of frontier settlement whose origins lie in the fact that neither of the governing powers on opposite sides of the border was disposed to assert control.

Conclusion
To summarise, we have here three contrasting settlements, all within 13 miles (21 kilometres) of Chester, which can only be fully understood in the wider context of the developing nature of the Anglo-Welsh

Looking at the Landscape

Figure 9: The street pattern of Threapwood, from OS 1st edn 6 inches to 1 mile, Cheshire, sheet nos LIX and IX, surveyed 1874: reproduced by permission of CALS and the owner/depositor to whom copyright is reserved. (Not to scale.)

frontier at the times they were formed. As an illustration of 'form following function' they would delight any modernist designer, but they also demonstrate History as both continuity and change: change because the role of the frontier at any particular time helped to determine the morphology of each of these settlements, and continuity because key elements of that morphology have persisted into the twenty-first century.

Endnotes
[1] *Annales Cestrienses*, ed. R.C. Christie (RSLC, 1887), 72–73.
[2] H.C. Darby, *Domesday England* (Cambridge, 1977), 336, 359 (leaving aside Lancashire, most of which was omitted, and Rutland).
[3] See, for example, G.J. White, 'Open Fields and Rural Settlement in Medieval West Cheshire' in T. Scott and P. Starkey, eds, *The Middle Ages in the North-West* (Oxford, 1995), 15–35; A.D.M. Phillips and C.B. Phillips, eds, *A New Historical Atlas of Cheshire* (Chester, 2002), 52–53.

[4] R. Coates, 'The Lyme', *Journal of the English Place-Name Society*, XXXVI (2004), 39–50.
[5] *Liber Luciani de Laude Cestrie*, ed. M.V. Taylor (RSLC, 1912), 65; G.J. White and J. Pepler, *The Magna Carta of Cheshire* (Chester, 2015), 22, 73–79.
[6] G. Barraclough, 'The Earldom and County Palatine of Chester', *THSLC*, CIII (1951), 23–57, at 52–53, 56–57.
[7] Barraclough, 'Earldom and County Palatine', 38–47; *VCH Ches.*, II, 6–41, 56–60.
[8] R.W. Barrett, Jr, *Against All England: Regional Identity and Cheshire Writing, 1195–1656* (Notre Dame, 2009), e.g. 7–9, 197–206.
[9] *DB Cheshire*, fo. 266 d. Villeins and bordars were categories of unfree peasant, the former normally with larger holdings than the latter.
[10] *DB Cheshire*, fo. 263 a.
[11] R. Swallow, 'Landscape of Power: Aldford Castle, Cheshire', *Ches. Hist.*, LII (2012–13), 5–28, at 6.
[12] I.D. Margary, *Roman Roads in Britain* (3rd edn, London, 1973), 297. The agger was the low linear mound on which the road surface had been laid.
[13] C. Hartwell, M. Hyde, E. Hubbard and N. Pevsner, *The Buildings of England: Cheshire* (rev. edn, New Haven and London, 2011), 94.
[14] Little Ness, Quatford, Smethcott and West Felton offer good examples of this arrangement in Shropshire and there are nearly 50 cases of churches within 220 yards of a motte in Herefordshire alone. See Ancient and Scheduled Monuments: England, Shropshire: <<https://ancientmonuments.uk/111771-motte-50m-south-east-of-st-martins-church-part-of-a-motte-and-bailey-castle-little-ness>>; <<https://ancientmonuments.uk/117209-motte-and-bailey-castle-90m-west-of-st-mary-magdalenes-church-quatford-bridgnorth>>; <<https://ancientmonuments.uk/106609-motte-and-bailey-castle-50m-to-the-west-of-st-michaels-church-smethcott>>; <<https://ancientmonuments.uk/117497-motte-castle-adjacent-to-st-michaels-church-west-felton>> all accessed 5/2/22; R. Morris, *Churches in the Landscape* (London, 1989), 248–53; J. Blair, *The Church in Anglo-Saxon Society* (Oxford, 2005), 387–90.
[15] J. Dodgson, *The Place-Names of Cheshire: Part IV* (Cambridge, 1977), 77.
[16] *Liber Luciani*, 63–64.
[17] *Calendar of Close Rolls, Edward I: 1272–1279* (London, HMSO, 1900), 281.

[18] S. Reynolds and G. White, 'A Survey of Aldford Castle' (plan by W. Cocroft), *Cheshire Past*, no. 4 (1995), 14–15; Geophysical Surveys of Bradford, 'Aldford Castle, Cheshire: report on Geophysical Survey', unpubl., 1996 (CCC report R2492); S. Ward, ed., 'Aldford Castle Cheshire 2000, Excavation Interim Report': Chester Archaeology Evaluation & Assessment Report no. 61, Chester City Council, unpubl., 2001 (CCC report R2348); S. Ward, 'Aldford Castle Cheshire 2002, Excavation Interim Report': Archaeological Service Evaluation & Assessment Report no. 66, Chester City Council, unpubl. 2003 (CCC report R2472).
[19] M. Shaw and J. Clark, *Cheshire Historic Towns Survey: Aldford Archaeological Assessment* (Chester, 2003), 4–5.
[20] Shaw and Clark, *Aldford Archaeological Assessment*, 8–9.
[21] CALS, D7404/1: A Map of part of the Township of Aldford & Churton … by Tho. Badelade, 1738.
[22] E.g. B.K. Roberts, *The Making of the English Village* (Harlow, 1987), 26–28, 174–75.
[23] Yorkshire Dales National Park Authority: Castle Bolton, Wensleydale – Conservation Area Character Appraisal: <<https://www.yorkshiredales.org.uk/wp-content/uploads/sites/13/2019/10/castle_bolton_conservation_area_character_appraisal_03-11-99_with_map-2.pdf>> accessed 21/5/21.
[24] P.H.W. Booth, 'The Corporation of Holt, the Manor of Farndon and the Bridge over the Dee', *Archaeologia Cambrensis*, CXLVI (1997), 109–16, at 109.
[25] D. Pratt, 'The Medieval Borough of Holt', *TDHS*, XIV (1965), 9–74, at 13; Booth, 'Corporation of Holt', 109.
[26] D. Pratt, 'The 1563 Charter of Holt', *TDHS*, XXIII (1974), 104–25.
[27] Booth, 'Corporation of Holt', 109–14; on different views on the date of the present bridge structure, cf. E. Hubbard, ed., *The Buildings of Wales: Clwyd* (Harmondsworth, 1986), 183 (under Holt) and Hartwell et al., *Buildings of England: Cheshire* (rev. edn), 359 (under Farndon).
[28] Clwyd Powys Archaeological Trust Historic Settlement Survey – Wrexham County Borough, Holt: <<https://www.cpat.org.uk/ycom/wrexham/holt.pdf>>; Wrexham Heritage, Holt Castle: <<https://www.wrexham.gov.uk/english/heritage/holt_castle/index.htm>> both accessed 11/10/19.

[29] Wrexham Heritage, Holt Castle: <<https://www.wrexham.gov.uk/english/heritage/holt_castle/index.htm>> accessed 11/10/19; British Listed Buildings, Holt Castle: <<https://britishlistedbuildings.co.uk/300001595-holt-castle-holt#.Yf1mjfjLeUk >> accessed 4/2/22. On the Principality of Chester, see R.R. Davies, 'Richard II and the Principality of Chester, 1397–99' in F.R.H. du Boulay and C.M. Barron, eds, *The Reign of Richard II* (London, 1971), 256–79.

[30] *Calendar of Ancient Correspondence concerning Wales*, ed. J.G. Edwards (Cardiff, 1935), 84.

[31] Pratt, 'Medieval Borough of Holt', 38, 55.

[32] Booth, 'Corporation of Holt', 112.

[33] K. Lilley, 'The Landscapes of Edward's New Towns: Their Planning and Design' in D. Williams and J. Kenyon, eds, *The Impact of the Edwardian Castles on Wales* (Oxford, 2009), 99–113; Archaeology Data Service: <<https://archaeologydataservice.ac.uk/archives/view/atlas_ahrb_2005/atlas.cfm?town=holt&CFID=7992650a-1d13-4b39-9c2f-1f5133171fa3&CFTOKEN=0#b2>> accessed 13/10/19, from which the quoted extract which follows is taken.

[34] Pratt, 'Medieval Borough of Holt', 53.

[35] M. Aston and J. Bond, *The Landscape of Towns* (London, 1976), 89–91.

[36] M.W. Beresford and J.K. St Joseph, *Medieval England: An Aerial Survey* (2nd edn, Cambridge, 1979), 179–83.

[37] Dodgson, *Place-Names of Cheshire: Part IV*, 61.

[38] TNA, C 1/1325/26: Court of Chancery, Six Clerks Office, Early Pleadings and Proceedings, Richard II to Philip and Mary, Lloyd v. Verch David ap Res., 1553–55.

[39] The quotations from Warburton, the Lord Chancellor and Pennant are all reproduced from Threapwood History Group, Threapwood Past: <<http://www.threapwoodhistory.org/threapwoodpast.html>> accessed 4/5/22.

[40] Threapwood History Group, Threapwood Past: <<http://www.threapwoodhistory.org/threapwoodpast.html>> accessed 4/5/22; CALS, Local Studies Collection 206831: T. Cox, 'Parochial Notes respecting Threapwood, Flintshire'.

[41] Threapwood History Group, Church and Chapel, School: <<http://www.threapwoodhistory.org/threapwoodpast.html>> accessed 4/5/22.

[42] F.A. Latham, *Tilston, Shocklach and Threapwood* (Whitchurch, 2001), 79.

[43] Threapwood History Group, *Threapwood Past*: <<http://www.threapwoodhistory.org/threapwoodpast.html>> accessed 4/5/22. CALS, Local Studies Collection 204787: Order under Section 9 of the Welsh Church Act, 1914.
[44] CALS, CCP 2/47: *Local Government Act*, 1894: Joint Committee order for transfer of townships of Shocklach Church, Shocklach Oviatt and part of Threapwood to County of Chester, 1894–96; *Local Government Board's Provisional Orders Confirmation (No. 13) Act*, 1896, 59 & 60 Vic. c.236; Threapwood History Group, *Threapwood Past*: <<http://www.threapwoodhistory.org/threapwoodpast.html>> accessed 4/5/22.
[45] *Village Design Statement, Threapwood* (2013), 4: <<http://www.threapwoodparishcouncil.co.uk/wp-content/uploads/2015/11/Threapwood-Village-Design-Statement-Adopted-12-December-2013.pdf>> accessed 4/2/22. On Threapwood, cf. G.J. White, 'Notes from the Editor and List of Abbreviations', *Ches. Hist.*, LXI (2021–22), 5–9, at 5–8.

Colour Plates

Plate 1: St John's church, Threapwood, an early nineteenth-century 'civilising' addition to the dispersed settlement (2022). Photograph: Graeme White.

Looking at the Landscape

Plate 2: Cringlemire (2018). Photograph: Mike Taylor.

Colour Plates

Plate 3: Early nineteenth-century listed buildings in Whitchurch and Ellesmere (2022). Photographs: Robert Ginder.

Plate 4: An early illustration of Chester Station from *Bradshaw's Guide* (Creative Commons ref. CC BY-SA 4.0).

Colour Plates

Plate 5: The Queen Hotel – a fine example of a railway hotel (2022). Photograph: Chris Pilsbury.

Plate 6: Neston Carnegie Library in 2014. The oval window in the gable is now largely obscured by trees. Photograph: Vanessa Greatorex.

Colour Plates

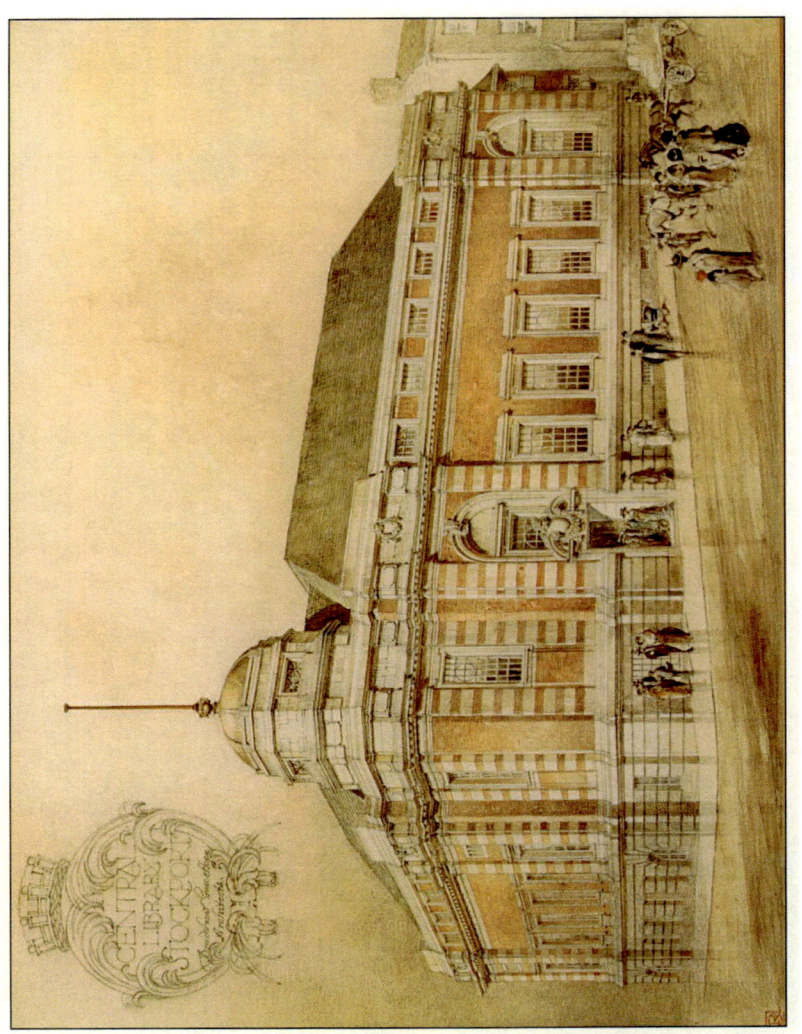

Plate 7: A 1909 perspective drawing of Stockport Central Carnegie Library by Roger Oldham of Bradshaw Gass & Hope. Hope Archives, scanned by Lingard, Public Domain.

Plate 8: Malpas town centre (2022) showing how the clustering of older buildings in the centre of the town distracts from the presence of modern buildings hidden from view downhill. Photograph: Graeme White.

3

CRINGLEMIRE – TAMING A LAKELAND LANDSCAPE

Maggie Taylor

Introduction

Cringlemire takes its name from the six-acre field on which it was built. Great Cringlemire was one of six lots on the Little Lowther estate that came up for auction at the Low Wood Hotel, Windermere, on 14 August 1860. James Nicholson of Thelwall Hall near Warrington attended and subsequently purchased this field with a view to building a second home there. The story of this landscaping and building project came to light in a collection of documents relating to the manor of Thelwall.[1] This paper traces the transformation of an exposed field overlooking Lake Windermere that involved negotiating a tricky social as well as natural landscape. Cringlemire still stands today (Plate 2) with new developments in its grounds, surrounded by mature shrubs and woodland trees some of which were part of a later garden design by Thomas Mawson.[2]

The Cheshire Connection

On the death of Thomas Abree Pickering in 1837, having no direct heirs, the bankrupt Thelwall estate was devised to his solicitor, William Nicholson.[3] The Nicholsons, Peter, the father, and sons William and James were all partners in a Warrington legal practice. They also served in the Territorial Army: Peter and William in the 3rd Royal Lancashire Militia and James in the King's Cheshire Yeomanry Cavalry. In 1843, as lord of the manor and patron of the old chapel dedicated to All Saints, William laid the foundation stone of the new church building. Shortly after, on his conversion to the Catholic faith, William left for Woolston on the other side of the River Mersey and his younger brother, James, took over the manor and estate of Thelwall and patronage of the church. Between them, the Nicholsons worked to improve the fortunes of the estate and were active in supporting the local community, its church and school.

In September 1852, James married Elizabeth Jones-Parry of Edern in North Wales. Her uncle, Revd William McIver, was rector of St Mary's at Lymm, some three miles (five kilometres) from Thelwall. James and Elizabeth probably met when she was visiting her relatives and large family there. In 1857, James and Elizabeth paid for the addition of a chancel at All Saints' with a brick vault beneath for members of the Nicholson family. The chancel reredos was dedicated to the memory of Elizabeth's parents, Revd John Jones-Parry and Margaret McIver.[4]

James and Elizabeth were living at Thelwall Hall, built in 1755 for Thomas Pickering, and it is easy to imagine the Nicholsons wanting another 'project' to interest them. It was a time when many professionals and businessmen were moving out of their residences in town to build more modern and fashionable homes in rural areas, away from all the noise and industrial pollution. Having no children, James and Elizabeth had the freedom to be creative in other ways, planning a new, more manageable property for use at their leisure and as an investment. A rebuild of Thelwall Hall would be inconvenient and by 1857, their expenditure on All Saints' new chancel with the Nicholson vault beneath was finished. A second home in a fashionable location was an exciting prospect and they now had the funds to do it. Their search area seems to have extended to the Lake District, as by this time brother William had moved to Southport and was Recorder at Lancaster Crown Court. James and Elizabeth probably made occasional visits there and beyond, thanks to the new railway connections. From 1854 they would have been able to take the train from Thelwall station to Warrington and connect with services to Preston, Kendal and Windermere.

Cringlemire – Taming a Lakeland Landscape

The Nicholsons were local pioneers in the search for a Lake District site on which to build a country retreat. Ten years later, in 1870, James Fenton Greenall of Grappenhall Hall in the neighbouring parish, commissioned Alfred Waterhouse to design Lingholm on the western shore of Derwentwater.[5] James was a partner in Parrs Bank and a member of the Greenall family of brewers. William Long, a tannery owner of Grappenhall, may have influenced Greenall's choice of architect with his new family home, Thelwall Heys, designed by Waterhouse in 1864. In 1899, William Long built Cleabarrow at Windermere, with a garden that was also designed by Thomas Mawson in 1900.[6]

Incomers
In 1847, the coming of the railway to Windermere opened up the Lake District to trade and tourism in a landscape lauded by the Romantic Movement. This was not a development welcomed by William Wordsworth who wrote *On the Projected Kendal and Windermere Railway*:

> Is there no nook of English ground secure
> From rash assault?[7]

Improved transport connections combined with the Lake District's natural beauty whetted the appetites of business and professional classes for a second home in the area and there were those willing to sell them the land on which to build. This Victorian influx might be seen as yet another wave of 'incomers' that have left their mark on this landscape over the centuries.

Great Cringlemire is situated on a hilly slope rising from 100 to 150 metres (approximately 330 feet to almost 500 feet) above Lake Windermere. It sits in the crook of two ancient track ways: to the south-west, a Roman road and to the east, an ancient packhorse trail (see Figure 1, overleaf). Research using Lidar technology has traced the Roman route from Watercrook Fort, Kendal to Galava at Waterhead, Ambleside.[8] This road passes Cringlemire on a steep

Looking at the Landscape

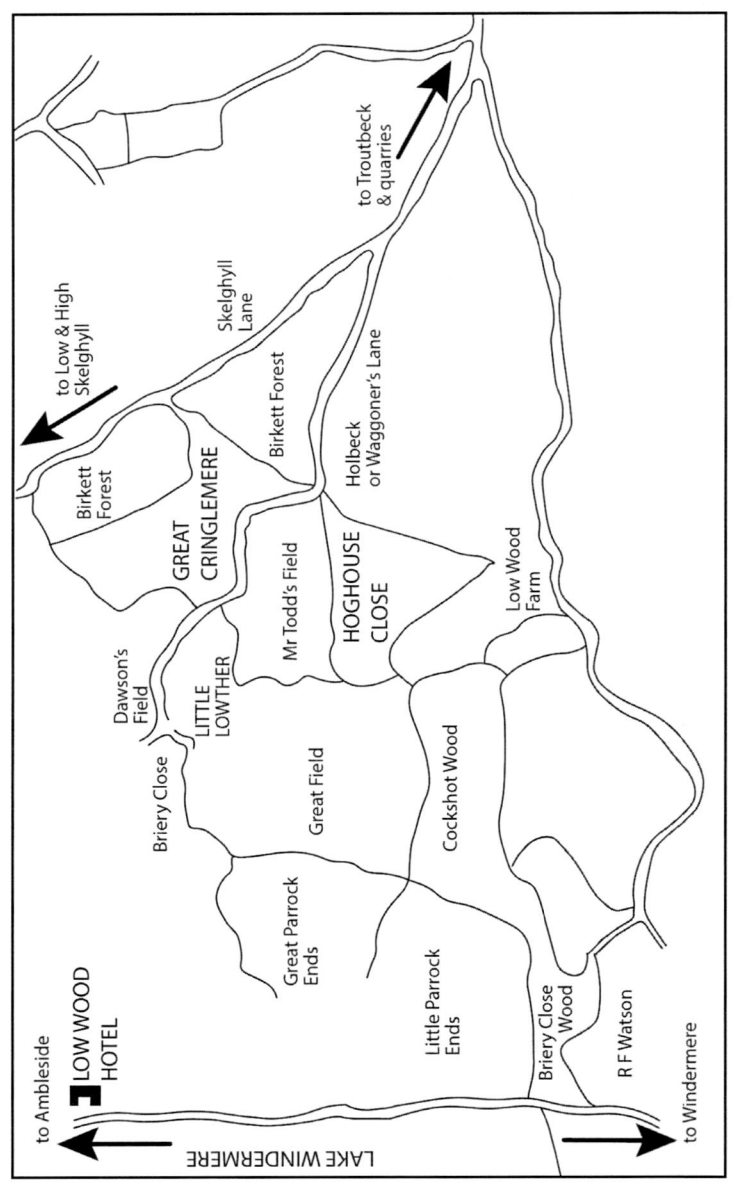

Figure 1: Little Lowther Estate (taken from a sketch by P. Sherwen).

track that has all the hallmarks of Roman engineering to negotiate steep gradients. To the east is the higher-level packhorse trail from Troutbeck. This goes up to Low Skelghyll (the site of the former Packhorse Inn) and on to Ambleside via High Skelghyll. Place- and field-names in the area reflect Anglo-Saxon and Scandinavian settlement. Cringlemire is the only field-name on the Little Lowther estate that derives from the Old Norse: *kringla* – a circle, twist or bend and *myrrh* – a muddy patch.[9] However, many place-names in the area such as Birthwaite, Claife, Wray, Clappersgate, Ambleside and even the name of Lake Windermere itself are Old Norse in origin.

The eighteenth and nineteenth centuries saw significant developments in transport networks in the Lake District with the growth of mining, quarrying, gunpowder manufacture and the woollen trade. In 1763, the Kendal to Ambleside turnpike opened the lower level route that runs near the eastern shore of Lake Windermere. This passed the Low Wood Inn which was originally a tenanted holding occupied by 'builders and slayters' with a quarry on site, then carriers, and eventually, innkeepers. The Low Wood achieved recognition as a posting inn by the late 1700s offering livery, a change of horses and refreshments for travellers on the mail coach route. Wars, revolutions and political instability in Europe affected the Grand Tour market, leading to a greater interest in the landscapes of the Lake District and Scotland for an eighteenth- and early nineteenth-century 'staycation'. The Low Wood Inn was ideally placed to meet this demand, becoming even more popular thanks to the paintings and poetic works of the Romantic Movement. Constable, Turner, Ruskin and William and Dorothy Wordsworth were among the visitors to Low Wood, not least to enjoy and record the vista over Lake Windermere to the fells and the Langdale Pikes in the distance.[10]

By 1845, the Low Wood Inn had become the Low Wood Hotel reflecting the clientele they sought to attract. But Low Wood was not just providing services for travellers and tourists. From 1828 it was also where the Petty Sessions Court was held and, later, the manor court of the earls of Lonsdale that regulated agricultural affairs and tenancy matters. The Low Wood Hotel was becoming an important legal and business hub for the area and an obvious place for the auction of the Little Lowther estate that lay behind it. It was also the place where documents of public interest could be seen. After the auction, letters from the Nicholsons' architect, Miles Thompson, state that the plans, specifications and invitation to tender for the Cringlemire contract would be available for public inspection at the hotel as well as his office in Kendal.

Customary Tenure

The auction notice that appeared in the press (Figure 2) sets out the lots by name and acreage. It mentions that the whole estate is of customary tenure held under the earl of Lonsdale, lord of the manor of Troutbeck, by payment of the yearly customary rent of 12s. 4d. and other dues and services. Customary tenure has long been a feature of land holding in Cumberland and Westmorland, whereby tenants are free to devise or sell their holding subject to payment of certain fees on any change of tenant or landlord as well as an annual charge.[11] This arrangement has its origins in the need

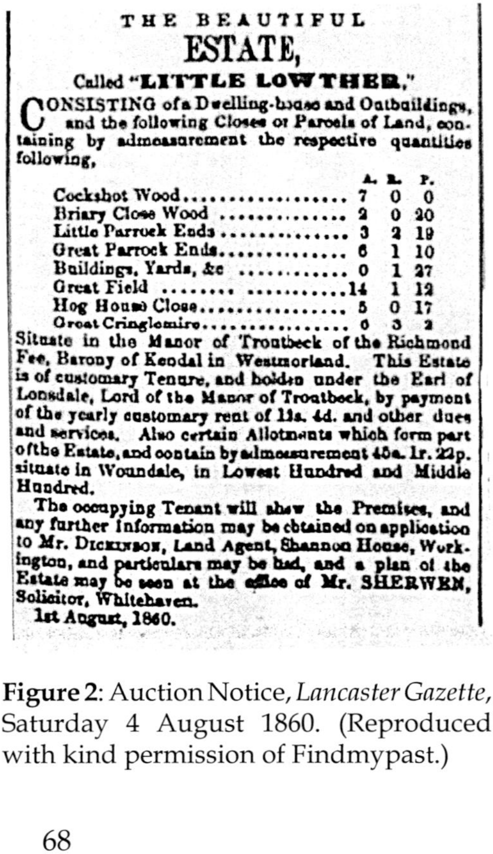

> THE BEAUTIFUL
> **ESTATE,**
> Called "**LITTLE LOWTHER**,"
> CONSISTING of a Dwelling-house and Outbuildings, and the following Closes or Parcels of Land, containing by admeasurement the respective quantities following,
>
> | | A. | R. | P. |
> |---|---|---|---|
> | Cockshot Wood | 7 | 0 | 0 |
> | Briary Close Wood | 2 | 0 | 20 |
> | Little Parrock Ends | 3 | 2 | 19 |
> | Great Parrock Ends | 6 | 1 | 10 |
> | Buildings, Yards, &c | 0 | 1 | 27 |
> | Great Field | 14 | 1 | 12 |
> | Hog House Close | 5 | 0 | 17 |
> | Great Cringlemire | 0 | 3 | 2 |
>
> Situate in the Manor of Troutbeck of the Richmond Fee, Barony of Kendal in Westmorland. This Estate is of customary Tenure, and holden under the Earl of Lonsdale, Lord of the Manor of Troutbeck, by payment of the yearly customary rent of 11s. 4d. and other dues and services. Also certain Allotments which form part of the Estate, and contain by admeasurement 45a. 1r. 22p. situate in Woundale, in Lowest Hundred and Middle Hundred.
>
> The occupying Tenant will shew the Premises, and any further Information may be obtained on application to Mr. DICKINSON, Land Agent, Shannon House, Workington, and particulars may be had, and a plan of the Estate may be seen at the office of Mr. SHERWEN, Solicitor, Whitehaven.
>
> 1st August, 1860.

Figure 2: Auction Notice, *Lancaster Gazette*, Saturday 4 August 1860. (Reproduced with kind permission of Findmypast.)

for landlords to call their tenants to arms in the event of raids from across the border. In return for this service and obligation, customary tenure offered some security to tenants' families and the local community.

The 2nd earl of Lonsdale, William Lowther, was unmarried with debts and expenses incurred by his love of opera and opera singers and the children they bore him, all of whom he recognised and supported. The Little Lowther estate was a comparatively small pocket of land in the Lonsdale portfolio and, being ideally placed to appeal to this new market of people seeking to build in a fashionable location, could generate much-needed funds from the sale and a modest annual income.

Selecting a Site

On seeing the advertisement in the press, James Nicholson wrote to the earl of Lonsdale's agent requesting further details of the site and the forthcoming auction. Mr Peter Sherwen of Whitehaven replied on 10 August 1860 forwarding a plan of the Little Lowther estate (Figure 1) stating that:

> The Property has good building sites commanding Views of Windermere Lake, & the Lake Mountains. It is proposed to offer the Estate for Sale in six different Lots, & the whole will then be put for Sale, & which ever way brings the highest Price, the Purchaser will of course be disclosed. (Underlining in source.)

What type of auction was this – to auction it in lots then auction it as a whole to get the best price? This practice is not common today but in the past it was used to give estate landowners control of the process and protect the interests of existing tenants.[12]

A plan of the area accompanied Sherwen's letter. Nicholson had very little time in which to visit the site and make arrangements to attend but he had long enough to appraise himself of other interested parties, in particular Mr John Brookes of Little Lowther. It appears there was some agreement between them not to compete for the same lots to avoid inflating the price for each one. A possible land-swap was mooted before the auction: Cringlemire for Hoghouse Close as Nicholson was undecided as to which would be the best site. In the aftermath there seems to have been some heated written exchanges between them regarding Hoghouse Close and Todd's Field that was adjacent to it (see Figure 1). Brookes sought to secure his existing boundaries with the purchase of Todd's Field but if the land-swap were to go ahead, it only made sense if Nicholson could purchase some two acres of Todd's Field to create a more impressive entrance to a property built on Hoghouse Close. Mr Todd attempted to play one party off against the other, upping the price and making conditions, such that stalemate was reached and none of the parties went ahead.

Why all the fuss? After the auction, the architect, Miles Thompson of Kendal, received instructions from James Nicholson to visit both sites and report on their relative merits. The main issues for Thompson were the availability of water, stone and shelter. His letters indicate a strong preference for Hoghouse Close on the grounds that it was more sheltered. Cringlemire lacked stock timber for shelter but it did have 'good, sound stone for building purposes'. Thompson submitted sketches in red on the original map, identifying access points and where a house could be located on each field to get the best view of Lake Windermere. He then awaited further instructions from Nicholson following his meeting with Brookes to sort out their differences over Todd's Field and any land-swap. No further mention is made of Hoghouse Close after 7 September 1860 and a visitor there today would find the field just as it was in 1860.

For the rest of September the Nicholsons visited other properties in the area designed by Thompson and began to specify their requirements. This was probably not their first encounter with his style since they may have stayed at the Windermere Hotel on previous visits to the area. This purpose-built hotel had been commissioned by the Kendal and Windermere Railway Company and built by Abraham Pattinson of Bowness.[13] Thompson and Pattinson had worked together on a number of projects that included public buildings as well as domestic residences, so it was not surprising that Pattinson subsequently bid for the Cringlemire contract and secured it. On 29 September 1860, Thompson forwarded two sets of plans and elevations, one for a larger property, the other a slightly smaller one. He requested the Nicholsons look at the plans carefully and suggest any modifications at this point, it being easier to change lines on a drawing than when building work was underway.

Sadly, these plans are not among the Nicholson papers and it has not been possible to establish which of the two designs they selected. The only records of floor plans for Cringlemire are to be found in Kendal Archive Centre.[14] However, the first set, dated May 1893, was prepared by Joseph Pattinson, architect of Windermere for Henry Martin, a merchant from Halifax. The second, dated July 1910, was prepared for his son, Thomas Martin, by W. Mason, FRIBA, architect and surveyor of Ambleside and Windermere. The first set was particularly helpful in clarifying the orientation and layout agreed by the Nicholsons.

A Change of Land Use
What was the setting for this new venture? The sketch map (Figure 1) along with the place- and field-names of the auction lots indicate this was a working pastoral landscape.[15] Cockshot Wood (OE) suggests a place for hunting woodcock while Great and Little Parrock Ends (OE) were paddocks used for grazing. Great Field suggests common land for growing crops, but 'Great', in this context, might simply reflect its size. The other place- and field-names are good descriptors of distinctive features or their particular use. As we have seen, Cringlemire (ON) describes 'a circular patch of wet and boggy ground' or a 'circle, twist or bend with boggy ground'. Briery Close (OE) was probably so-called for its wild roses while Hoghouse Close (OE) indicates a shelter for 'hoggs' or 'hoggets', the name given to one-year-old sheep. These young sheep would be

kept separately from the rest of the breeding ewes for another year or two before going to the ram.

An interesting feature of Hoghouse Close and Cringlemire is that both have a 'funnel' situated at the higher level where a narrow gate gives on to a lane – Holbeck Lane in the case of Hoghouse Close and Skelghyll Lane for Cringlemire. These funnel arrangements are particularly useful for handling livestock, confining them to a narrow space with hurdles so they could be checked and sorted before going to market or on to the fells. It would suggest these fields could be used for lairage[16] on the packhorse routes or for overwintering livestock. This is confirmed in a letter from Thomas Fleming of Ecclerigg Farm who was the sitting tenant on Great Cringlemire at the time of the auction.

Before any site preparation could begin, some agreement had to be reached between the parties about vacating the site. Fleming wrote:

> In answer to your enquiry about the Field on the Little Lowther Estate, I have given due consideration and I find it will put me to great inconvenience to give up possession at this time of year As I keep these Fields purposely for Wintering young stock after coming from the High Pastures in the Autumn, but rather than disappoint you I will give up all possession if you will allow me to have the field until the 12th day of October 1860 by giving me £10-0-0 … in the meantime Mr Grier may trench in the Field providing the Fences are not pulled down so as to let the Cattle or Sheep stray on the Road.[17]

The timing is interesting here as the date coincides with the annual livestock sales at Ambleside.

The Mr Grier mentioned in this letter is John Grier, nurseryman, florist and seedsman of Waterhead, Ambleside. In Harriet Martineau's *Complete Guide to the English Lakes* of 1854, he features in the Directory and the Advertisements section listing the plant species offered.[18]

The 1861 census locates Grier at Gale Howe, Below Stock and in 1871 on Lake Road, Ambleside. His nursery gardens of ten acres were probably in the vicinity of the present-day Hayes Garden Centre and the large car park across the road from Waterhead Pier.[19]

Cringlemire – Taming a Lakeland Landscape

   The taming of Great Cringlemire owes much to Grier, not only for his knowledge of plants and landscape design but also his patience in dealing with neighbours' concerns and conveying them to James Nicholson as the project got underway. It was Grier's responsibility to secure the boundaries by repairing the stone walls as necessary. He also had to break through them to relocate the access from Skelghyll Lane to a point on Holbeck Lane more convenient for a residence. With this in prospect, it seems plans were already underway to widen the road here that Thompson only learned of after the auction. This was to rumble on until December 1860 when the Surveyor of the Highways came to discuss payment. Having just purchased the land, James Nicholson was about to lose some of it for the common good! The parties seem to have come to an agreement and the timing was right because Arthur Jackson, the 'waller', had yet to start work on the stretch abutting Holbeck Lane.

   There was something about the shape of Great Cringlemire that seemed to offend the senses of James Nicholson and his architect. On each side of the funnel arrangement were fields belonging to Birkett Forest (Figure 1). If these could be acquired it would mean a straight run of walling up to Skelghyll Lane on either side. Another advantage would be access to a spring, the source of water running through Great Cringlemire. Nicholson seems to have had an eye to straightening the circular wall to the west that separated Cringlemire from Dawson's field although his architect pointed out he would be losing more land if he did. Negotiations over these proposed land exchanges were protracted and complicated; Birkett Forest died, his estate being managed by trustees until his son came of age. Dawson of Crag House, Troutbeck was often away with his regiment in Gibraltar or Ireland leaving his mother or sister to deal with matters on his behalf and they were inclined to rebuff all approaches. It took some time to resolve these issues as neighbours came to terms with Nicholson's intentions for a totally different use for the site: a new house with a kitchen garden and pleasure grounds that would take some two to three years to complete.

Looking at the Landscape

John Grier, as the one person regularly on site in the early days of this development, wrote to Nicholson to express the locals' concerns about his plans to use wire fencing rather than traditional stone walls. Metal and wire fencing may have been satisfactory around Thelwall's comparatively well-sheltered fields with their trees and hedgerows. In the more exposed Lake District landscape, stone walls have provided essential protection for livestock in all weathers for centuries. Nicholson may have felt Cringlemire offered an opportunity for 'land improvement' or perhaps he just wanted to support a thriving Warrington industry but neighbours' concerns centred on possible damage to Nicholson's property and the risk to their animals of 'noxious shrubs'. This was not a criticism of Nicholson's plans for pleasure grounds but concern for the health of their livestock and their pockets. Plants like laurel and rhododendron can poison and kill sheep and cattle if ingested. Any loss arising from this and having to pay for damage to any new planting scheme was to be avoided. The matter was settled to the satisfaction of all parties with stone boundary walls, not wire fences or wooden hurdles. Good walls make good neighbours!

Establishing a well-stocked and productive kitchen garden was a priority along with providing quick-growing trees and shrubs for shelter. For Grier, the project was starting at an ideal time for planting, especially fruit trees, it being their dormant season from October to March. An early start would ensure they were established and could supply the house when it was ready for occupation in two to three years' time. The delays caused by land exchange negotiations, the proposed road widening scheme and deteriorating weather conditions were frustrating. But first, the stony ground had to be prepared.

The Local Geology

Using stone extracted from the site made sense in terms of saving time, money and energy.[20] The foundations and cellars had to be dug out and a kitchen garden area prepared that was to measure 30 by 50 yards (28 by 48 metres). Any stones of appropriate size found in the course of 'trenching' could be used for boundary walls, for the kitchen garden walls and drainage purposes. They might even be used for building the house if they were of the right quality. Thompson had certainly seemed to imply this was possible from his initial reconnaissance missions. Some stone would have been surface-gathered, some re-used from making a breach in the wall on Holbeck Lane, while other material may have been taken from an outcrop on site; mention was made of a quarry two fields away above Cringlemire on Birkett Forest's land. Grier's first account includes gunpowder for blasting and bills from local carriers mention 'carting of stons' [sic] in 1861 and 1862. Abraham Pattinson's account for March 1862 includes 78 cartloads of stones brought from a quarry in Troutbeck for 'building and gateways'.[21]

What was the underlying geology of this site? The whole of the Little Lowther estate sits on rocks of the Windermere Supergroup that include strata of the Upper Ordovician and Silurian period.[22] These are made up of mudstones, siltstones and sandstone and their porous nature is such that they tend not to be suitable for general building purposes but some strata have been found to be well suited to a particular use. For example, quarries at Troutbeck working the Wray Castle Formation produced substantial quantities of thick Lakeland roofing slates.[23] At Low Skelghyll, larger stones and slabs from the Brathay Formation could be found.[24] These were the raw materials available and much would depend on the eye of the craftsmen to select the best for a particular purpose or situation.

Importing better stone from elsewhere would be expensive and bricks would have to be transported from Preston. So the architect's skill in anticipating problems arising from this mix of location, weather, orientation and material quality would be crucial. The specifications would need to incorporate features into the design of the house and its setting to secure a satisfactory outcome.

Building Cringlemire

The demands of the client and design preferences of the architect for this 'pretty little villa'[25] meant the building would be oriented to the west. This would give the best possible views of Lake Windermere but the worst possible exposure to the elements. The only ways to 'design out' the problem would be to employ particular construction techniques and materials best suited to local weather conditions alongside providing protection with a shelterbelt of trees and shrubs. The locals certainly knew there would be problems. In a letter to Nicholson, dated 19 September 1860, Thompson wrote:

> I find neither Fleming nor Dawson like the exact spot where you are going to build for being too high, and wanting shelter; the formen [sic] jokingly said some day you will find the House, or some of it blown into Birkett Forrests Field, but both admit the view is the finest there.[26]

Perhaps this was Thompson's way of reminding his client that the location would not have been his first choice!

Thompson and Pattinson were well versed in the vernacular architecture of their locality and features such as extended roof overhangs or 'watershot' masonry would be familiar to them as a means of managing porous stone and the high rainfall of the Lake District.[27] Certainly many of Thompson's designs are characterised by large overhanging roofs and decorative bargeboards, verandahs and a front door leading into a porch or vestibule with a further door leading into a hallway, making use of glass above doorways to allow light in.

Lime mortar and plaster were used. While these materials allow stonework to breathe, the mortar can wash out in driving rain and lime plaster will absorb moisture. Pattinson's accounts for 1862 record quantities of Portland cement. This cement is hydrophobic, but the mortar does not allow the stonework to breathe. Whichever mortar was used, any water ingress around chimneys, windows and doors would eventually rot the woodwork and cause damage to the interior fabric and decoration. These problems arose during the build and at various times during the Nicholsons' ownership. In March 1869, William Dixon, joiner and cabinet-maker of Ambleside, reported that most of the walls in the upper rooms and beneath the chimney stacks were completely wet. He attributed the problem to poor quality stone for the chimneys combined with a most unusual winter for rain and storms that had affected many properties in the neighbourhood. Various solutions were proposed, such as modifications to window closures and catches and Dixon even suggested rendering the chimneys, if not the whole building, with Portland cement.

A number of properties in the area like Townend at Troutbeck, have used cement rendering to address problems of porous stone quality and water ingress. This tends to be a relatively temporary, cosmetic solution requiring regular maintenance with a coat of lime-wash or paint. Sadly, this can also exacerbate problems of damp patches on the internal fabric and decoration of the property. Cement rendering does not seem to have been adopted at Cringlemire.

Weather Conditions
The letters from Thompson and Grier make frequent mention of the weather as the cause of delays and problems subsequently experienced with the building once it was occupied. Was the weather an excuse for absenteeism, bad workmanship or based on actual fact? The project was hampered by snow at the start but the main culprit seems to have been the rain. The Lake District has the highest annual rainfall of anywhere in England but there are variations across the region and over time.[28] Thanks to amateur meteorologists, Lake District records go back to the 1780s. For Windermere, the record starts in 1866. During the five-year period 1866–70, the mean annual rainfall was 71.96 inches. The wettest years were 1866 (80.96 inches) and 1868 (80.21 inches). The mean annual rainfall during the subsequent five-year periods, 1871–75 and 1876–80, fell to 68.84 and 64.34 inches respectively. However, there were individual years such as 1872 and 1877 when the annual

rainfall exceeded 85 inches. The wettest months of the year for Windermere were December through to February and the lowest rainfall from April/May to July.[29] This suggests delays to the start of the building programme could be attributed to adverse weather conditions. Heavy precipitation during the winter months of subsequent years would go on to pose maintenance problems for Cringlemire throughout the Nicholsons' tenure.

Another factor, affecting the availability of workmen, was that many of them were agricultural labourers picking up casual work at Cringlemire – clearing the site, trenching or providing carting services from local quarries. At certain times of year the community priority would be to help with seasonal work at harvest time or help with 'the gather' – bringing sheep down off the fells for shearing, tupping or for the annual sales.

The weather was always going to be an issue for any building situated in this particular locality but some of the problems might be attributed to matters of communication and organisation. There seemed to be no one permanently on site with day-to-day responsibility for overseeing the project. It was largely a matter of trust. The Nicholsons were dependent on the local knowledge and judgement of their architect and builder in the employment of craftsmen and sub-contractors. The joiners and carpenters, plumbers, painters and glaziers, plasterers, bell hangers, masons and wallers, cabinet-makers, blacksmiths and carters were all drawn from around Windermere – from Bowness, Hawkshead, Ambleside, Low Skelghyll and Troutbeck. Progress depended on their availability at the right time in the building sequence but this was not always possible.

John Grier's presence on site in all weathers in the earliest days of the project was crucial to getting the project off the ground as neighbours shared issues of local concern with him so he could seek a decision from James Nicholson. Grier's services in this respect do not figure in his bills so it is understandable he felt aggrieved when challenged over the volume and cost of plants, trees and shrubs as well as other materials and services itemised in his first account. Most of the plants had to be purchased in advance and 'heeled in' at Cringlemire until the time when they could be planted in their proper place in the kitchen garden or pleasure grounds. The result was more administrative work for Grier as he was obliged to get confirmation from James Nicholson before any future work or purchases were undertaken. James always went through every account in great detail, challenging them where he felt he had been overcharged or was paying for materials that he himself had provided. In the case of Grier's first bill, Nicholson's mood was probably tempered by the fact that he had to make the final payment on his land purchase at that time.

How Long Did it Take to Build Cringlemire?
From the correspondence between Thompson, Grier and the Nicholsons, we can begin to piece together the story of this building project and progress on the gardens. In November 1860, Thompson and Grier had pegged out the Holbeck Lane entrance and the carriage road leading up to the site for the house. Grier was also getting underway with a shelterbelt of laurels in preparation for Pattinson's men coming up to build a shelter for the labourers and their equipment. Rain and snow hampered progress in these early stages but the accounts reveal that Nicholson paid for a 'rearing treat for the workmen' in May 1861, suggesting the roof was now on and the structure secured. In September 1861, the Nicholsons stayed at the Low Wood Hotel as the house was not yet ready for occupation but Thompson hoped they might expect occupancy in early spring 1862. That same month, the Nicholsons made decisions on the interior decoration for the house and on the choice of a kitchen range. Sadly, bad weather caused further setbacks as Thompson's letter of 14 December 1861 reveals; while he could report that the walls and roof were dry, a good deal of water had come into the casements with the strong driving winds and there was damp to the south and west fronts of the building.

Looking at the Landscape

Things took longer than the Nicholsons had hoped and Thompson's report seemed to spur them to action. On 4 January 1862, Edward Severn of Laskey Lane in Thelwall was sent to keep an eye on progress and report back. Accompanied by a man called Roberts and a load of luggage, they arrived to find the place 'in a very unfinished state'. In March that year, Thompson reported trouble with the windows and, as we have seen, this problem was to crop up again in subsequent years. In February 1863, the final bills were submitted and Thompson's task was to do a final check, visiting the site to assess each item for quality, counting slabs and measuring wall lengths among other matters of detail before advising the Nicholsons that the accounts were fair and correct. On 16 April, the parties attended a settlement meeting where the final accounts were presented.

Taming a Lakeland Landscape
It took over three years to transform Great Cringlemire from a field to a desirable residence overlooking Lake Windermere. The site presented tremendous challenges being at an elevation that was difficult to access, exposed to the weather and in a locality that did not offer the most suitable stone for building. Despite this, the house still stands today although much modified and extended along with further properties built in the extensive grounds.

It took an army of labourers, wallers and plasterers to build the house with men, horses and carts transporting stone from nearby quarries. Pattinson's contract was for £550 and there were other sub-contractors' bills to add but the records are incomplete. At the outset, Miles Thompson had advised the Nicholsons that costs could be in the region of £1,000–£1,500. As to the gardens, it took 32 men to landscape the site under Grier's direction at a cost of approximately £301. Nearly 5,000 trees, shrubs, fruit and nut trees and canes were planted over this three-year period. Once the building was occupied, Grier's business continued to provide maintenance services for a few more years, particularly with pruning and training fruit trees in the kitchen garden.

The property was staffed with a housekeeper and a manservant. Also, Thomas Davies was employed as gardener and handyman; his entertaining letters give insights into local life as well as the state of Cringlemire and its grounds. The Nicholsons used the house for their own enjoyment at certain times of year as bills from the Low Wood Hotel testify – bills for carriage from the station, to and from churches in Troutbeck and Ambleside, boats to Wray Castle, hire of ponies and also beer, wine and spirits. The property was also let for one guinea a day and there are letters from visitors on settling their account, commenting on their time at Cringlemire that usually included reference to the weather and the courtesy (or otherwise) of the staff.

The story of Cringlemire is told through an 'in-tray' of letters, notes, bills and receipts sent to the Nicholsons. Elizabeth pre-deceased James, but his death notice appears in the Chester, Warrington and Ulverston press of July and August 1899 describing him as 'of Thelwall Hall and Cringlemire'.[30] Clearly, both residences were important to the Nicholsons. Thelwall Hall was demolished in the 1950s; the only trace of the capital house of that manorial estate is a platform of scrub in Elizabeth Park but Cringlemire survives as the Nicholsons' legacy in the Cumbrian landscape today (Plate 2).

Endnotes
[1] CALS, DDW 3765/76/4, DDW 3765/76/5, DDW 3765/77/4: Collection of letters, notes, bills and receipts relating to the building of Cringlemire, 1860–1872.
[2] Kendal Archive Centre, WDB 86: Thomas W. Mawson. For further reading see J. Waymark, *Thomas Mawson: Life, Gardens and Landscape* (London, 2009), 18, 42, 43.
[3] M. Taylor, *No Mean City* (rev. edn, Thelwall, 2021), 161–62.
[4] M. and M. Taylor, *The Log of Admiral John Parry Jones-Parry: From Cadet to Lieutenant 1845–1858* (Thelwall, 2021), 100–1, 171.

[5] B. Cooke, *The Story of Warrington – The Athens of the North* (Kibworth Beauchamp, 2020), 295.
[6] N. Froggatt, oral communication, 21/2/22.
[7] W. Wordsworth, 'On the Projected Kendal and Windermere Railway' Sonnet, October 1844: <<www.bl.uk/onlinegallery/onlineex/kinggeorge/p/027add000044361u00278000.html>> accessed 27/7/21.
[8] D. Ratledge, The Roman Road from Watercrook to Ambleside, Margary 70f (2017), Roman Roads Research Association: <<www.romanroads.org/gazetteer/Cumbria/M70f>> accessed 14/12/21.
[9] A.J.L. Winchester, *Lake District Field-Names: A Guide for Local Historians* (Lancaster, 2017), 44, 50.
[10] M. Berry and R. Yuen, *A Sunlit, Intimate Gift … Low Wood: Three Hundred Years of Lakeland History, A Tribute to the Tri-centenary of the Low Wood Hotel 1702–2002* (Windermere, 2002).
[11] Customary Tenure: <<https://www.lancaster.ac.uk/fass/projects/manorialrecords/manors/whatis.htm#CustomaryTenantright>> accessed 5/12/21.
[12] S. Cleaver, Estate Agent, oral communication, 5/12/21.
[13] D. Matthews, great-granddaughter of Abraham Pattinson, personal correspondence, 27/5/16.
[14] Kendal Archive Centre, WDB 133/2/192: Cringlemire alterations for Henry Martin, May 1893; alterations for Thomas Martin, July 1910.
[15] Winchester, *Lake District Field-Names*, 40–56.
[16] Lairage is a place where cattle or sheep may be rested on their way to market (or slaughter).
[17] CALS, DDW 3765/76/4, DDW 3765/76/5, DDW 3765/77/4: full description see endnote 1.
[18] H. Martineau, *A Complete Guide to the English Lakes* (Windermere, 1854), xi, 215.
[19] 1861 Census, Ambleside District 2, Below Stock. Schedule No.157, Gale Howe, John Grier, nurseryman, gardener of 10 acres employing eight labourers and two boys: <<https://ancestry.co.uk/imageviewer/collctions/8767/images/WESRG9_3964-0325>> accessed 1/3/22.
[20] S. Denyer, *Traditional Buildings and Life in the Lake District* (The National Trust, 1991), 148–63.
[21] CALS, DDW 3765/76/4: Abraham Pattinson's accounts, March 1862.

[22] *Strategic Stone Study: A Building Stone Atlas of Cumbria and the Lake District*, English Heritage, 2013: <<https://cumbria.gov.uk/elibrary/Content/Internet/538/755/1929/177716/42117103947.PDF>> accessed 14/12/21.
[23] *Strategic Stone Study*, English Heritage.
[24] D. Cooper, oral and email communication, 12/12/21.
[25] CALS, DDW 3765/76/5, see endnote 1.
[26] CALS, DDW/3765/76/5: Extract from letter to James Nicholson from Miles Thompson, 19 Sept. 1860.
[27] R.W. Brunskill, *Traditional Buildings of Cumbria: The County of the Lakes* (Yale, 2010), 157.
[28] P.A. Barker, R.L. Wilby and A.J. Borrows, 'A 200-year Precipitation Index for the Central English Lake District', *Hydrological Sciences-Journal-des-Sciences Hydrologiques*, XLIX (5) (October 2004), 769–70.
[29] G.J. Symons, *Rainfall tables of the British Isles for 1866–1880 M.O. 47*: <<https://library.metoffice.gov.uk>recordview>index>> Archive reference: MET/2/1/3/48. Online access METDLA/3/4 Search for No. 268 – Windermere, The Wood, Observer – Rev. G. Crewdson accessed 17/12/21.
[30] *Chester Courant*, 31 July 1889, 6. *Warrington Observer*, 27 July 1889, 5. *Soulby's Ulverston Advertiser and General Intelligencer*, 1 Aug. 1889, 6. Available: <<https://www.findmypast.co.uk>> accessed 21/2/22.

4

EARLY NINETEENTH-CENTURY GROWTH IN THREE NORTH SHROPSHIRE MARKET TOWNS AND THE INFLUENCE OF THE ELLESMERE CANAL

Robert Ginder

This study originated during research carried out for a *Victoria County History* publication on Wem.[1] The research focused on trade directories and revealed a major increase in the number of traders between the 1790s and 1830s – the period of the Napoleonic Wars and the subsequent slump and recovery. One significant factor was the Ellesmere Canal; this opened fully in 1805, traversing north Shropshire, and connecting it with the port of Chester and the Mersey, and with coalfields and mineral sources along the Welsh border. Trinder had noted that 'the five market towns of north Shropshire … all owed some of their nineteenth-century prosperity to canals'.[2] Whitchurch and Ellesmere, along with Wem, were the three towns benefiting specifically from the Ellesmere Canal at this stage, as the other towns, Market Drayton and Newport, were not added to the canal system until much later. Although the Ellesmere Canal originally had more strategic ambitions, it was promoted principally as an agricultural waterway with traffic mainly in coal, lime, grain and malt, as well as building materials and commercial goods. As it was known that Ellesmere became a significant malting centre for barley in this period,[3] and the trade was also significant in Whitchurch and Wem, the influence of local agriculture seemed worth investigating. These factors stimulated the present study into the canal, its trade, business growth in the three towns and agricultural developments in the area, including the influences these had upon each other, in the period from the 1790s to the 1830s.

Three North Shropshire Market Towns and the Ellesmere Canal

Early Canals in the Region

The canal age commenced with the opening of the Duke of Bridgewater's short canal from his coal mines in Worsley to Manchester in 1762, which was later extended to the Mersey at Runcorn, giving a connection to Liverpool.[4] The Duke, along with his brother-in-law, Earl Gower, was also involved in a canal from the Bridgewater through Cheshire and the Potteries to the Trent, thus linking two major rivers, and providing routes to the Midlands and the east coast (Figure 1, overleaf). This Trent and Mersey Canal (T&M) opened fully in 1777.[5] Earlier, in 1772 the Severn at Stourport was also connected to the Trent, and to canals in Birmingham and the Black Country.[6] These early canals were generally successful, reducing the price of coal and other bulk materials dramatically compared with road transport, spurring industrialisation and providing handsome profits for their investors.

A notably less successful example was the Chester Canal, proposed to combat competition for the city from the upcoming port of Liverpool by connecting the lower Dee to the T&M at Middlewich; this gave access to Manchester and the Midlands, with a branch to Nantwich.[7] Although the proposed junction with the T&M faced strong objections, a line to Nantwich was completed in 1779, but no work was done on the branch to Middlewich. Although Nantwich was a thriving market and gentry town, serving the passing trade on the London to Chester turnpike, this isolated stretch of canal fell far short of the original objective of connecting Chester's port to an extensive hinterland, and little trade was forthcoming. In spite of this and other difficulties, the canal company just managed to keep the canal open, encouraged by the prospect of a beneficial junction with the proposed Ellesmere Canal.[8]

In Shropshire, the earliest canals to be constructed were industrial ones, to transport raw materials between the coal mines, quarries and industrial sites in the east Shropshire coalfield and to ship their products down to the River Severn.[9] The final addition to

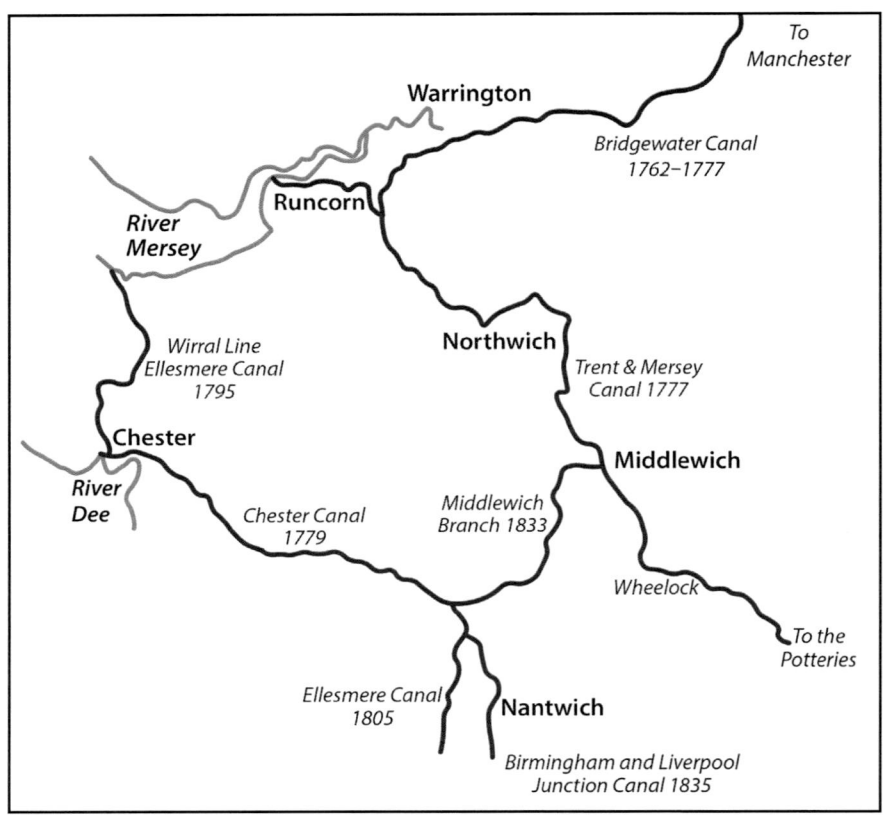

Figure 1: Regional Canal Network.

this system, completed in 1796, was a link to Shrewsbury, to supply the town with coal and limestone.

The Ellesmere Canal
In 1791 a more strategic project known as the Ellesmere Canal was proposed to link Shrewsbury and the upper Severn with the lower Dee at Chester, and then cross the Wirral to the Mersey estuary. It would pass through north Shropshire and close to the mineral

sources and coalfield industries along the border of north-east Wales, supplying both county towns.[10] A south-westerly branch was proposed from the canal's centre near Ellesmere to quarries and mines near Llanymynech, together with a north-easterly branch towards Prees (near to Wem) and to Whitchurch. It was an ambitious scheme requiring many locks, long tunnels and high-level aqueducts to cross the Dee and Ceiriog and to reach Chester. It was nevertheless received enthusiastically, with the initial share offering substantially oversubscribed at the inaugural meeting chaired by the canal duke. An alternative less ambitious eastern route was not favoured when the leading canal engineer William Jessop was appointed to overview the challenging western route. Thomas Telford, then the county surveyor for Shropshire, was appointed to act as 'General Agent, Surveyor, Engineer and Overlooker of the Works'.

The Wirral section, opening first in 1795, was a broad waterway linking the Chester Canal with the Mersey estuary at Whitby (which became known as Ellesmere Port), enabling river craft, including passenger boats, to pass between Chester and Liverpool, and generating revenue to help finance construction of the rest of the canal. This section took water from the Chester Canal, on the understanding that the two canals would eventually meet. The Llanymynech branch was completed in 1796 and by 1797 the section south of the aqueducts was complete to Weston Lullingfields and work on the Whitchurch branch had started. However, the viability of the canal as a supplier to Shrewsbury and Chester was now doubted, due to competition with the newly opened Shrewsbury Canal on one hand and from horse-drawn tramways on the other. The expense of the remaining lock construction and tunnelling was also a major consideration, while Telford's famous Pontcysyllte aqueduct, pioneering the use of iron and requiring many years' work, was a major constructional challenge. Hence, no further work was done south of Weston or northwards beyond the Pontcysyllte basin, apart from a feeder channel to the Dee Falls above Llangollen.

Looking at the Landscape

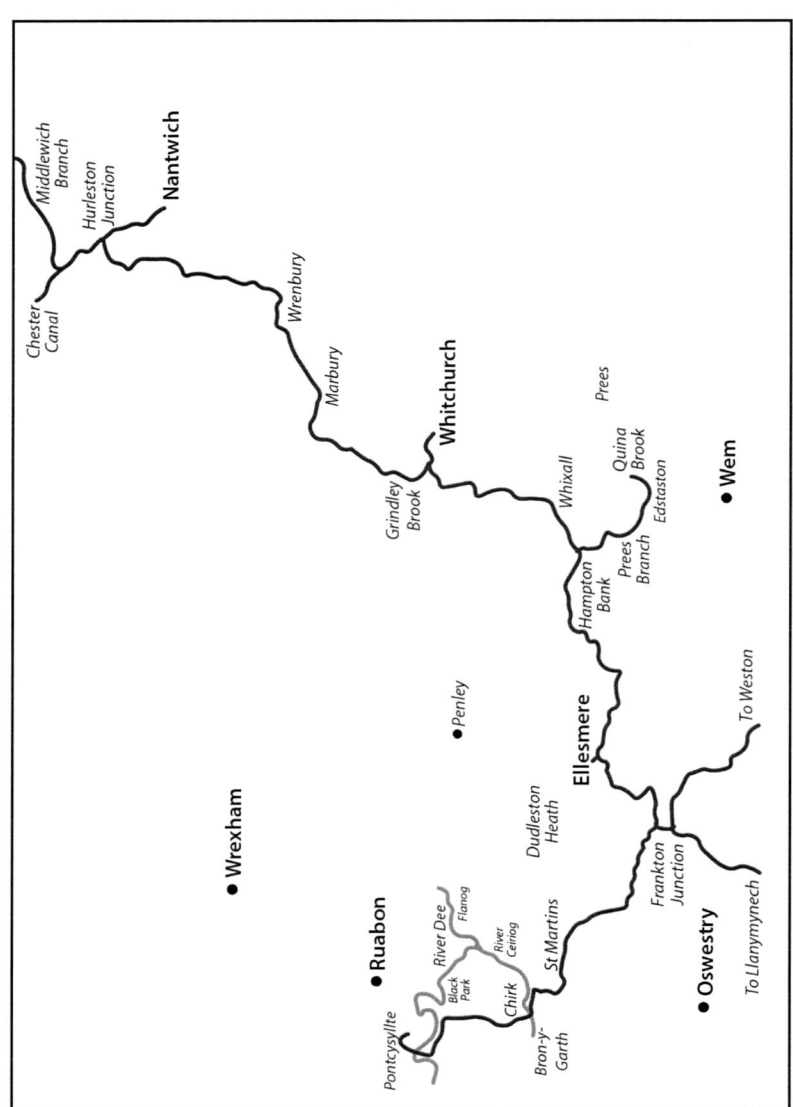

Figure 2: Ellesmere Canal.

Three North Shropshire Market Towns and the Ellesmere Canal

Instead, it was decided to extend the Whitchurch branch to meet the Chester Canal at Hurleston near Nantwich, which was achieved in 1805; the same year as the Pontcysyllte aqueduct opened (Figure 2, opposite).

The lack of direct connections to Shrewsbury and Chester robbed the canal of much of its intended purpose. While some commercial traffic was still expected, the canal was now promoted mainly as an agricultural waterway, supplying Welsh coal and other bulk materials, particularly agricultural lime, to rural north Shropshire, and taking produce to market. Lime kilns were sited at close intervals along the canal, supplemented by banks of several kilns at key locations, including the canal termini at Weston Wharf and Quina Brook near Wem, the closest points to Shrewsbury.

Trade on the Canal

The canal soon became busy with traffic in coal, lime, building materials, agricultural produce and commercial goods. Toll receipts for 1808/9 reveal that lime traffic (limestone, lime coal and burnt lime) was by far the most significant, earning about twice as much as fire coal.[11] Lower down the list came grain and malt, timber and commercial goods, followed by building materials and bark. Referring to Edstaston Wharf, on the Prees branch near Wem, Trinder stated that:

> By 1810 it was a busy centre for sundries traffic with direct services to Chester ... connecting to Liverpool and Manchester. In 1816 pig and bar iron, and iron castings were being dispatched, as well as locally produced grain and malt, and there was a heavy inward traffic in shop goods for the Coalfield.[12]

Although the canal never reached Shrewsbury, there was a road connection from Edstaston, which enabled the wharf to operate as a canal port for the county town. Its significance is indicated in Pigot's trade directory entry for Shrewsbury in 1822, which listed services using the Ellesmere Canal, via Edstaston Wharf, alongside others to destinations on the Severn and on the Midlands canal system.[13] By 1835 several road carriers offered regular services between Shrewsbury and Edstaston, making the wharf one of the county town's best served wagon destinations; one carrier ran daily services from his Shrewsbury warehouse 'to meet Swanwick and Co.'s Fly Boats for Liverpool and Manchester'.[14] This particular service would probably have taken advantage of the eventual opening of the Middlewich branch of the Chester Canal in 1833, which gave a direct route for narrow boats from the Ellesmere Canal to Manchester and the Midlands, without transhipment on to river flats at Chester. Shrewsbury was by then a significant transport hub, boasting many stagecoach services and over 40 carrier destinations in 1835, some served by several operators.[15] Pigot's directories of 1822, 1828 and 1835 for Whitchurch, Ellesmere and Wem indicate a range of canal carriers offering regular services to destinations including Nantwich, Chester, Liverpool and Manchester.[16]

There was a downturn in traffic following Telford's additions to the regional canal network in 1835, which connected the Chester Canal from near Nantwich to the Birmingham canal system, with a branch through Newport to the Shrewsbury Canal. This forged better links between Shrewsbury, the east Shropshire coalfield industries, Chester, Manchester and the Midlands, effectively bypassing the Ellesmere Canal, although its agricultural traffic and some commercial trade continued.[17]

Descriptions of the Towns
Whitchurch, Ellesmere and Wem were essentially rural market towns with little or no manufacturing industry and their economies depended mainly upon agriculture, with the towns functioning largely as suppliers of goods and services to their farming communities. They were all large parishes, with many townships and chapelries; Whitchurch and Wem extended over approximately 20 square miles (about 50 square kilometres) and Ellesmere had about twice this area.

Three North Shropshire Market Towns and the Ellesmere Canal

Though fundamentally rural in character, these towns would not have been unaffected by the several booming industrial areas in the vicinity. The east Shropshire coalfield and associated industries were nearby; the Potteries a little further afield, while the cotton mills of Lancashire were not far distant. These areas, with their rapidly growing populations, would have provided a ready market for Shropshire's agricultural produce, along with alternative employment possibilities for any surplus labour.

The three towns will be considered in turn using information from the census and trade directories. As well as population figures, the 1831 census gives employment data under various broad occupational headings, both agricultural and non-agricultural down to parish level.[18] Whilst only male workers aged over 20 (accounting for about a quarter of the population) are included, this does indicate the relative importance of the various sectors. Trade directories list the prominent individuals and businesses, including professionals, traders and service providers, in each town using a much wider range of categories. The main sources used are the Universal British Directory (UBD) of the 1790s, which is the most comprehensive source for the start of the period,[19] and Pigot's directories of 1822, 1828, 1835 and 1842.[20] The latter are generally regarded as being the most reliable for the early nineteenth century, although there are reservations, particularly about the 1822 issue.[21]

Comparisons between the UBD and Pigot's directories give useful trends, but should not be over-interpreted quantitatively due to possible inconsistencies in the way the data was gathered and the different business categories used. It should be noted that these directories focus mainly on the towns (i.e. the main urban areas) rather than parishes, although there are a few entries from adjacent villages, and hence few farmers are listed. Further qualitative information on the towns and their surrounding villages is taken from Bagshaw's later directory of 1851.[22]

The directories give brief descriptions and valuable insights into town life. For example, Whitchurch was described briefly as 'a pleasant and populous market town' in the 1790s, but by 1835:

> The town contains some neat streets and respectable houses. The trade is principally in malt and hops; shoes are manufactured for Manchester and some other markets; nails and fire bricks are likewise made here; and there are lime kilns and corn mills in the neighbourhood. The situation of the town contributes much to its prosperity, and the continual passing of travellers infuses into it considerable life and spirit, and promotes the success of three excellent Inns. ... The country around here is fertile, and in an excellent state of agriculture ... while the Ellesmere Canal comes close to the centre of the town.[23]

In 1851, Bagshaw noted that:

> The town is well built ... there are many good inns and shops and respectable private residences. ... [The Market Hall] ... is a spacious building of brick ... [under which] the corn market is held. The fairs and markets are well attended by the agriculturists of ... both ... Shropshire and Cheshire ... commercial intercourse is facilitated by the Ellesmere and Chester Canal.[24]

While some allowance must be made for the different approaches of the directories, it is clear that the later correspondents had much more to write about, and that the vitality and prosperity of the town had increased, spurred on by its prime position on a main thoroughfare from London to Chester and Liverpool, as well as by the canal. This impression is reinforced by the number of entries in the directories which grew by about 70% to almost 300 by 1835. (This includes professionals but not nobility, gentry and clergy.) This growth is much greater than the 40% increase in population of the parish between 1801 and 1841. The evidence thus suggests a substantial increase in demand for goods and services arising from greater prosperity, the availability of a wider range of goods, and growth of the passing trade.

Significantly, both Pigot and Bagshaw comment on the canal, which was extended to the town centre in 1811, following release of land by the earl of Bridgewater. The canal arm ended in a basin, with warehouses and wharves. Several businesses depending on the canal were evident here in 1835, including lime, coal and timber merchants, nail makers, a steam mill (a four-storey building of 1826 which still survives in much altered form) and a maltster. There was also a canalside gas works on the edge of town, a brick and tile maker and, by 1837, William Smith's iron foundry, which later became one of the town's largest employers. A canalside community had developed nearby at Grindley Brook where the staircase of three locks obliged traffic to pause; this included two taverns, a blacksmith, a plough maker and Thomas Whittingham's boat-building concern.

Turning now to Ellesmere, the UBD of the 1790s dismissed it quite briefly, but significantly noted the Ellesmere Canal then under construction: 'This place has little to boast of, except its situation. The principal trade is that of malt, the barley of the neighbourhood being remarkably good. ... A new canal is nearly cut to this town.' By 1835, one is struck by the contrast:

> The town has an aspect of great respectability and comfort: it has lately been lighted with gas, and the houses are in general neat and well built. The principal trades of Ellesmere are tanning, skinning, and malting; the barley of the neighbourhood being very good, a corresponding demand for the malt is generally experienced. A respectable boat building concern is carried on here, belonging to Messrs. Tilstons, who also have a considerable timber trade. ... This place has of late been much benefited by a navigation, called the Ellesmere Canal.[25]

By 1851, Bagshaw observed that:

> The town now contains several respectable inns, and many good houses and shops, in all the different branches of the retail trade. The malting business is extensively carried on. Mr. John Frumston's is one of the largest establishments in the county. The cultivation of barley being particularly attended to in the neighbouring country, causes the farmers usually to attend the market here, which is held on Tuesday.[26]

Looking at the Landscape

As was the case for Whitchurch, it is evident that the town was prospering and had seen many improvements since the 1790s, although passing trade seems to have been less influential due to Ellesmere's position on a relatively minor route. The impression of growth is reinforced by the increase in the number of trade directory entries between the 1790s and 1835 to nearly 200, an increase of 70%. This greatly exceeds the 20% growth in the parish population between 1801 and 1841, to reach a total of 7,080. The emphasis on malting in the above extracts underlines Ellesmere's early involvement and continuing significance in the trade. In 1835, many central streets, particularly Scotland Street, had a number of malt houses, possibly laid out along burgage plots,[27] and conveniently situated for the canal to bring barley to town as well as to export malt to markets. Much of Ellesmere parish belonged to the Bridgewater estate and the earl was responsible for building a large timber yard near the town arm of the canal. There was also a coal wharf, warehouses, a gas works, several work sheds and the Bridgewater Iron Foundry, making products for the estate and the canal.[28] The wharf became the town's commercial centre, with the canal company offices and maintenance works situated nearby (Figure 3, opposite, and 4, overleaf).

Bagshaw also referred to the canalside lime kilns at Hampton Bank near Welshampton (Figure 5, overleaf):

> The township [of Lineal] is intersected by the Shropshire Union Canal and the turnpike road from Ellesmere to Wem. There are lime works here which were formerly carried on to a very considerable extent, the canal affording facilities for sending that commodity to distant parts of the country.[29]

There was no lime burner listed locally and it seems that Hampton Bank was already falling into disuse by 1851. However, other canalside kilns were still active, including those at Quina Brook, Weston Wharf, Whixall Wharf and Grindley Brook.

Three North Shropshire Market Towns and the Ellesmere Canal

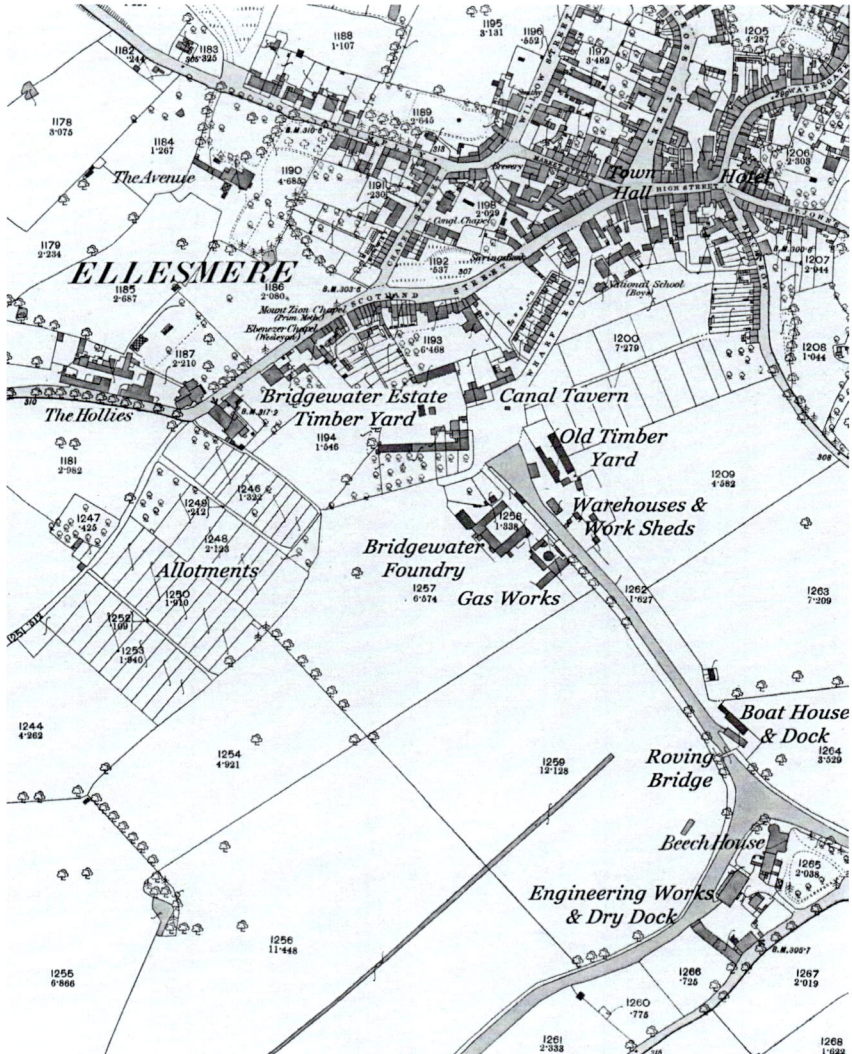

Figure 3: Town Canal Arm at Ellesmere. (OS 1st edn, 25 inches to 1 mile (not to scale), Shropshire, sheet no. XIII.2, 1875, reproduced with permission of the National Library of Scotland.)

Figure 4: Ellesmere Canal Wharf and former canal company buildings (2022). Photographs: Robert Ginder.

Figure 5: Lime kilns at Hampton Bank (2022). Photograph: Robert Ginder.

Three North Shropshire Market Towns and the Ellesmere Canal

A particular feature of Ellesmere parish was that a much greater proportion of its non-agricultural workers lived outside the town than was the case for Whitchurch or Wem.[30] This is suggestive of a significant enclave of such workers in one or more of the out-lying villages. The large chapelry of Dudleston, consisting of four townships with a total population of over 1,200, lying between Ellesmere town and the neighbouring parish of St Martins, appears to be a likely candidate. For Dudleston, Bagshaw stated as follows:

> originally built upon unenclosed land … generally [with] a small plot, or a few acres of land attached … two manufactories of bricks, tiles and brown earthenware …[for which] coal is got at the Flannag colliery. … The pits … are within … St Martin's parish, but the underground works extend into this chapelry.[31]

This suggests an open, partly squatter settlement, which was probably a focus for a variety of cottage industries or a home for casual workers in the local manufactories, on the surrounding estates, on the canal, in the maltings, or in the nearby coal mines. This settlement could thus account for a significant number of rural non-agricultural workers within Ellesmere parish.

Finally we turn to Wem. It was described in the 1790s as merely 'a market town'.[32] By 1835, the description had expanded and mentioned the canal, along with three inns which served stagecoaches going between Chester and Shrewsbury:

> The place has no manufactures, and the trade is chiefly confined to … supplying its inhabitants and those of its immediate neighbourhood (which is very respectable) with articles of ordinary consumption. There are several tanneries and malting concerns, and three respectable posting inns … [at Prees] there is also traffic in lime, coal and slate carried on by means of the … canal.[33]

Bagshaw's comments of 1851 underline the continuing importance of the canal to Wem, although Edstaston Wharf was no longer served by scheduled canal or road carriers:

there are … many good houses and shops, and several respectable private residences of more modern erection … The traffic of Wem is facilitated by a branch of the Ellesmere canal, which terminates near to Edstaston, about two miles from Wem. It is chiefly used for the conveyance of coal. Mr. John Brown, coal, slate, lime, and guano merchant, has a wharf here.[34]

By 1835 settlements had developed at Edstaston Wharf and at neighbouring Quina Brook. These included three taverns, a blacksmith, a tailor, a shopkeeper and two coal merchants, including Messrs Ireland and Davies who were also lime burners and brick and tile makers. Evidence of Edstaston Wharf (Figure 6), its warehouses and the bank of five lime kilns at Quina Brook is still apparent. The latter must have been a considerable enterprise, attracting significant business and traffic from the surrounding area.[35]

Spurred on by the various activities at Edstaston Wharf and Quina Brook, its passing trade, as well as its malting and leather businesses, Wem experienced a large increase in the number of traders from less than 80 in the 1790s to over 180 in 1835: thus improving its initial very low level of service provision to one more comparable with Whitchurch. This growth greatly exceeded the 33% increase in parish population, which reached 4,119 in 1841.

Figure 6: Edstaston Wharf and associated canal buildings (2016). Photographs: Robert Ginder.

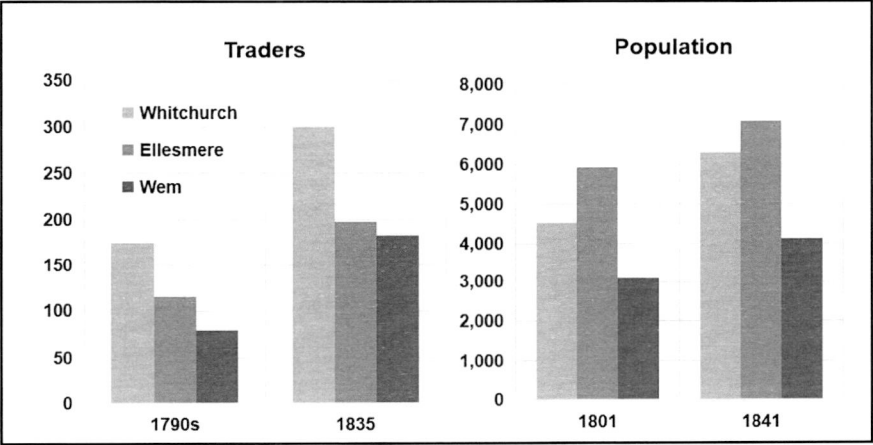

Figure 7: Traders and population growth in Whitchurch, Ellesmere and Wem.

Comparisons Between the Towns

As indicated previously, the number of traders in all three towns increased much faster than their populations between the 1790s and 1835, and Wem's growth rate of 130% greatly exceeded the figure of 70% for Whitchurch and Ellesmere. This is illustrated in Figure 7. In considering these figures, it should be remembered that each trade directory entry refers to a single business. These would have varied greatly in size, from those involving a single person through to family businesses and those having several employees, such as builders, timber merchants and brick makers. The generally small size of the businesses is indicated by comparing the numbers employed in retail and handicraft given in the 1831 census with the corresponding number of traders in the 1835 directory; this gives an average of about two adult male workers per entry.[36]

In order to analyse the trade directory data further, business sectors have been defined that account for about 70% of the trade entries in the 1790s and about 75% in 1835. The four leading sectors

Looking at the Landscape

across all three towns in order of their size in 1835 were: food and drink, professional services (teachers, attorneys, surgeons, etc.), clothing (including drapers) and hostelries (inn and tavern keepers, but not including victuallers and beer-sellers with unnamed premises).[37] These sectors accounted for about half the trade entries. Apart from the hostelries sector, all had grown at more than the average rate for each town from the 1790s to 1835, resulting in each taking a slightly larger share of the total, as can be seen in Figure 8 (opposite). The inns and taverns sectors grew less than average, thus their proportions of the total were reduced. However, it seems likely that several hostelries, particularly coaching and posting inns, were enlarged or rebuilt to cope with the increase in passing trade. The inns supplied refreshment and accommodation for travellers, as well as fresh horses, stabling and feed, thus providing considerable employment and business for the towns.

The remaining sectors were leather (fellmongers, tanners, curriers, bootmakers and saddlers); malting and milling; and building (bricklaying, joinery, plastering, painting and glazing, etc.). These showed more varied behaviour that differed between the towns (Figure 8, opposite). The number of leather traders grew by only a small amount in absolute terms for Whitchurch and Ellesmere, and so this sector shrank relative to the total. However, in Wem the leather sector maintained its share. This was almost certainly associated with an increase in tanning, as discussed below.

The building sector was significant only in Ellesmere at the start of the period and subsequently grew at near the average rate for this town. However, Figure 8 shows that this sector expanded substantially more in Whitchurch and to a lesser extent in Wem. The relatively large building sector in Ellesmere initially was probably connected with ongoing improvements to the Bridgewater estate as well as to the town fabric and canal infrastructure, which occurred earlier than elsewhere. As Bagshaw stated:

> The Duke of Bridgewater is deserving of notice in this place, as having been possessed of large estates in Ellesmere and its neighbourhood,

Three North Shropshire Market Towns and the Ellesmere Canal

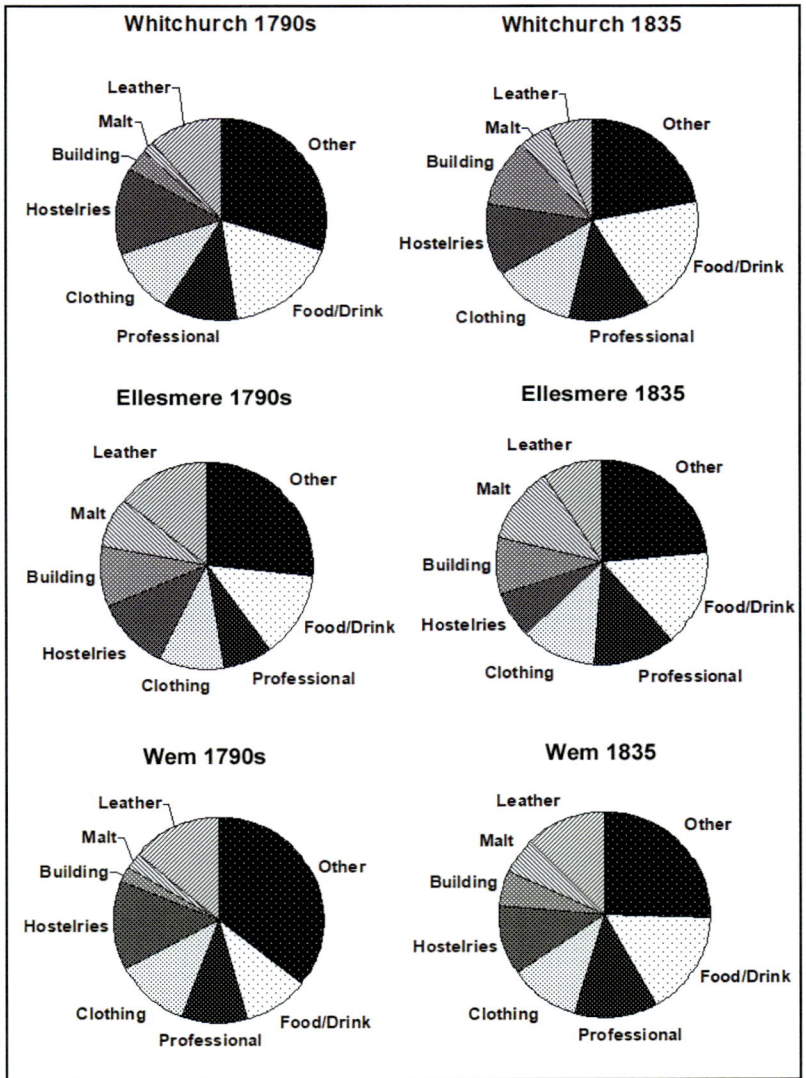

Figure 8: Trade sector comparison in Whitchurch, Ellesmere and Wem between 1790s and 1835.

and as being distinguished for his public spirit, and for the vast plans he formed and executed for the improvement of his estates. He died in 1803 ... .[38]

The duke and his successor the earl would also have had significant influence in Whitchurch where they had substantial holdings. The strength of the building trade is consistent with the high proportion of listed buildings dating to the early nineteenth century. Each town has numerous structures that were either built, extended or remodelled at this time (Plate 3).[39] It seems likely that the building trade also flourished in rural areas. In discussing two villages in Whitchurch parish, Bagshaw commented that: '[The village of Ash Parva is] studded with respectable farmhouses, with commodious outbuildings adjoining ... [in Tilstock] there are some extensive farms, with good farm houses.'[40]

With regard to malting, this was initially of significant size only in Ellesmere, but mushroomed subsequently in all the towns. Around 1830, our three towns accommodated a peak number of about 50 maltsters between them (Figure 9, opposite) supplemented by additional (unlisted) ones in their surrounding villages. There were similar numbers in Shrewsbury and in the east Shropshire coalfield towns, which would have received much of their barley from north Shropshire. Shropshire's towns accommodated over 300 maltsters in 1830, the third highest number of any English county, following Yorkshire and neighbouring Staffordshire.[41] However, the counties serving the London market would have been more significant on a national scale with considerably more malt houses (rather than maltsters) than Shropshire.[42] The number of maltsters in north Shropshire declined later, probably due to amalgamations and the erection of larger malt houses typical of the Victorian period as the original small buildings became uneconomic (Frumston's establishment in Ellesmere was remarked on earlier). Bagshaw listed 27 maltsters in our three study towns in 1851, with seven more in their rural villages, mainly within Ellesmere parish, plus another five in the neighbouring parishes of Welshampton and

Three North Shropshire Market Towns and the Ellesmere Canal

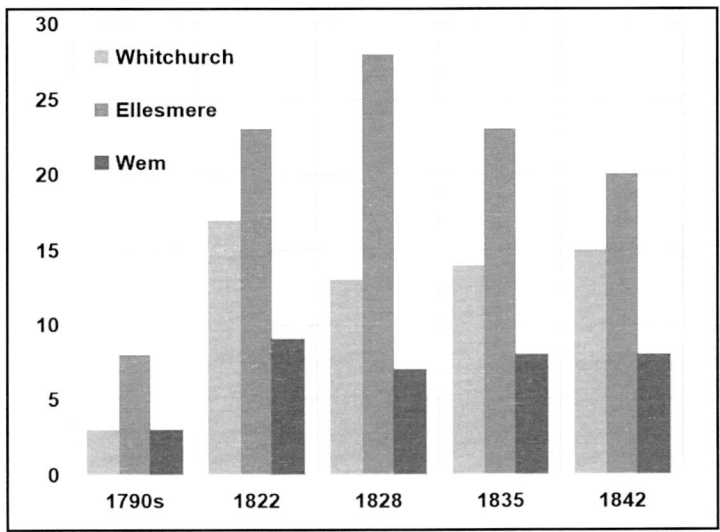

Figure 9: Number of maltsters in Whitchurch, Ellesmere and Wem.

Prees.[43] Most of these rural maltsters also had other occupations, such as farming or inn-keeping, and their malt houses were probably quite small, serving only local needs. By 1851, the total number of maltsters in Shropshire's market towns had fallen to about 150, with about 100 more in other towns and villages.[44] The decline was hastened by a shift in grain production towards eastern counties where growing conditions were more favourable. While the malting sector was always relatively small in terms of the number of businesses, it was important in bringing income into the three study towns (much north Shropshire malt was destined for Lancashire), providing employment and reinforcing connections between the towns and their agricultural hinterlands.

Further insight into activity in the towns comes from the carrier and stagecoach services listed in the directories.[45] Whitchurch lay on a main route between London and Chester and had a long history as a staging post for both coach and carrier services.[46] In the 1790s, it had three road carriers, going to London, Birmingham and Manchester every week, but by 1835 this had increased to 11 services per week, with destinations now including Chester, Newport, Shrewsbury and Stone but no longer London. In the 1790s, Ellesmere and Wem had just one weekly wagon each, serving Wrexham and Manchester respectively, though Wem also had a twice-weekly cart to Shrewsbury. By 1835, Ellesmere had six wagons per week, including services to Chester, Liverpool and Shrewsbury, while Wem had four (not including those serving Edstaston), going to Whitchurch and Shrewsbury. In the 1790s, there were four stagecoach services a week from Whitchurch to both London and Birmingham, three from Ellesmere, travelling between Chester and Shrewsbury, but none from Wem. By 1835, Whitchurch was visited by two services each day travelling between Liverpool and Birmingham via Chester. A significant change was an additional route between Chester and the increasingly important coaching hub of Shrewsbury. This route had three services per day, which called at Whitchurch and Wem, one of them on its way between Liverpool and Cheltenham. Ellesmere was visited by three daily services linking Chester and Shrewsbury; two of them travelling between Liverpool and Cheltenham or Bristol. The role of the Shropshire towns as coaching stops was thus significantly increased. One important factor was the growth in traffic to Ireland via the ports of Chester, Liverpool and later Holyhead (aided by Telford's improvements to the road passing through Shrewsbury), subsequent to the unification with Ireland in 1801.[47]

It should be noted that a considerable growth in traders as indicated above was not unusual during this period, but was more commonly associated with rapidly growing industrial or resort towns. Our three towns appear to have prospered at a time when other non-industrial rural towns were stagnating or dwindling, despite the vicissitudes of the Napoleonic Wars and their aftermath. The large increase in traders noted for Wem may be due to several factors. Firstly, it may have been more of a backwater in the 1790s with no stagecoach service and having a particularly low level of service provision. Secondly, three tanneries had been established there by 1835, compared with two in Ellesmere and one in Whitchurch, stimulating its leather trade in general and expanding export possibilities for its products. Thirdly, there was the stimulus of new stagecoach services and finally, the important canal terminus at Edstaston with its lime, coal, stone and brick merchants. The increased status of Wem is underlined by Trinder's comment that it 'was the smallest Shropshire town to have all the characteristic market town industries' in 1851.[48]

The business growth described above was consistent with increased prosperity and growing demand for all kinds of goods and services in these towns. Improved connections by canal would have helped to widen the range of goods on offer, including items imported via Ellesmere Port and Bristol (via the River Severn), and also to reduce the costs both of bringing in bulk commodities such as coal and building materials, and of exporting local products to market. The inns, some of the shops and particularly the maltings and mills would have been supplied from the surrounding countryside, whose inhabitants came to the towns to satisfy many of their needs, particularly on market days. The economic fortunes of the towns and the surrounding countryside would thus be strongly interlinked, prompting the discussion of local agriculture, and the influence of the canal upon it, that follows.

Agriculture in North Shropshire
Farming was a major influence on the economy of north Shropshire. This is underlined by figures from the 1831 census which indicate about 42% of male workers were in the agricultural sector in Whitchurch parish, 50% in Ellesmere and 47% in Wem – all considerably greater than the national average of 30%. Moreover, the proportion of adult male workers classified as farmers in our three parishes was about 50% higher than the national average. There were significant advances in agriculture in the area, typical of

the wider agricultural revolution, during the late eighteenth and early nineteenth centuries, spurred by high demand (and hence high prices) for grain due to bad harvests and the Napoleonic Wars. Enclosure was a significant aspect and was often a precursor to other improvements. Although Shropshire was an area of old enclosure, a considerable area of about 40 square miles (approximately 104 square kilometres), almost all common waste, was enclosed in the north of the county from the 1760s to 1820, either by parliamentary Act or private agreement. The more fertile, heavy clay soils and peat mosses were dealt with first, despite high drainage costs, followed by the less fertile but more easily tackled heathlands, contributing to very few commons being left by 1820.[49]

The 1831 census indicates that there was a higher proportion of 'large farmers' in our area (employing labourers) than was the case nationally.[50] The census figures indicate that the average area of such farms in our three parishes (which would account for the vast majority of the acreage) was about 140 acres. However, some farms were clearly much larger. Bagshaw states: 'The sizes of the farms are various, but large farms of from 400 to 800 acres are much more numerous than in the adjoining counties'.[51] Larger farms were beneficial because they encouraged landlords and their wealthier tenant farmers to invest in improvements.[52]

Northern Shropshire abounded in wetlands: meres, mosses, mires and moors, which were often waterlogged for much of the year.[53] Better drainage in the form of improved river flows, ditches and land drains was thus often incorporated in enclosure schemes. Key examples of parliamentary enclosure are: Bagley (Baggy) Moor (1777), near Weston Lullingfields, and the neighbouring Fenn's and Whixall Mosses (1777 and 1823 respectively), all of which were near the canal.[54] Bagshaw referred to similar work in the Wem townships of Coton and Edstaston: 'The soil ... has been much improved by draining and superior cultivation.'[55] It was reckoned that virtually all the 'carrs' of north Shropshire were reclaimed between 1750 and

1850, accompanied by a significant increase of around 30% in the arable acreage.[56] The tithe returns *c.*1836 indicated that the land in the vicinity of our three study parishes had an arable proportion that was amongst the highest in England.[57] The reclaimed areas often suffered from high levels of soil acidity and combating this required the application of lime. Liming increased cereal yields, particularly of barley which was highly sensitive to excessive soil acidity and waterlogging, and it was also effective on pasture land and in reclaiming acidic lowland heaths.[58] The turnpiking of the road from the lime quarrying area of Bron-y-Garth to Wem in 1771 is a good example of the importance attached to bringing lime to the area.[59]

As Plymley commented *c.*1800:

> There is much draining done by the best farmers, both with stone and wood … but in many situations … the materials … are very expensive. … The manure most in use, is lime, with which every part of this county is tolerably well supplied. It is principally spread upon arable land, and by that means the farmer can reserve the dung for the grass. … To the general use of it, some attribute the great improvements of our lands. … It is generally allowed, that upon bringing commons and old rough pastures into tillage, lime acts very beneficially.[60]

By 1851, Bagshaw recorded that:

> Great improvements by draining, enclosure, and superior management have been progressing for the last half century in most parts of the county … accomplished on many estates by the united efforts of the landlords and tenants.[61]

From the 1790s, alternative systems of crop rotation such as the use of turnips and clover as fodder crops between the corn cycles became more common.[62] This increased the number of animals that could be kept and hence the amount of manure available, whilst reducing the need for a fallow period or for dedicated pasture land.[63] Once again, barley yields are thought to have benefited significantly. The acreage under turnips is significant in this respect, and returns for

Shropshire in 1801 and 1831 showed a considerable increase from about 7% of arable to 17%.[64]

The potential influence of the canal on these improvements is apparent from Telford's contribution to Plymley's report, referring to the Ellesmere Canal:

> The advantages which the county is likely to derive from this canal … are the improvements in agriculture … from the cheap and expeditious conveyance of coal, lime, and slates, and the easy communication … [to] markets … improvements will extend to those lands which now lye waste, and increase … upon those … already under cultivation.[65]

There is good evidence that the various advances in agriculture were effective. Pigot's directory (1835) stated that 'The whole county is in general well cultivated, yielding great quantities of grain', whilst in 1851 Bagshaw noted: 'Barley and wheat in many parts are grown to a considerable extent'.[66] The *VCH* stated that 'During the years 1793 to 1815 there was a great extension of cereal farming, notably the growing of barley on the newly inclosed heaths of the north'.[67] However, the *VCH* does not address the important issue of liming, the role of the 'agricultural' Ellesmere Canal, or the significant link between agricultural advances and the major expansion of malting in north Shropshire.

Agricultural developments did not necessarily follow a smooth path. Grain prices fell dramatically at the end of the Napoleonic Wars, and farmers who had over-extended themselves during the good years faced problems. Comments in a Board of Trade report of 1816 illustrate this:

> some of the farmers' difficulties have arisen from their mode of living, which has been much beyond their station in life. … As soon as there was a depression in the market, [the Country Bankers] declined to advance any farther. The farmers, being called upon to repay the money suddenly … have not been able to stand the shock.[68]

The interdependence of canal trade and agriculture is illustrated by the Canal Company Report of 1817, which referred to the 'depressed

Three North Shropshire Market Towns and the Ellesmere Canal

Agriculture of the County having considerably affected the Revenue of the Canal. In the Articles of Grain and Malt a great Defalcation has taken place ...'.[69] Nevertheless, the thriving state of agriculture at the end of our period indicates that any setbacks were temporary. Whitchurch, Ellesmere and Wem clearly benefited from the local expansion of grain production and the cheap and convenient transport of coal, lime, grain and malt made possible by the Ellesmere Canal.

A Brief Comparison with Nantwich

Nantwich, just over the Cheshire border, was a thriving market town in the late eighteenth century. The UBD describes it as being 'one of the largest and best built towns in the county … adorned with many gentlemen's houses', and its thriving trade and position 'on the great thoroughfare to Ireland' were highlighted.[70] However, Nantwich, unlike the towns of north Shropshire, failed to grow commercially during the subsequent period of the Napoleonic Wars. This appears to be because its hinterland was primarily dairying country and did not participate in the boom in grain production needed to feed the rapidly growing national population. Cheshire farmers tended to be conservative and improvements in drainage and crop rotations do not appear to have been widespread.[71] Fields were generally treated with marl rather than lime because it was cheaper and more readily available, although less effective. Platt, in his history of Nantwich of 1818, commented on the limited use of liming, blaming this on its poor availability and high price.[72] It appears that lime coming from the Welsh borders via the Ellesmere Canal was not regularly used, the nearest canalside lime kiln being about five miles (eight kilometres) away at Wrenbury. Also, waterlogging of the fields was a major concern and better drainage using clay tiles, which were not generally adopted until later on, was needed for liming to be fully effective. Platt also commented that the termination of the Chester Canal some distance from the town centre was a major disadvantage, and (vainly) proposed an extension through the town to join the T&M Canal at Wheelock.[73] This was in order to make lime more readily available, facilitate the export of cheese, which was the area's principal product, and generally improve Nantwich's commercial prospects.

The number of traders in the town did recover to the levels of the 1790s by 1828 and had grown by about 20% by 1835.[74] The latter growth may have been stimulated by the construction phase of the new canal link to the Midlands, which involved major works near Nantwich, and by the anticipation of increased business arising after its opening, which finally occurred in 1835. However, the growth was much less than in neighbouring towns in north Shropshire, and Nantwich's coaching trade had also fallen behind.

Conclusion
During the period from the 1790s to the 1830s, north Shropshire became a regionally significant grain producing area, spurred by high demand due to the rapidly growing national population. The arable area expanded and agricultural practices improved, boosting barley production in particular, leading in turn to a rapid growth in malting. The three north Shropshire market towns of Whitchurch, Ellesmere and Wem prospered, with the numbers of traders increasing much faster than population growth, in line with an increased demand for goods and services. Passing trade increased with many more coaching and wagon services. There was significant building activity with many listed buildings in the towns dating from this period. It is argued here that the Ellesmere Canal, which opened in stages between 1795 and 1805, had a significant influence, bringing in bulk commodities, such as coal and building materials more cheaply and conveniently, and transporting local produce to market. In particular, the availability of agricultural lime was increased and its cost reduced, contributing to improvements in soil fertility, particularly of land reclaimed by the widespread enclosure and draining of commons, meres and mosses. The influence of

the Bridgewater family, who were the principal local landowners, and also had significant canal interests, was an important factor. Nearby Nantwich, across the county boundary, failed to prosper in this period and lost its place as the principal town of the region. Its hinterland remained wedded to dairy farming, its agricultural practices little improved, and its canal connection not capitalised upon. The greater vitality and business growth in Whitchurch, Ellesmere and Wem owed much to the interlinked influences of agricultural developments, a rapid growth in malting and improved transport connections, particularly the Ellesmere Canal.

Endnotes
[1] J. Everard, J.P. Bowen and W. Horton, *The Victoria History of Shropshire: Wem* (London, 2019).
[2] B. Trinder, *The Industrial Archaeology of Shropshire* (1st edn, Chichester, 1996), 39.
[3] E.A. Wilson, *The Ellesmere and Llangollen Canal* (Chichester, 1975), 59.
[4] C. Hadfield, *The Canals of the West Midlands* (2nd edn, Newton Abbot, 1969), 19.
[5] Hadfield, *Canals*, 19–32.
[6] Hadfield, *Canals*, 28 and 49–50.
[7] Hadfield, *Canals*, 42–43.
[8] Hadfield, *Canals*, 44–45.
[9] R.K. Morris, *Canals of Shropshire* (Shrewsbury, 1991), 13–33.
[10] Hadfield, *Canals*, 166–83; Wilson, *Ellesmere Canal*, 1–23; Morris, *Canals of Shropshire*, 34–42; T. Pellow and P. Bowen, *Canal to Llangollen* (Nantwich, 1997), 7–25.
[11] Wilson, *Ellesmere Canal*, Appendices 2 and 3.
[12] Trinder, *Industrial Archaeology of Shropshire*, 182.
[13] *Pigot's National Commercial Directory for 1822, Shropshire* (London, 1822), 377.
[14] *Pigot and Co.'s National Commercial Directory for 1835, Shropshire* (London, 1835), 380: <<http://specialcollections.le.ac.uk/digital/collection/p16445coll4/id/217400/rec/12>> accessed 14/3/22.
[15] *Pigot's Directory 1835*, 379–80.

[16] *Pigot's Directory 1822*, 364–65, 379–80, 381–82; *Pigot and Co.'s National Commercial Directory for 1828–9, Shropshire* (London, 1829), 699–700, 677–79, 697–98: <<http://specialcollections.le.ac.uk/digital/collection/p16445coll4/id/233467/rec/8>> accessed 14/3/2022; *Pigot's Directory 1835*, 386–88, 356–57, 383–85.
[17] Hadfield, *Canals*, 183–89.
[18] A Vision of Britain through Time, historical statistics: Whitchurch: <<https://www.visionofbritain.org.uk/unit/10367517>>; Ellesmere: <<https://www.visionofbritain.org.uk/unit/10364632>>; Wem: <<https://www.visionofbritain.org.uk/unit/10367311>> all accessed 14/3/22.
[19] *The Universal British Directory of Trade, Commerce and Manufacture*, IV (London, 1791–98), 717–18, 744–46: <<https://play.google.com/books/reader?id=4QwH AAAAQAAJ&pg= GBS.PA 745-IA3&hl=en>> accessed 13/3/22; Universal British Directory, V (London, 1791–98), 57–59, available: <<https://play.google.com/books/reader?id=xtcAAAAYAAJ&pg=GBS.PA58&hl=en>> accessed 13/3/22. The UBD was published in five volumes and several editions between 1791 and 1798, with volume IV including Whitchurch, Wem and Shrewsbury and volume V (an appendix to the preceding volumes) including Ellesmere. The Ellesmere entry mentions the canal being under construction, suggesting that volume V post-dates the others.
[20] *Pigot's Directory 1822*, 364–82; *Pigot's Directory 1828–9*, 669–700; *Pigot's Directory 1835*, 343–88; *Pigot and Co.'s Royal National and Commercial Directory and Topography of Shropshire for 1842* (London, 1842), 1–54.
[21] N. Raven and T. Hooley, 'Industrial and Urban Change in the Midlands: a Regional Survey' in J. Stobart and N. Raven, eds, *Towns, Regions and Industries: Urban and Industrial Change in the Midlands c.1700–1840* (Manchester, 2005), 25–26.
[22] S. Bagshaw, *History, Gazetteer and Directory of Shropshire* (Sheffield, 1851), 219–40, 317–37, 337–64: <<http://specialcollections.le.ac.uk/digital/collection/p16445coll4 /id/224405/rec/4>> accessed 30/3/22.
[23] *Pigot's Directory 1835*, 386.
[24] Bagshaw, *Directory of Shropshire*, 356, 362.
[25] *Pigot's Directory 1835*, 356.
[26] Bagshaw, *Directory of Shropshire*, 219.

[27] A. Patrick, 'Strategy for the Historic Industrial Environment Report No.1, Maltings in England' (English Heritage, 2004), 8–9; this reference indicates that in towns it was common to find malt houses behind houses which fronted on to the main streets. These are commonly referred to as burgage plot maltings and were generally long and narrow, by the nature of the plots.

[28] Wilson, *Ellesmere Canal*, 57–58.

[29] Bagshaw, *Directory of Shropshire*, 237.

[30] This is based on comparisons for all three parishes between the proportions of adult male workers that were employed in agriculture, as indicated by the 1831 census, and the proportions of the parish populations that lived outside the town according to the 1841 census (which gives the populations of the 'towns', or principal urban areas, in addition to the parish figures).

[31] Bagshaw, *Directory of Shropshire*, 233–35.

[32] *Universal British Directory*, IV, 717–18.

[33] *Pigot's Directory 1835*, 382.

[34] Bagshaw, *Directory of Shropshire*, 322.

[35] *Pigot's Directory 1835*, 382.

[36] *Pigot's Directory 1835*, 382–85, 386–88; A Vision of Britain through Time, historical statistics: Whitchurch: <<https://www.visionofbritain.org.uk/unit/10367517>>; Wem: <<https://www.visionofbritain.org.uk/unit/10367311>> both accessed 14/3/22; The comparison is only appropriate for Whitchurch and Wem because the census results for Ellesmere include a considerable number of non-agricultural workers living outside the town.

[37] For some businesses, for example victuallers, beer-sellers and shop-keepers, judgement is involved in allocating them to appropriate sectors, resulting in some uncertainty in the final data. Thus attention should be focused on general trends in the results rather than the finer detail.

[38] Bagshaw, *Directory of Shropshire*, 220.

[39] British listed buildings: Whitchurch: <<https://britishlistedbuildings.co.uk/england/whitchurch-urban-shropshire#.YkV3qzXTUdU>>; Ellesmere:<<https://britishlistedbuildings.co.uk/england/ellesmere-urban-shropshire#.YjIMW3rP0dU>>; Wem: <<https://britishlistedbuildings.co.uk/england/wem-urban-shropshire#.YjIM-3rP0dU>> all accessed 30/3/22.

⁴⁰ Bagshaw, *Directory of Shropshire*, 356, 362.
⁴¹ Patrick, 'Maltings in England', Appendix B: County totals.
⁴² For example, Ware, a long-established malting centre in Hertfordshire, had about 20 maltsters in the 1820s but perhaps as many as 80 malt houses. See J. Brown, *The English Market Town* (Marlborough, 1986), 77.
⁴³ Bagshaw, *Directory of Shropshire*, 228–40, 255–56, 304–5, 326–37, 350–64.
⁴⁴ B. Trinder, *The Industrial Archaeology of Shropshire* (2nd edn, Woonton Almeley, 2016), 44. Bagshaw, *Directory of Shropshire*, 115–715.
⁴⁵ *Universal British Directory*, IV, 717–19, 744–46; *Universal British Directory*, V, 57–59; *Pigot's Directory 1835*, 357, 385, 388.
⁴⁶ D. Gerhold, *Carriers and Coachmasters: Trade and Travel before the Turnpikes* (London, 2005), 125.
⁴⁷ J. Quartermaine, *Thomas Telford's Holyhead Road, the A5 in North Wales* (London, 2003), xvi.
⁴⁸ Trinder, *Industrial Archaeology of Shropshire* (2nd edn), 37.
⁴⁹ P. Stamper, *The Farmer Feeds Us All* (Shrewsbury, 1989), 52; Baugh and Elrington, *VCH Shrops.*, IV, 168–231.
⁵⁰ A Vision of Britain through Time, 1831 census occupational categories: Whitchurch: <<https://www.visionofbritain.org.uk/unit/10367517/cube/OCC_PAR1831>>; Ellesmere: <<https://www.visionofbritain.org.uk/unit/10364632/cube/OCC_PAR1831>>; Wem: <<https://www.visionofbritain.org.uk/unit/10367311/cube/OCC_PAR1831>> all accessed 31/3/22.
⁵¹ Bagshaw, *Directory of Shropshire*, 22–23.
⁵² *VCH Shrops.*, IV, 168–231.
⁵³ M.D. Leah et al., *The Wetlands of Shropshire and Staffordshire* (Lancaster, 1998), 11.
⁵⁴ Shropshire Archives, X6000/37/4/16868: Copy from the Baggymoor Enclosure Award (1777); North East Wales Archives, QS/DE/1: Bronington Enclosure Award (1823); Shropshire Archives, QE/1/2/44: Enclosure Award: Whixall Moss, in the parish of Prees (1777).
⁵⁵ Bagshaw, *Directory of Shropshire*, 330, 331.
⁵⁶ T. Williamson, *The Transformation of Rural England 1700–1870* (Exeter, 2002), 126, 136.
⁵⁷ Williamson, *Transformation of Rural England*, 161.
⁵⁸ Williamson, *Transformation of Rural England*, 120–25.

[59] Shropshire Turnpikes: <<http://www.turnpikes.org.uk/map/Salop/turnpikes.jpg>> accessed 9/1/22.
[60] J. Plymley, *General View of the Agriculture of Shropshire* (London, 1813), 228, 32.
[61] Bagshaw, *Directory of Shropshire*, 22–23.
[62] Stamper, *Farmer Feeds Us*, 54.
[63] Williamson, *Transformation of Rural England*, 126.
[64] M. Overton, *Agricultural Revolution in England* (Cambridge, 1996), 98.
[65] Plymley, *General View*, 305–6.
[66] *Pigot's Directory 1835*, 343; Bagshaw, *Directory of Shropshire*, 22–23.
[67] *VCH Shrops.*, IV, 168–231;.[68] Board of Agriculture, *The Agricultural State of the Kingdom* (London, 1816), 265.
[69] Pellow and Bowen, *Canal to Llangollen*, 28.
[70] *Universal British Directory*, IV, 91–94.
[71] C.S. Davies, *The Agricultural History of Cheshire, 1750–1850* (Manchester, 1960), 107–19, 127–32.
[72] J.W. Platt, *The History and Antiquities of Nantwich in the County Palatine of Chester* (Liverpool, 1818), 9–12.
[73] Platt, *History and Antiquities*, 10–11.
[74] *Universal British Directory*, IV, 91–94; *Pigot's National Commercial Directory for 1822–1823, Cheshire* (London, 1823), 18–19; *Pigot's Directory 1828–9, Cheshire* (London, 1829), 42–45: <<http://specialcollections.le.ac.uk/digital/collection/p16445coll4/id/233467/rec/8>> accessed 14/3/22; *Pigot's Directory 1835*, Cheshire (London, 1835), 18–19.

5
'ESTIMATING THE EFFECTS OF THE RAILWAY ON CHESTER IS NOT EASY'
Chris Pilsbury

So states the *Victoria County History of Cheshire*.[1] But is this true? And if not, what were the possible effects and why are they so difficult to estimate? Understanding the problem is, perhaps, a matter of context.

Railways were undoubtedly the great facilitators of the early to mid-nineteenth century. The successful early railway entrepreneurs swiftly realised the potential economic benefits and profits of linking established cities or larger areas together using this fast, efficient and relatively cheap transport system. Although originally created for the transportation of heavy materials, such as coal, they were soon adapted to convey passengers. New coastal resort towns, such as Bournemouth, Blackpool and Morecambe[2] quickly sprang up; Middlesbrough, from a population of 31 in 1801, became one of the great steel producers of the world.[3] Secondary industrial growth was frequent and the railways were predominantly the catalyst. Would Cornwall still be an isolated mining and fishing county had it not been for the railway linking it to the rest of the country? Would the North Wales coastal resorts have existed without the railways? Would Burton-on-Trent have become the brewing capital of Britain without rail links? The railways undoubtedly played an enormous part in the development and success of Victorian Britain.

If, therefore, we are to estimate the effects of the railway on Chester we must also consider, amongst other things, its unrealised potential, along with its strengths, whilst also noting, unlike many other towns or cities in Britain, it had nearly two thousand years of history behind it.

'Estimating the Effects of the Railway on Chester is Not Easy'

At the start of the nineteenth century Chester was, in military, legal, ecclesiastical, political and social terms, a local capital, with good road communication for freight and passengers to places as far away as Lincolnshire or the west of England, as well as closer destinations.[4] Unfortunately, road travel at that period was expensive, very slow and potentially hazardous, particularly in winter. However, the rise of Liverpool and Manchester, the failure of the canal to Nantwich, the silting of the Dee and the consequent loss of the port and shipbuilding, along with the decline of other traditional industries such as the Irish linen trade and tobacco pipe manufacturing, had led to the economic decline of the city.[5] Bagshaw (1850) wrote, 'The modern history of the trade of Chester is rather the history of its decay. … It was at one time of great trade.'[6]

Table 1 (overleaf), based on census results, shows that throughout the nineteenth century the city's population, overall, declined relative to the region.[7] Only between 1841 and 1871 did a consistent relative population increase occur.[8] This can 'be attributed to the arrival of the railway'[9] and also suggests a rise in economic activity. The *VCH* says that this, 'was Chester's most successful period between 1762 and 1914'.[10] From 1871 the population increase was slower; in the four decades from 1871 to 1911 the city population grew at only 50% of its hinterland.

From being an important port on the Irish Sea, with good trade and strong links, within a few decades it fell very much under the shadow of two of the greatest cities in the north of England, Liverpool and Manchester, with their huge populations and resources. Neither was it generally able to compete economically with many of the Lancashire and Yorkshire cotton, industrial or coalfield towns. The city did have much unrealised economic potential, but this was perhaps less obvious than in many other settlements.

Firstly, it was located at the gateway to North Wales and the Welsh Marches with easy access to their mineral and agricultural products. Chester had always been an important nodal point from Roman times onwards. The newly built railway infrastructure

Table 1: The population of Chester relative to the region.[11]

Date	Population	Chester rise %	Regional rise %	Chester's increase relative to the region %
1801–11	17,344	7.8	15.8	0.5
1811–21	21,516	24.1	18.7	1.3
1821–31	23,029	7.0	19.3	0.4
1831–41	25,039	8.7	15.5	0.6
1841–51	29,216	16.7	12.0	1.4
1851–61	34,209	17.1	9.6	1.8
1861–71	39,757	16.2	9.8	1.7
1871–81	42,246	6.3	12.1	0.5
1881–91	44,002	4.2	10.5	0.4
1891–01	47,975	9.0	10.9	0.8

The region referred to in the table above comprises: Cheshire, Flintshire and Denbighshire. The average increase of Chester's population throughout the nineteenth century, 1801–1901, relative to region is 0.94% (1.0 = parity with region).

enlarged and reinforced Chester's area of influence greatly, particularly along the North Wales coast.

Secondly, the historic city centre with its unique Rows, Walls, Cathedral and links with the Romans was a great attraction, as was the river for boat trips. This was at a time when leisure travel linked with statutory paid or unpaid holidays and rapid transport links was in its infancy, but one which was to become increasingly important throughout the second half of the nineteenth century and continues to be so to this day.

Thirdly, the acquisition of land by the railway companies released relatively large quantities of money to the corporation. This

'Estimating the Effects of the Railway on Chester is Not Easy'

newly acquired financial strength must be seen in conjunction with some influential and rich landowners such as Lord Curzon, the earl of Kilmorey, and the fabulously wealthy marquis of Westminster. These individuals all held large undeveloped areas of land on the city outskirts and this subsequently led to the development of the important suburbs of Curzon Park, Kilmorey Park, Handbridge and Saltney.

Fourthly, the location of the railway infrastructure in Chester is not always clear. It did not destroy or even impinge on historic buildings. Other than the station and the extensive triangle of lines to the west of it, but well to the north of the historic centre, there were few large and intrusive industrial areas or buildings. The few that did exist were generally to the north of the station, away from the city. Other than the Roodee Viaduct, many of the rail approaches to the station are hidden in cuttings or tunnels. Only at the Water Tower, the north-west angle of the walls, have the tracks crossed within the walls and then only for a very short distance.

Chester Station and the Centre

Described by Pevsner as 'One of the most splendid early railway stations, extremely long, and, at least in its central part … excellently held together',[12] Chester (General) Station, Grade 2* (1847), is situated well to the north of the city centre, but within walking distance of it (Plate 4). It was designed by Francis Thompson (1808–95) and built by Thomas Brassey (1805–70);[13] the Clerk of Works was George Grove (1820–1900).[14] It was constructed in the hamlet of Flookersbrook, the watercourse of that name being partly culverted beneath the station, and took just 12 months to build. Bagshaw (1850) described the hamlet of Flookersbrook as 'a populous hamlet which contains some good houses, pleasantly situated half a mile [0.8 kilometres] north-east from Chester, and is partly in the township of Hoole and partly in Newton'.[15] It was built as a successor to two temporary stations situated at the north end of Brook Street. They were owned by separate railway companies a short walk from each other and were thoroughly inconvenient for passengers.[16] Access to the city was via Brook Street and Cow Lane Bridge. Several hotels and inns sprang up along this street; the earliest was perhaps the Liverpool Arms – now Lloyds of Chester – which was quite close to the original two stations. Writing in 1856, Thomas Hughes gives an excellent description of 'our noble' station, which 'Twenty years ago ... were

Figure 1: An example of Victorian railway publicity, 1897. Source: Chris Pilsbury.

'Estimating the Effects of the Railway on Chester is Not Easy'

but plain kitchen gardens and uninteresting fields'.[17] Within a short time, large numbers of visitors were coming to Chester on railway excursions. The *Cheshire Observer* reported that during Whit Week of 1858 over 52,000 excursion passengers 'arrived and departed from the station'.[18]

Today the principal road approach to the station is along City Road which, at the station end, passes between the splendid Grade 2 Queen Hotel (1860),[19] shown in Plate 5 and similarly listed Town Crier (1865).[20] This must be one of the finest station approach roads in the country, and the hotels make an excellent and enviable ensemble with the station. Both establishments were built on land belonging to the Chester Railway Station Joint Committee (CRSJC). The former hotel was for first class travellers and the latter for others and servants. The Queen Hotel was joined to the station by a covered walkway. Unfortunately, with the exception of the Ionic style English Presbyterian Church of Wales, a Grade 2 building (1864) at the city end of the road, most of the remaining buildings are of quite indifferent quality architecturally.

City Road was built on land owned by the Railway Station Joint Committee up to the canal and beyond, to the south, by the city corporation. As early as Spring 1847[21] the CRSJC was considering the construction of the road. However, it was not until June 1862 that the corporation received an estimate of £13,000 for building the road, exclusive of the canal bridge, estimated at £2,000. The CRSJC, consisting of representatives of the Great Western Railway (GWR), London and North Western Railway (L&NWR), Chester and Holyhead Railway (C&HR) and the Birkenhead and Chester Railway (B&CR), appear to have been very enthusiastic about building the road, but there was a problem. The corporation was unwilling to pay for the canal bridge, which was later estimated at £3,200. In August, the companies offered to lend the corporation the money at 4% p.a. This seems to have been rejected as, by October of the same year, the Directors of the GWR were asking the corporation to contribute £3,000 towards the cost of the bridge in return for which the GWR would 'consent to abandon the reversionary right to £2,947 10s. 0d.' paid to the Grosvenor Bridge Commissioners on 16 October 1850. This was also agreed by the L&NWR.[22]

It may have been expected that City Road would develop into a commercially thriving thoroughfare, expanding the commercial centre of Chester; however, this did not happen, although, unsurprisingly, the road contained a large number of hotels.[23] Within the historic city centre, during the later 1850s and throughout the 1860s, we see an explosion of high-quality buildings nearly all of which are still in use today. Arguably, it is at this point that we can see the foundations of the modern city being laid down. Some of the major developments within the walls at this time included:

- The new Browns of Chester department store in Eastgate Street. This business had such a fine reputation that it was sometimes described as 'the Harrods of the North'. It dates to 1858 (Grade 1).[24]
- The City Market, the facade of which was in a rather fantastical rococo/baroque style. This joyfully exuberant facade, constructed in 1863, was destroyed by the city corporation in 1967.
- Chester Town Hall, built between 1865 and 1869, was a replacement for the Exchange building destroyed by fire in 1862 (Grade 2*).
- The Grosvenor Hotel built by the marquis of Westminster as a replacement for the Talbot Hotel. It was completed in 1865 (Grade 2).
- The transformation of Eastgate Street from a Georgian thoroughfare into what we see today.

Extramural developments included:

- The Queen Hotel, adjacent to the station and built 1859–60 (Grade 2).
- The Albion Railway Hotel, currently The Town Crier. This is also adjacent to the station and built 1865 (Grade 2).

'Estimating the Effects of the Railway on Chester is Not Easy'

- Grosvenor Park, given to the city by the marquis of Westminster and designed by Edward Kemp, 1865–66 (Grade 2).
- The first suspension bridge between the Groves and Queen's Park, 1852. Instigated by Enoch Gerrard 'projector and proprietor of Queen's Park'.[25] This was demolished in 1923 and replaced in the same year by Chester Corporation.

Beyond the historic city centre, the suburbs of Hoole, immediately to the north of Chester Station and Saltney, to the south-west, grew rapidly from what had essentially been a few scattered dwellings into substantial suburbs.

Saltney

The suburb of Saltney, situated about one and a half miles (2.4 kilometres) south-west from Chester city centre, lies partly in Cheshire and partly in Flintshire. The area within Flintshire is built entirely on former salt marshes, drained when the River Dee was canalised in the eighteenth century. A 1732 Act of Parliament allowed the digging of a channel along the estuary towards Chester in an attempt to save the port from silting up. The River Dee Company was incorporated in 1740 to undertake this work, but was much criticised in the local press for, seemingly, being more enthusiastic about reclaiming land for profit than pursuing its statutory obligation to maintain navigation into the port of Chester. Prior to the work, the land route from Chester into North Wales was indeed dangerous at certain states of the tide. Celia Fiennes, writing in 1698, states 'by the castle you crosse over a very large and long bridge over the River Dee ... Cross this river by this bridge enters [sic] Flintshire and so crossed over the marshes, which is hazardous to strangers'.[26] The less hazardous, and possibly the more frequented, route was via Balderton and Higher Kinnerton.

    The two-thousand or so acres of the Saltney Marshes were enclosed in 1781 following the passing of an Enclosure Act in 1778.[27] The future suburb of Saltney lies on the eastern fringes of the marsh.

Looking at the Landscape

The tithe maps of the late 1830s and early 1840s show that much of the former marsh land reclaimed from the Dee was laid down to arable or pasture. There were some dwellings in Higher Saltney, as that part lying to the east of the border, and therefore in Chester, was called. The only significant buildings appear to be Poor House Farm and Saltneyside Farm, both of which can be seen on the 1910 OS map, plus another unnamed dwelling, which appears to have several outbuildings.[28] The fields on the former tidal marshes in Flintshire, part of which became known as Saltney Town, were almost entirely rectilinear. Here too there were only a few scattered dwellings, with the notable exception of a row of 15 cottages adjacent to Balderton Brook at the Stone Bridge and another larger dwelling, listed as House, Buildings, Yard and Lane, of about three acres in extent. This was located slightly to the north of the cottages, towards the river, at the end of what subsequently would become Bridge Street, and adjacent to the river embankment upon which the railway later would run.[29] This area would subsequently develop into the small partially self-contained community of Saltney.

The principal landowners in Higher Saltney were: Earl Howe; the mayor and citizens of Chester; the trustees of the will of Sir John Cotgreave of Netherleigh, Handbridge; and the Bakewell family. Over the county border, on the former salt marshes, there was a much more varied landownership, perhaps reflecting the more recent availability of the land. The marquis of Westminster possibly held the greatest acreage; certainly this was true close to the county (and national) boundary in the east.

It was through this sparsely populated,[30] rural, perhaps even desolate landscape that the railway was to run and to be the catalyst for the creation of Chester's only truly industrial area.

The first proposal to build a railway into Saltney was made in 1839[31] by the North Wales Mineral Railway (NWMR). The company was incorporated by Parliament in 1844. It proposed a line from Ruabon, Denbighshire, to wharves on the Dee at Saltney, for the transhipment of coal and other heavy mineral goods, principally to

'Estimating the Effects of the Railway on Chester is Not Easy'

Ireland and Liverpool. Nearby, at what was to become Saltney Junction, it would also connect with the proposed Chester and Holyhead Railway (C&HR). By November 1844, the NWMR was putting pressure on the C&HR to complete the two mile (3.2 kilometre) section of the line between Saltney Junction and Chester, thus providing the NWMR access to Chester, which was already in the process of becoming a regional railway hub. Access to Chester would also give tacit support for a proposal to create the Shrewsbury, Oswestry & Chester Junction Railway (SO&CJR)[32] by extending the NWMR line southwards to Shrewsbury and northwards to Chester. This latter railway was authorised by Parliament in June 1845. Subsequently the line was absorbed by the Great Western Railway, giving access to Wolverhampton and beyond, with far reaching consequences for Saltney.

Most of the land over which the C&HR and the NWMR crossed between Saltney and Chester, and within the city boundaries, was owned by Chester Corporation, as was much of the surrounding land. These holdings would thus allow the city, financially at least, to profit well from the forthcoming railway development.

Under an enabling Act for a railway, the route was fixed and the required land was compulsorily purchased by the promoters, the former owners negotiating a fair price for the land. The Saltney Lands Committee, also known as The Tower Field Committee, was established to represent the interests of the corporation and oversee the sale of the various plots to both the C&HR and SO&CJR. In March 1845 they instructed John Stewart of Liverpool, 'an eminent surveyor and accountant', to value some of the corporation estate in Saltney. His estimated value of the various plots was between £60 and £240 per acre; the committee met on 11 December 1845 and decided to charge £340 per acre![33]

The NWMR and the city corporation moved swiftly to agree on the price of several parcels of land, as speed was of the essence for the former party. By 14 June agreement had been reached to purchase one plot for £3,800, with immediate possession: this had previously been rented to the Guardians of the Poor at £6 p.a.,[34] whilst two other parcels of land to both the north and south of the turnpike were also released. That to the north, consisting of just under 11 acres, was sold for just over £3,684.[35] Not all went the way of the corporation. Earlier, in mid-February 1845, the directors of the NWMR complained regarding the city valuation of £4,677 17s. 6d. for 'The Sands of Saltney' which 'altogether exceeds that to which several experienced surveyors employed ... have reported to them as the full and liberal value'. They then offered £2,500. Obviously, the negotiations continued, as, by 11 June, in a letter to Finchett Maddock, the city town clerk, the NWMR offered a revised figure of £3,700 which appears to have been accepted.[36] It seems that the city valuations were frequently somewhat higher than the NWMR was willing to accept.

In September 1846, the *Chester Courant* reported that the port was importing sleepers, timber and iron fillets, these almost certainly related to the construction of the new line towards Chester.[37] The development of Saltney as an industrial suburb of Chester was moving ahead swiftly. On 4 November the line southwards towards Shrewsbury was opened, as was Saltney Station, which was situated on the south side of Chester Street adjacent to the railway bridge.

The construction of the two mile (3.2 kilometre) section northwards to Chester did not always go particularly smoothly. It was built by the C&HR from Saltney Junction, a little to the north of Saltney, to Chester Station and over which the SO&CJR[38] had negotiated running rights, thus giving them access to the city. There seem to have been frequent accusations of encroachment on to corporation land from members of the Saltney Lands/Tower Field Committee, and from the builders there were complaints regarding difficulty of access. In a letter from the C&HR, dated 7 December 1846, to the town clerk, it was testily stated 'The claim is to the bed of the River Dee ... I beg to observe that this is claimed by the Crown.'[39] By the end of 1846 things appeared to be going from bad to worse. A letter from a legal practice of Lincoln's Inn Fields to the town clerk states the 'Plaintiffs do not intend to take further proceedings'. Few details have yet been found, but it appears to be a dispute over which land had or had not been paid for.[40] According to The Tower Field Committee, there were also problems regarding the stability of the embankment between the Water Tower and Crane Street; they considered that it was built too steeply and likely to collapse. However, the tunnelling under Upper Northgate Street seems to have progressed smoothly, perhaps because the members of The Tower Field Committee did not wish to venture underground.

The arrival of the railway into Saltney was the catalyst for rapid expansion. Industrialists very quickly realised its huge potential with its excellent transport links, both land and water, availability of suitable industrial land and owners willing to sell, particularly the marquis of Westminster and Chester Corporation. Meanwhile, the building of a siding across the turnpike, towards the riverbank and along it enabled about a mile or so (1.6 kilometres) of river frontage to become available for industrial development.

Eventually the Shrewsbury and Chester Railway Company[41] purchased just over 25 acres from the city for the sum of £7,484.[42] Some of this may have been along the riverbank and was possibly extra land beyond that which was included in the enabling Act. With the absorption of the SO&CJR by the Great Western Railway, Saltney wagon works subsequently became one of the three principal maintenance and manufacturing works for GWR freight vehicles. It was to become a major employer in Saltney and, by 1864, 354 men were employed there.[43] As early as August 1848 the Lords of the Treasury were contacted by the city corporation regarding the sale of land 'for the purpose of increasing annual income'. A letter from the Treasury to the corporation states that they – the city – had already sold over 25 acres to the SO&CJR for just over £7,484.[44] In another letter to the Treasury, dated 26 April 1850, seeking permission to sell more land on leasehold, it was stated 'a great demand has lately arisen for Dwelling houses in Saltney in consequence of several large works having been established there and your petitioners are advised to sell the same in lots for building purposes ... for the utmost value'.[45] The lots were to be about a quarter of an acre each and the rental would be '£5 per cent per annum on the ... purchase money'.[46] Finchett Maddock, town clerk, stated the council intended to sell just over 13 acres of Saltney Marsh Estate and some 'waste ground called Hough Green'.[47] The industrial areas were generally confined to the west of the railway, in Flintshire, whilst much of the housing, at least initially, was to the east of the railway in Cheshire.

In August of 1847 Henry Wood personally wrote to the corporation asking to purchase 1.5 acres of land, 'a low wet piece', on which to build 'for a manager and Clerks, cottages with gardens' and also for 'the reception of refuse that will be created in my new works'.[48] The new works were Henry Wood & Co.'s Dee Iron Works otherwise known locally as the Chain & Anchor works.[49] It was probably the first of the major employers, other than the railways, to establish in Saltney. Located across Boundary Lane from the new railway sidings to which it had a link line,[50] the works was also connected by a railway siding to the wharves along the riverbank. A year later, in 1848, H. Wood & Co. was eliciting support for their proposed new licensee at The Anchor, a public house that had been built by the company (Figure 2). This may seem strange, but drinking water was easily polluted by effluent and his foundry workers required a large liquid intake.[51] This was probably the earliest of what was to

Figure 2: The Anchor, Saltney. This was probably Saltney's earliest public house. Photograph: Chris Pilsbury.

'Estimating the Effects of the Railway on Chester is Not Easy'

become 13 public houses in total at Saltney, although not all traded simultaneously.[52]

Between 1850 and 1856 the city corporation held a series of annual land sales to the east of the railway line. The terms of sale were quite strict: the land was sold leasehold; dwellings had to be constructed within three years of the purchase and 15 feet (4.6 metres) from the road; sewers were to be built at the builder's expense and privies were to be constructed at the back of the plot, which was to have a nine foot (2.75 metres) high surrounding wall. Although the records are incomplete, at least five acres were sold under these terms. This area, comprising Cable Street, Wood Street and Curzon Street, was demolished in the late 1960s, although a few houses at the southern end of Curzon Street still remain.

The riverbank, served by a siding, connected the mainline across Chester Road via a level crossing, and became the site of several large industrial concerns. Proctor & Rylands moved their Bone Manure Works from Birmingham in 1856. By the late 1870s there were three refineries distilling oil from Flintshire Cannel coal[53] and in 1913, C. & H. Crichton opened a shipyard for the construction of 'High Class Light Draft Shipbuilding'.[54]

In the two middle decades of the nineteenth century, the city corporation went to very considerable lengths to promote the city as a nodal point for the railways in general, and as an industrial centre situated in Saltney. There is no doubt they were successful.

In 1856 Thomas Hughes wrote:

> since the cutting of the two great railways … Saltney has rapidly risen in importance and population. A large ironworks and coal trade have been established, new streets have sprung up … and the number of inhabitants is now computed at about 3,000.[55]

Hoole

To the immediate north of the railway station lies the suburb of Hoole, described in 1850 by Bagshaw as a 'township and scattered village … in 1841 had 47 houses and 294 inhabitants containing, some genteel houses'.[56] By 1871 the population had grown to 2,032.[57] The *Post Office Directory* of 1878 states that the land was principally worked by market gardeners.[58]

From the early 1850s the local press frequently had advertisements for building land for sale in Hoole, invariably freehold, as the owners realised the financial potential of their land in close proximity to the new station.

By the early 1870s most of the development was within a relatively small area: close to and to the north of the station and to the south-east of Hoole Road. To the north-west of the road the principal landowner was the earl of Kilmorey. Here, other than a few relatively high-status dwellings, there was little development until the early twentieth century. To the south-east of Hoole Road landownership was much more varied. The tithe award of 1838–39 shows among the principal landowners members of the Hamilton family, Thomas Walker and Macclesfield School, but there were several others with significant holdings including the earl of Shrewsbury and Mrs Elizabeth Brassey.[59] It is here, immediately to the south-east of Hoole Road, we find the early urban development

Figure 3: A Hoole streetscape. Photograph: Chris Pilsbury.

of Hoole. Facing Hoole Road are some fine, large dwellings. Behind these, running generally at right angles, we find long runs of terraced houses built directly on to the streets. Much of this housing was of working-class or lower middle-class status, but was generally of a good quality and, unlike at Saltney, is extant (Figure 3, opposite).

Much of the necessary infrastructure was developed, as to some extent were the streets, in a rather piecemeal manner; there appears to be little overall planning, although the suburb seems to have developed outwards from Faulkner Street. Neither did the streets follow the original field boundaries with the exception of the rear alleyways of William Street, Edna Street and Prescott Street, which mainly follow the boundaries of the northern part of the Bishop's Field. This area was developed for housing from about 1897.[60]

Hoole needed to be self-sufficient, principally because it was quite a distance from the city, the roads were poor and could be impassable in places. Purpose-built shops were not erected specifically and it seems at first that provision was often made by converting the fronts of houses. The Anglican parish church, All Saints, built on land given by Mrs Martha Hamilton, was not consecrated until December 1867.[61] However, a Mission House had been built in 1855 when much of Hoole was part of Christ Church, Newtown parish. This building was also used as an elementary school, initially for boys, but, from sometime before 1865, for girls also. Nonconformist denominations arrived in the suburb a little later.

Unlike Saltney, there was little or no industrial development, except within areas occupied by the railway. Hoole developed entirely as a dormitory suburb of Chester, and particularly for the station, providing homes and accommodation for those who worked there or for the several railway companies associated with it. Many would have required nearby accommodation as the station was active throughout the day and night. There are many references to railway workers in the census returns. Similarly, Hoole was convenient for rail commuters.

The importance of the railway station to Hoole is suggested by several memorials, or petitions, presented by the citizens to the joint owners of the station from 1889 onwards, requesting a direct entrance into the station from Hoole. There is some evidence that at least three were sent. In one, 197 petitioners described Hoole Bridge as 'long and disagreeable' and the route 'along the south side of the station … is frequently almost in an unusable condition and has no flagged or other footpath'. The petition also mentioned sharing the bridge with cattle for which 'There is no protection for pedestrians'. Whilst the Joint Committee of the station agreed to build a bridge, the conditions attached were unacceptable to the Hoole Local Board. Eventually, when the Royal Agricultural Show was held in Hoole in 1893, the entrance and footbridge were built[62] and opened on 15 June of that year.[63] This remained open until 1 February 1965. Subsequently there was much debate in the local press regarding the error of closure; the argument ran on for several years in the local press and council meetings; however, the entrance remained closed.[64] The bricked-up up evidence of it can still be seen in the wall at the start of Hoole Bridge.

Hoole today is a successful and lively suburb of the city. It has a wide range of local shops, public houses, schools and restaurants, plus an enviable number of societies and clubs.

Summary
Were the effects brought by the railways difficult to estimate? Not in this author's opinion.

The purchasing of land by the railway companies released relatively large sums of money into the local economy. The financial input this provided could only have had a beneficial effect and must have facilitated, at the very least, the partial rebuilding of the city centre and elsewhere.

The railways transported many hundreds of thousands of visitors to the city over the years, again bringing new money and business into the city. Chester developed a very important tourist industry, assisted by good transport links, which thrives to this day.

The railways were instrumental in giving Chester two new suburbs: one industrial and one dormitory. The port was reinvigorated about a mile (1.6 kilometres) downstream at Saltney, and from 1913 it facilitated the return of shipbuilding at Crichton's shipyard, also in Saltney.

Over a century and a half later, Chester continues to benefit from the building of the railway. Its arrival directly and indirectly reinvigorated the economy and businesses of the city and also facilitated the construction of several fine public buildings and hotels. At the same time Chester avoided the urban blight often associated with nineteenth-century railway development. It can be strongly argued that the railway has undoubtedly been a beneficial influence on the landscape of Chester whilst not damaging or impinging upon those very important, notable and admired aspects of the city's past, such as the medieval street plan, the Rows and the Walls.

Endnotes

[1] *VCH Ches.*, V i, 172.
[2] Named Morecambe by the Lancashire & Yorkshire Railway.
[3] J. Simmons, *The Railway in Town and Country* (Newton Abbot, 1986), 145–46.
[4] J. Broster, *A Walk Round the Walls of Chester* (6th edn, Chester, 1821), 97–101.
[5] *VCH Ches.*, V i, 172–77.
[6] S. Bagshaw, *History, Gazetteer and Directory of the County Palatine of Chester* (Sheffield, 1850), 76.
[7] The region comprised: Cheshire, Flintshire and Denbighshire.
[8] There was a small rise between 1811–21 of 0.3%.
[9] *VCH Ches.*, V i, 185.
[10] *VCH Ches.*, V i, 186.
[11] Table 1 is taken from *VCH Ches.*, V i, 171.
[12] N. Pevsner and E. Hubbard, *The Buildings of England: Cheshire* (Harmondsworth, 1971), 159. See also C. Hartwell, M. Hyde, E. Hubbard and N. Pevsner, *The Buildings of England: Cheshire* (rev. edn, New Haven and London, 2011), 248.

[13] Born near Aldford, educated at The King's School, Chester. Referred to as 'one of the greatest railway contractors of his generation', in J. Simmons and G. Biddle, *The Oxford Companion to British Railway History* (Oxford, 2000), 43.

[14] George Grove: first principal of The Royal College of Music 1883. Founding editor of Grove's *Dictionary of Music and Musicians* (1st edn 1878, now online). Partly instrumental in forming The Associated Board of the Royal Schools of Music. Knighted May 1883.

[15] Bagshaw, *Directory of Chester*, 154.

[16] *Chester Chronicle*, 25 Dec. 1846.

[17] T. Hughes, *The Stranger's Handbook to Chester and its Environs* (Chester, 1856), 10.

[18] *Cheshire Observer*, 5 June 1858.

[19] Morris & Co.'s *Directory and Gazetteer of Cheshire* (1864), page 6 gives a construction date of 1858/9. See also *Chester Chronicle*, 30 Nov. 1861 for details of a catastrophic fire at the hotel which virtually destroyed it.

[20] Formerly The Albion, previously Queen Railway Commercial Inn (OS 1st edn 25 inches to 1 mile, Cheshire, sheet no. XXXVIII, 1875, surveyed *c.*1873).

[21] CALS, ZCCB 34: Railway Lands Committee 12 Mar. 1847, 252.

[22] CALS, ZCCF4: Chester City Files, 1862.

[23] Phillipson and Golder, *Directory for Chester* (Chester, 1933–34), 126–27.

[24] Virtual Chester website: <<http://www.virtualchester.org/view/view_location.php?id=22>> accessed 14/7/21 and 'Browns of Chester: Sad demise of "the Harrods of the North"', BBC News: <<https://www.bbc.co.uk/news/uk-england-merseyside-57111826>> accessed 15/2/22.

[25] <<https://www.chesterwalls.info>> accessed 15/9/21.

[26] C. Fiennes, *The Journeys of Celia Fiennes* with an introduction by J. Hillary (1st edn, London, 1983), 208.

[27] J. Hemingway, *History of the City of Chester, from Its Foundation to the Present Time: With an Account of Its Antiquities, Curiosities, Local Customs, and Peculiar Immunities; and a Concise Political History* ... II (Chester, 1831), 236.

[28] Cheshire Tithe Maps online: <<https://maps.cheshireeast.gov.uk/tithemaps/>> accessed 17/6/21.

[29] Welsh Tithe Maps online: <<https://places.library.wales>> accessed 18/6/21.

'Estimating the Effects of the Railway on Chester is Not Easy'

[30] 1841 census returns give the population on the Chester side of the border as 23.
[31] J. Dixon and G. Picard, *Railways around Saltney* (1st edn, Saltney, 2006); P. Boughan, *The Chester and Holyhead Railway,* I (Newton Abbot, 1972), 69.
[32] This was the successor to the NWMR.
[33] CALS, CCF/13/9: Railway Lands Committee, 1845.
[34] CALS, CCF/13/20: Railway Lands Committee, 1846.
[35] CALS, CCF/13/28 and 29: Railway Lands Committee, 1846.
[36] CALS, CCF/13/44: Railway Lands Committee, 1846.
[37] *Chester Courant,* 23 Sept. 1846.
[38] By this time the NWMR had been incorporated into the SO&CJR. This was later incorporated into the Great Western Railway.
[39] CALS, CCF/13/62: Railway Lands Committee, 1846.
[40] CALS, CCF13/64: Railway Lands Committee, 1846.
[41] Formerly named the SO&CJR.
[42] CALS, ZCHDM/1: Hough Green and Saltney Marsh. Letter from Treasury of 7 March 1849.
[43] PRO RAIL 250/266: page 266. T. Wood *Saltney Carriage & Wagon Works Great Western Study Group* (Chester, 2007), 13.
[44] Equivalent to about £972,000 today.
[45] CALS, ZCHDM/1: Hough Green and Saltney Marsh. 26 Apr. 1850.
[46] CALS, ZCHDM/1: Hough Green and Saltney Marsh. 26 Apr. 1850.
[47] CALS, ZCHDM/1: Hough Green and Saltney Marsh. 12 June 1851.
[48] CALS, ZCCF/13/78: Railway Lands Committee, 1847.
[49] Saltney Local History Group, *Saltney and Saltney Ferry: A Short Illustrated History* (Chester, Tiverton, 1988), Unnumbered.
[50] Welsh Tithe Maps: <<www.places.library.wales>> accessed 30/8/21.
[51] It was not until the next decade that John Snow discovered the link between cholera and polluted drinking water.
[52] J. Dixon, *Saltney Pubs and Licensees* (Chester, 1990), 12.
[53] A Flintshire coal with a high oil content.
[54] J. Dixon and G. Packard, *J Crichton and Co. Shipbuilders* (Chester, 2002), 3. Letter dated 30 May 1905.
[55] Hughes, *The Stranger's Handbook,* 71.
[56] Bagshaw, *Directory of Chester,* 153.
[57] *Post Office Directory of Cheshire,* 1878, 199.
[58] *Post Office Directory of Cheshire,* 1878, 199.

[59] CALS, EDT 205: Plemstall and Chester St John Tithe Award: <<https://maps.cheshireeast.gov.uk/tithemaps/>> accessed 17/6/21.

[60] It was here that Chester Football Club played from 1885 until 1898: their first ground. C. Sumner, *On the Borderline: The Official History of Chester City F.C. 1885–1997* (Harefield, 1997), 124.

[61] *Cheshire Observer*, 28 Dec. 1867. This gives a good account of the donations, etc. leading to the building of the church.

[62] *Cheshire Observer*, 9 Mar. 1889, 13 Apr. 1889, 14 Dec. 1889, 29 Dec. 1890, 2 May 1891, 1 Jan. 1892, 9 June 1892. *Chester Chronicle,* 29 Apr. 1893, 3 June 1893.

[63] *Chester Chronicle,* 3 June 1893.

[64] *Cheshire Observer,* 1 Jan. 1965, 8 Jan. 1965, 15 Jan. 1965, 8 Oct. 1965, 18 Nov. 1966, 5 Jan. 1968 as a few examples of the discussions.

6

CARNEGIE LIBRARIES IN CHESHIRE

Vanessa Greatorex

What is the best gift which can be given to a community?
… a free library occupies the first place …
Andrew Carnegie, 1889[1]

Introduction

The Scottish-American steel magnate Andrew Carnegie (1835–1919) never forgot his humble beginnings or his gratitude for being given access to a businessman's personal library at a crucial phase in his life. After amassing a fortune he focused on philanthropic projects, which included augmenting local community funding for the construction of over 2,500 public libraries all over the world. These are collectively known as Carnegie Libraries and are celebrated not only as free, accessible repositories of knowledge and entertainment, but also for the diversity of their architecture.

However, after the initial injection of cash Carnegie did not provide any funding for the ongoing maintenance costs of libraries in the UK, as a consequence of which some have now been repurposed or demolished, while others are under threat of closure.

This paper outlines Carnegie's background, the legislative context in which Carnegie Libraries were built and the factors affecting library design, before briefly describing the Carnegie Libraries which were created in Cheshire and concluding with some comments about their future prospects.

Andrew Carnegie: Background, Philosophy and Motivation

Andrew Carnegie was born in a single-storey house in Dunfermline in Scotland on 25 November 1835. His father was a damask weaver called William and his mother, Margaret, sewed soles on to

Figure 1: Andrew Carnegie (1835–1919), advocate and benefactor of free public libraries, photographed in April 1905 by F.B. Johnston (Library of Congress).

leather boots for a local shoemaker and ran a food shop from the family home. Despite their strong work ethic, respect for education and belief in equal opportunities – William was a local leader of the Chartists and one of five weavers in Dunfermline who pooled their books to create the town's first circulating library – they did not send Carnegie to school until he agreed to go at the age of seven. From that point self-motivated, he found school 'a perfect delight',[2] and was highly regarded by his schoolmaster, Robert Martin, despite often arriving late after fetching the family's daily water supply. By the age of 10 he was also running shop errands for his mother after school. When increasing mechanisation reduced the family to poverty, Carnegie left school at the age of 12 and, with his parents and younger brother, embarked for America on 17 May 1848. The family settled in Allegheny City (now part of Pittsburgh), where Andrew Carnegie went to work in a bobbin factory, earning $1.20 a week. Keen to forge a better life for himself and his family, he attended evening classes in double-entry bookkeeping and was taught to declaim by an elocutionist. His new skills enabled him to become a messenger and clerk in a telegraph office before progressing to telegraph operator and secretary to the superintendent of the Pittsburgh division of the Pennsylvania Railroad.[3]

During this time he borrowed books from the personal library of Colonel James Anderson, founder of Free Libraries in Pennsylvania, who on Saturday afternoons allowed working boys to borrow one book each a week from his collection of 400. Carnegie later erected a monument to him and acknowledged that it was this generosity which inspired him to instigate the Carnegie Library scheme in order to enable people to acquire knowledge, even if they had received little formal education.[4]

In his mid-twenties he succeeded his boss as railroad division superintendent, and also made profitable investments in coal, iron, oil and railroad companies. Having founded Keystone Bridge Company the previous year, he left his railroad job in 1865 to focus on entrepreneurial activities. In 1873 he co-founded his first steel company. It was the start of a highly efficient and profitable steel empire underpinned by his ownership of raw materials, factories, transportation infrastructure and communication networks, all of which were consolidated in 1892 as Carnegie Steel Company. In 1901, having decided it was time to stop accumulating wealth and instead focus on spending his surplus millions on good causes, Carnegie and his partners sold the business to the banker John Pierpont Morgan (1837–1913) for $480 million.[5]

A prolific writer of speeches, articles, pamphlets and books, Carnegie believed in improving conditions for all people in all walks of life and declared that the rich should administer their 'surplus wealth for the good of the people'.[6] Championing 'the well-doing and industrious poor',[7] he maintained not only that philanthropical actions should take place during an individual's lifetime but that:

> In bestowing charity the main consideration should be to help those who will help themselves; to provide part of the means by which those who desire to improve may do so; to give those who desire to rise the aids by which they may rise; to assist, but rarely or never to do all.[8]

He had already been practising what he preached since the 1870s,[9] but it was not until 27 July 1881 that his mother laid the foundation stone of the first free public library building to be funded by Carnegie. The people of Dunfermline elected to name the building Carnegie Library after him. The architect wanted to put Carnegie's coat of arms above the door, but as the family did not have one Carnegie suggested instead a rising sun with rays and the motto 'Let there be light'.[10]

Between 1881 and Carnegie's death on 11 August 1919 over 2,500 Carnegie Libraries – including 380 in the United Kingdom – were established across six continents, sometimes in existing premises but usually in brand new, custom-made buildings[11] principally constructed in Anglophone countries.

Table 1: Carnegie Libraries across the World

Europe	UK, Ireland, France, Belgium, Netherlands, Serbia
North America	USA, Canada, Barbados, St Lucia, St Vincent, Dominica, Trinidad
South America	Guyana
Africa	South Africa, Seychelles, Mauritius
Asia	Malaysia
Oceania	Australia, New Zealand, Fiji

With the enactment of the Public Libraries Act in Britain on 23 December 1919, the penny rate was abolished and the responsibility for libraries was transferred from boroughs to county councils,[12] making it more straightforward for local authorities to provide and run public libraries regardless of the number of residents in a community and without having to hold referenda or court the support of ratepayers. Perhaps it is no coincidence that Andrew Carnegie, the most munificent of all library philanthropists, had died several months earlier.

Cheshire's Carnegie Libraries

In the traditional county of Cheshire (extending from Wirral in the west to areas now categorised as parts of Greater Manchester in the east) nine libraries received funding from the Carnegie Foundation. In order of opening, these were Knutsford (1904), Runcorn (1906), Neston (1907), Birkenhead South (1908), Birkenhead North (1909),

Birkenhead Central (1909), Ellesmere Port (1910), Wallasey (1911) and Stockport Central (1913).

The Influence of Legislation on the Location of Cheshire's Carnegie Libraries

It is noticeable that all of Cheshire's Carnegie Libraries were in Wirral or on the fringes of the county or in relatively small towns like Knutsford. This can be explained by a combination of civic history, legislation, population, local aspirations and the presence – or absence – of both benefactors and public-spirited motivators.

As far as can be gleaned from extant documents, Cheshire's first public library owed its existence to Geoffrey Downes, a Fellow of Queens' College, Cambridge, who had founded a chapel near his family home in the dispersed settlement of Pott Shrigley in east Cheshire. In his will of 20 June 7 Henry VII (1492), he mandated that, with the exception of the Mass Book, any of the volumes he had given to the chapel could be borrowed by the family's heirs 'or any other Gentleman, either for to read or to take a Coppy thereof' for 13 weeks, provided the borrower left 'sufficient plege to keep them safe, and bring them again att the day assign'd'.[13] Although women, children and non-gentry were not granted the same opportunity, it is possible that under the aegis of 'Gentleman' borrowers they were able to access the chapel's books.

Nearly 200 years passed before the county town of Chester could boast a similar facility, when a bequest by Dean Arderne in 1691 'for the Clergy and City' gave literate members of the public access to books in the cathedral library.[14] In the ensuing centuries this was supplemented by various subscription libraries within the city walls,[15] but other Cheshire communities could not consult or borrow books free of charge from a public repository until the Public Libraries Act of 1850 gave English and Welsh local authorities of boroughs with at least 10,000 inhabitants the right to finance free public libraries by levying a rate of one halfpenny in the pound from local ratepayers. In 1853 the Act was extended to include

Looking at the Landscape

Scotland and Ireland, and in 1855 more boroughs became eligible to construct free public libraries when the mandatory minimum number of inhabitants was halved to 5,000 and the rate was doubled to a penny. The money raised could only be spent on buildings – not books – and, despite the increase to the so-called 'penny rate', both the backing of local MPs and significant additional funding from public subscriptions and wealthy benefactors were essential to galvanise a community into action, garner public support and cover construction costs. Nevertheless, by 1900 there were 295 public libraries in Britain,[16] several of which were located in Cheshire's larger towns, including Macclesfield (opened in Park Green in 1876, thanks to the efforts of David Chadwick, MP),[17] Northwich (opened on Witton Street in 1885 with the assistance of John Brunner of Brunner Mond & Co. Ltd)[18] and Nantwich (opened in Pillory Street in 1888, courtesy of the combined efforts of Samuel Harlock, MP, public subscriptions and – again – John Brunner, who had reputedly said on being taken as a boy to the opening of the William Brown Library and Museum in Liverpool, 'Perhaps some day I shall be a rich man and give a free library like Sir William Brown').[19] Hence a number of the county's eligible communities did not need Carnegie funding because, thanks to the efforts of prominent residents and benefactors with local connections, they had already succeeded in establishing satisfactorily commodious public libraries without it.

The choice of location for Cheshire's Carnegie Libraries depended not only on the willingness of eligible communities to apply for funding but also on the availability of a suitable site and the co-operation of local landowners and ratepayers. In many instances, lack of space prevented Carnegie Libraries being built in the convenient heart of the community's principal shopping area. As a consequence, Cheshire's Carnegie Libraries tended to be extensions of existing edifices or built from scratch on plots of land on the edge of town. Neston's Carnegie Library, for instance, was built on a field between Neston and Parkgate on land donated by the Russell family who lived opposite,[20] while, despite being styled the

'Central' Library, Wallasey's Carnegie Library (formerly a private house) is situated in a park in the Earlston residential area some distance from the town centre and therefore a long walk away if you live on the other side of town. Other Carnegie Libraries, such as Birkenhead North, were upgrades of late Victorian reading rooms (carefully controlled spaces where books and newspapers had to be fetched from the shelves by the librarian and could only be read on the premises).

Design

One benefit of the legislative requirement for communities to contribute towards the construction costs was that it empowered them to make their own decisions about the location, architects, builders, materials and appearance of the library which they had raised money to build. Carnegie's role was limited to injecting cash, hence there was no 'official' Carnegie Library style. Nevertheless, Prizeman et al. have identified certain typical features, such as glazed domes and fire-proof stairs,[21] which prevailed in many libraries of the period, not just those part-funded by Carnegie. Architectural fashions undoubtedly influenced the taste and preferences of both those applying for funding and the architects hired for the job, as did various publications – such as Burgoyne's *Library Construction: Architecture, Fittings and Furniture*,[22] Champneys's *Libraries: A Treatise on their Design, Construction, and Fittings*[23] and Edwards's *Memoirs of Libraries, including a Handbook of Library Economy*[24] – which expatiated on suitable elements for libraries[25] and the best way to run them. It was not uncommon for architects to design more than one Carnegie Library, as occurred in the case of Birkenhead Central and Ellesmere Port (both designed by Sproat & Warwick) and Stockport (whose architect had previously designed Bolton's Carnegie Library). Large windows and roof lights were favoured to admit plenty of daylight, grander libraries had separate rooms for serious readers, reference books, meetings and children, and it was considered essential for librarians to have a good all-round view of the library to reduce the risk of theft. With an eye to the budget, local materials tended to be preferred. In Cheshire this principally meant red brick, sometimes embellished with stone or terracotta elements. Despite internal modernisation and reorganisation to accommodate self-service equipment, it is clear that many Carnegie Libraries across Britain still owe a great deal to such precepts even though there is considerable variation in their footprints, height and ornamentation.

Brief Descriptions of Cheshire's Carnegie Libraries
The descriptions below, presented in the chronological order in which the Carnegie Libraries opened, are based on information gleaned from a combination of site visits, primary sources and secondary sources, many of which can be accessed online. Particularly useful resources for those in search of further information include: British Listed Buildings,[26] Historic England,[27] Shelf-Life (a project funded by the Arts and Humanities Research Council to assess the current state of Carnegie Libraries in the UK and determine whether a systematic revitalisation programme is needed),[28] the Cheshire section of 'The Carnegie Legacy in England and Wales: Libraries Funded by Andrew Carnegie',[29] and documents held by Cheshire Archives and Local Studies.

Knutsford
- Opened: 1904.
- Location: Brook Street, Knutsford.
- Carnegie grant: £1,500.
- Architect: Alfred Darbyshire of Manchester.
- Status: Grade II listed building.
- Current use: Day nursery.

Described by Pevsner and Hubbard as 'Elizabethan, asymmetrical, with mullioned and transomed windows',[30] Knutsford's Carnegie Library is built of red brick with buff terracotta dressings and a Welsh

Figure 2: Knutsford Carnegie Library in March 2022, 20 years after its closure and subsequent conversion into a day nursery. Photograph: Vanessa Greatorex.

slate roof. Although it did not open until 1904, deeds held by CALS indicate that land had been set aside for a library in Brook Street on the outskirts of the town as early as 1868.[31] The library's irregular L-plan layout consists of two main ranges connected by an entrance bay. Its front elevation features a handsome, four-light mullion and transom window with diamond-latticed glazing beneath a lintel bearing the words 'Public Free Library'. The pyramidal roof on the left side of the building is punctuated by a row of dormer windows. The single-storey, flat-roofed entrance range to the right has a wide arched doorway surmounted by a heavily decorated panel with ball finials and the date 1904. Set back from this is a single bay with a sloped roof. In its heyday the larger range, with its high, hammer-beamed roof, constituted the adult library, while the lower single bay contained the children's library.[32]

It was designated a Grade II listed building on 12 February 1999 and remained in use as a library until 2002. Its listing fortuitously led to the premises being repurposed as a children's day nursery.

Looking at the Landscape

The replacement library, run by Cheshire East Council, was opened in 2002 in Toft Road near the Town Hall. It houses the Mrs Gaskell Whitfield Collection and is open for 44 hours a week.[33]

Runcorn
- Opened: 1906.
- Location: Egerton Street, Runcorn.
- Carnegie grant: £3,000.
- Architect: James Wilding.
- Status: Grade II listed building (13 June 2007).
- Current use: Empty.

Runcorn's first free library opened in Waterloo House on Egerton Street in 1882, but occupied only part of the building, which was also used as the Town Hall. Carnegie's donation of 1904 enabled a purpose-built reverse L-shaped library to be constructed on an adjacent plot. Its two-storey Victorian Gothic frontage is built of Runcorn red sandstone, while the single-storey rear range is red brick.[34] The entrance bay juts further forward than the rest of the front elevation. Its upper storey has a six-light mullion and transom window containing Mackintosh-style stained-glass windows, and its arched doorway is surmounted by a five-light window inscribed, in capital letters, with the words 'free library and reading room'. The front elevation of the two-storey bay to the right has three

Figure 3: Runcorn Carnegie Library in 2014, two years after its closure. Photograph: SteHLiverpool, cc licence.

four-light mullion and transom windows of varying width on the lower floor and one eight-light mullion and transom window; the upper lights of the windows in this bay contain stained glass, but the lower lights are plain. A carved foliate and floral frieze separates the two storeys across the entire frontage, and the roof is surrounded by a parapet. Inside there is a tiled mosaic floor and cast-iron spiral staircase to the upper storey. Green and dark brown enamelled brick dados decorate the walls.[35] Despite its attractive appearance, it is not mentioned by Pevsner and Hubbard, who in their original edition high-handedly write off the entirety of Runcorn as 'miserable to look at'.[36] However, this was rectified in the revised edition through a generous entry of over five lines:

> Attractive Free Style Elizabethan in red sandstone, with a low porch tower, mullioned-and-transomed windows with shallow ogee heads and an entrance arch with mouldings dying into the jambs. Nice Art Nouveau glass and other details.[37]

The grand opening of Runcorn's Carnegie Library took place on 1 December 1906. It was downgraded to a branch library in 1981 when Halton Lea Library opened in Runcorn Shopping City. Although the Carnegie Library was designated a Grade II listed building on 13 June 2007, this was not enough to prevent its closure in 2012, when a new branch library opened in Granville Street. Both the new libraries are run by Halton Borough Council. The smaller branch library is open for 35 hours a week, while, boosted by its commercial neighbours in Shopping City, the central library's facilities include meeting rooms and a café, enabling it to remain open for 44.5 hours a week.[38] A plan put forward by Runcorn and District Historical Society to convert the Carnegie Library into a local studies centre was thwarted by the expense.[39] In 2020 Signature Housing Group submitted a planning application to refurbish the library as a community centre with meeting rooms, clinics, employment and advice services and – appropriately – a library,[40] but this is contingent on approval being granted for the demolition of the adjacent Waterloo House in order to create 36 supported living apartments to be known as Carnegie Court.[41]

Neston
(Plate 6)
- Opened: 1907/8.
- Location: Parkgate Road, Neston.
- Carnegie grant: £1,200.
- Architects: Green, Knowles & Russell.
- Current use: Library.

Despite the parish vicar's assertion that 'the level of literacy in Neston did not justify a reading room', the town's progressive schoolmaster, Dr Riddock, had set one up in his school by 1882 to complement the Literary and Debating Society he had founded in 1881. The book collection – complete with volumes donated by the newly enlightened vicar – was relocated to the Town Hall in 1890, but Queen Victoria's death in 1901 was seized as an opportunity to forward plans for a brand new purpose-built library as a 'fitting tribute' to her memory. Dr Riddock applied for Carnegie funding, which was duly granted provided the usual conditions of a suitable site and the levy of the penny rate could be met. As a memorial to the late Dr Russell, the Russell family of Vine House in Parkgate Road offered to donate the field diagonally opposite their home,[42] a substantial eighteenth-century brick residence which was granted Grade II listed building status in 1962.[43] This is several minutes' walk from the centre of Neston and the nearest railway station. Since Frank Russell of the local firm Green, Knowles & Russell was not only the architect who designed the library but also the son of the owner of Vine House,[44] it is logical to surmise that, in conjunction with the impetus provided by Dr Riddock and the demise of the long-reigning Queen, the success of the project owed much to the Russell family's local influence.

The library is constructed of red brick and features an octagonal domed cupola with eight windows. In addition to a triangular pediment above the door, the front elevation has three bays, one of which contains the reference library and local history books. Several rectangular windows are set into each wall and an oval window in the left gable admits extra light. Despite its attractive yet practical design, it is not mentioned in the 1971 edition of Pevsner's *Buildings of England: Cheshire*, but the 2011 edition describes it as 'a typical Carnegie library, i.e. Baroque with a little dome'.[45] Some experts would contend that such features owe more to the pattern-books and era in which it was built than to the Carnegie connection.

There appears to be doubt about the official opening date of the library, with some sources citing 6 December 1907 and others 3 January 1908.[46] Until the appointment of a paid librarian in 1934 the library was open for only two and a half hours a week, spread across three different days, and users were not permitted to browse the shelves unattended.[47] Now run by Cheshire West and Chester Council (CWaC), it is open for six days a week for 47.5 hours[48] – a decided improvement on its original opening hours.

The library is not a listed building, though perhaps it should be, given its rarity as one of the few remaining purpose-built free libraries in Cheshire which has retained its original use for more than a century. Its survival may in part be due to the absence of other public libraries in either Neston or Parkgate and the existence of a small car park and additional free parking on adjacent roads.

Birkenhead South, North and Central

For a couple of decades Birkenhead enjoyed the distinction of hosting three Carnegie Libraries – Birkenhead South, Birkenhead North and Birkenhead Central – all now demolished.

Birkenhead North, on the corner of Price Street and Pensby Street, began life as a reading room in 1856, making Birkenhead the first unincorporated borough to utilise the 1850 Public Libraries Act. The following year its collection was relocated to premises above the

Looking at the Landscape

Figure 4: Birkenhead Central Carnegie Library, demolished nearly a century ago to make way for the Mersey Tunnel. Drawing, produced by W. Edwardes Sproat and Eldon Warwick, originally published in *The Architect*, 1 November 1907.

Table 2: Birkenhead's three Carnegie Libraries

	Birkenhead South	Birkenhead North	Birkenhead Central
Opened	1908	1909	1909
Location	Grove Road, Rock Ferry	Price Street	Market Street South
Carnegie grant	£2,500	£2,500	£15,000
Architects	J.R. Mewton	A.W. Street	Sproat & Warwick
Status	Demolished	Demolished	Demolished

new Post Office in Conway Street, which became so popular that in 1861 it had 130,000 visitors, including 80,000 described as 'working class'. This led to the opening of a purpose-built central library on Hamilton Street in 1864. Thirty years later the 1877 extension of Birkenhead's boundaries, the acquisition of more stock, and the growing popularity of reading prompted the reopening of the Price

Street premises – which survived as a library until the 1980s[49] – and the establishment of a new branch library in Rock Ferry.[50] When further improvements were deemed desirable, Carnegie agreed to provide £15,000 for a new central library on Market Street and to contribute a further £5,000 towards the cost of rebuilding the two branches,[51] even though Birkenhead North was less than a mile and Birkenhead South less than two miles from the new Central Library.

The Market Street building contained lending, reference and children's libraries, a reading room, a lecture hall and over 95,000 volumes,[52] and was considered to be of outstanding architectural merit with stone-trimmed red-brick elevations, large windows, an ornately carved portico and a dome. None of this mattered in 1929, when it was demolished to make way for the Birkenhead entrance to Queensway Mersey Tunnel. The lending stock was moved back to the 1864 Hamilton Street library, the reference stock was stored in a disused shipyard canteen, and the compensation of £55,000 – £40,000 more than Carnegie's grant – was used to fund a new central library in Borough Road. This was opened on 18 July 1934 by George V, fresh from his inaugural drive through the new tunnel,[53] and can now be accessed by the public 42 hours a week.[54] Its proximity to the other two libraries undoubtedly contributed to their closure. Rock Ferry was provided with a new library, but that, too, is now facing the axe unless more funding can be found.[55]

Ellesmere Port
- Opened: 1910.
- Location: Carnegie Street.
- Carnegie grant: £1,500.
- Architects: W. Edwardes Sproat & Eldon Warwick.
- Current use: Offices.

Despite, a century later, being defamed by Hartwell et al. as 'a bit of a shed',[56] when Ellesmere Port's Carnegie Library was built it was considered so important that the street in which it was located was

Figure 5: Ellesmere Port Carnegie Library in March 2022, now occupied by offices. Photograph: Vanessa Greatorex.

named after it. Now that street is just a car park and, after a brief period as an Assembly of God Pentecostal Church, the library has been repurposed as offices.[57] Although it has not been designated a listed building, its front elevation is pleasingly symmetrical. The central doorway is surmounted by an intricately carved Baroque escutcheon featuring the word 'Library'. Above this is a curious device which looks like a cross between a wishing well and a mini spire but is actually a wind-driven fan ventilation system. Hartwell et al. describe it as a 'shrunken cupola'.[58] The doorway is flanked on each side by a single-storey range featuring three large windows. The chief building material is brick, punctuated by decorative stone accents at the corners and around the door. Its much larger, two-storey replacement, located near a shopping precinct and other amenities in Civic Way and designed by Richard H. Kelly of Gornall, Kelly & Partners, was opened in 1962 and is somewhat unfairly described as 'architecturally poor' by Pevsner and Hubbard.[59] Run by CWaC, it is currently open for 48 hours a week.

Carnegie Libraries in Cheshire

Wallasey Central
- Opened: 1911.
- Location: Earlston Road.
- Carnegie grant: £9,000.
- Architects: R.B. MacColl & George Edward Tonge of Manchester.
- Current use: Library.

Contrary to the impression implicit in its name, Wallasey Central Library is not located in the town centre. It is described by Shelf-Life as 'purpose built'[60] though stated by those with local knowledge to be an extension of Earlston House, a red-brick residence built *c.*1840 'in the Tudor style'[61] and converted into the site's first library – known as New Earlston[62] – after being purchased by the council in 1898.[63] Its frontage is on Earlston Road, a quiet boulevard with plenty of parking spaces. It backs on to a leafy park and there is a children's playground to the left of the frontage.

The Shelf-Life researchers describe it as 'one of the least altered and best-preserved examples of a substantial symmetrical Carnegie library in the UK',[64] a description clearly based on the front elevation and the interior since it blithely disregards the quirky irregularity

Figure 6: The impressive frontage of Wallasey Central Carnegie Library in September 2021. Photograph: Vanessa Greatorex.

of the rear of the building – the legacy of its previous incarnation as a house. The front elevation is lavishly decorated with stone, particularly around the windows and ornately carved doorway, which is surmounted by the words 'Public Library'. On the other façades the use of stone is less lavish and there is considerable variation in the size of the windows. Inside it is light and airy, with decorative moulding and coving, glazed roof lights and fresh-air inlets under the ground-floor windows – a feature also present in the Carnegie Library in Cradley Heath in the West Midlands.[65]

The stock is shelved on the original bookcases, although they are no longer arranged in the radial pattern which graced the library in its earliest years.[66] Green glazed tiles decorate the walls of the staircase to the upper floor, where the reference library is located, along with meeting rooms, models of ships connected with the area and a framed letter dated 10 August 1908 confirming the Carnegie grant.[67] Although combining spacious elegance with practicality, its ground floor was not in the best state of repair during a site visit in September 2021, peeling wallpaper and damaged plaster demonstrating exactly why, despite their architectural merit and contribution to the cultural and social life of their respective communities, other Carnegie Libraries in need of renovation have fallen into disuse or been repurposed as offices or nurseries. Notwithstanding its maintenance requirements, in January 2022 Wallasey Central Library – now run by Wirral Council – received a reprieve amid a raft of other library closures in the peninsula[68] and remains a valuable public amenity which is open for 42 hours a week.[69]

Stockport Central
(Plate 7)
- Opened: 1913.
- Location: Corner of St Petersgate and Wellington Road South.
- Carnegie grant: £15,000.

- Architect: Arthur John Hope of Bradshaw, Gass & Hope.
- Status: Grade II listed building.
- Current use: Library.

In 1875 a reading room opened above Stockport Market's cheese hall, but poor ventilation and complaints about the stench led to its closure in 1890.[70] Residents had to wait more than 20 years for a new library, situated near the Town Hall on the prestigious new Wellington Road South (part of the A6 between Derby and Manchester). The foundation stone of Stockport's Carnegie Library was laid on 1 August 1912,[71] the architect having been selected because of his work on Bolton's Carnegie Library, which had opened in 1910.[72] Variously described as 'neo-Baroque',[73] 'Edwardian Baroque'[74] and 'Very free William-and-Mary, with a corner dome',[75] the last Carnegie Library to be built in Cheshire is set on a partially visible stone plinth designed to simultaneously contain the library's L-shaped basement and solve the issues inherent in building on a slope in a creative way. Above the plinth, the elevations consist of orange brick with Portland stone dressings and an octagonal Portland stone cupola with a zinc-clad dome and flagpole.[76] Inside, the stairwell is lit by windows with stained-glass panels featuring the surnames of English writers such as John Milton (1608–1874) and Charles Dickens (1812–1870). A vast glazed dome, or laylight, supported by Ionic columns is one of its most celebrated features.[77]

On 26 April 2017, just over a century after it opened, the library became a Grade II listed building.[78] Run by Stockport Metropolitan Borough Council, it is currently open 51 hours a week[79] and hosts a reference library, a lending library and a local history library. However, despite its architectural distinctions, its cultural value, and its proximity to both the Grade II listed Town Hall built in 1908 and Stockport's main shopping zone in the Merseyway precinct, its function as a library is due to end in 2023. The closure is fiercely opposed by thousands of residents[80] but, partly as a consequence of the Government's pledge of £14.5 million Future High Streets funding to repurpose vacant retail units, the Council is determined to forge ahead with plans to transfer the library to 'a brand new learning and discovery space' in empty shops in Merseyway, claiming that the money must be spent on rejuvenating the High Street and therefore cannot be used to refurbish the Carnegie Library.[81] Although – in view of the building's Grade II listing – the Council has pledged not to demolish or abandon the building, sell the freehold or allow the building to be converted into residential accommodation and has promised that public access to the building will be retained regardless of its future use,[82] critics of the project say the most suitable use for the Central Library is as a library and ask, 'How can such a vital building, which was gifted to the people of Stockport, shut with no plan made for what might happen to it in future?'[83]

The Future of Cheshire's Carnegie Libraries
Notwithstanding the Public Libraries and Museums Act of 1964, which requires local authorities to 'provide a comprehensive and efficient library service',[84] there is a debate around the future of all public libraries in Britain, not just those part-funded by the Carnegie Foundation. In 2014 Wirral Councillor Phil Davies described libraries as a 'vital frontline service',[85] an assertion supported not just by the 35–51 hours which those in Cheshire remain open each week but also the range of services they offer, such as rhyme and story times for pre-schoolers, book clubs, local history sessions, craft activities, computer access, printing and scanning facilities and free WiFi, as well as the opportunity to borrow and consult books, magazines and a wide range of digital resources.[86] However, although the Chartered Institute of Public Finance and Accountancy (CIPFA) reported the existence of 3,583 library branches in Britain in 2019, cuts in library expenditure have led to failures to modernise, fewer computer terminals (down from 42,125 in 2011 to 36,564 in 2019–20) and reduced stock. Comparing the data from 2005 with that from 2019–20, CIPFA noted that the number of visits to libraries across England, Wales and Scotland fell from 335 million to 215

million, the total number of books loaned dropped from around 323 million to 166 million, and the number of books stocked by public libraries decreased from 103 million to 75 million. By March 2020 – when public libraries were closed because of COVID-19 lockdown restrictions – 88.1% of the British public had access to a smartphone, enabling them to access knowledge and digital books online and reducing reliance on reference and reading facilities in public libraries. This has led to claims that the money spent on physical buildings could be allocated more effectively to expanding the range of electronic books available to borrowers.[87] Added to this, books are far cheaper in relation to the average salary than they were when the first Public Libraries Act was passed in 1850, and the abolition in 1997 of the Net Book Agreement – which, since 1899, had prevented books being sold at a discount[88] – has made them even more affordable. This has further diminished reliance on libraries for access to publications, especially at a time when the desire to avoid infection has made people more reluctant to use communal items.

Cheshire's Carnegie Libraries have inevitably been affected by the general downturn in public library usage and the devaluation of such institutions in public perception. Professor Oriel Prizeman, principal investigator of Shelf-Life, says, 'Arguably, the very act of provision of a service such as a library takes away responsibility and sets up an awkward form of ownership',[89] while Andrew Carnegie himself warned:

> An endowed institution is liable to become the prey of a clique. The public ceases to take interest in it, or, rather, never acquires interest in it. The rule has been violated which requires the recipients to help themselves. Everything has been done for the community instead of its being only helped to help itself.[90]

However, while the physical deterioration of Cheshire's extraordinary Carnegie Libraries may be regarded as a tragedy by lovers of historic architecture, the philanthropist who was forced through poverty to leave school at the age of 12 would undoubtedly consider it no bad thing that lifelong learning is now far more readily available to all, day or night, thanks to new technology and the replacement of demolished or repurposed libraries with facilities offering longer opening hours and a wider range of services.

Endnotes

[1] A. Carnegie, 'The Best Fields for Philanthropy', *The North American Review*, CXLIX, issue 397 (Dec. 1889), 653–64, reprinted in A. Carnegie, *The Gospel of Wealth* (New York, 1889, 2017), 16–37, at 24: <<https://media.carnegie.org/filer_public/0a/e1/0ae166c5-fca3-4adf-82a7-74c0534cd8de/gospel_of_wealth_2017.pdf>> accessed 1/9/21.

[2] A. Carnegie, *Autobiography* (London, 1920), 18.

[3] Carnegie, *Autobiography*, 7–84. See also 'Andrew Carnegie': <<https://www.history.com/topics/19th-century/andrew-carnegie>> accessed 29/11/21.

[4] Carnegie, *Autobiography*, 45–53.

[5] Carnegie, *Autobiography*, 85–263. See also 'About Andrew Carnegie' in Carnegie, *The Gospel of Wealth*, 38; and 'Andrew Carnegie': <<https://www.history.com/topics/19th-century/andrew-carnegie>> accessed 29/11/21.

[6] Carnegie, 'The Best Fields for Philanthropy', *The Gospel of Wealth*, 20.

[7] Carnegie, 'The Best Fields for Philanthropy', *The Gospel of Wealth*, 21.

[8] Carnegie, 'Wealth', *The North American Review*, CXLVIII, issue 391 (June 1889), reprinted in Carnegie, *The Gospel of Wealth*, 1–15, at 13.

[9] 'About Andrew Carnegie' in Carnegie, *The Gospel of Wealth*, 38.

[10] Carnegie, *Autobiography*, 215, 266.

[11] 'About Andrew Carnegie' in Carnegie, *The Gospel of Wealth*, 38. 'Shelf-Life': <<https://carnegielibrariesofbritain.com/>> accessed 1/9/21. 'Carnegie Library': <<https://en.wikipedia.org/wiki/Carnegie_library>> accessed 1/9/2021.

[12] Public Libraries: <<https://www.politics.co.uk/reference/public-libraries/>> accessed 29/11/21.

[13] J.M. Dodgson 'A Library at Pott Chapel (Pott Shrigley, Cheshire), *c*.1493', *The Library*, s5-XV, 1, March 1960, 47–53: <<https://doi.org/10.1093/library/s5-XV.1.47>>. I am indebted to Professor Graeme White for this reference.

[14] E. Edwards, *Memoirs of Libraries, including a Handbook of Library Economy*, 2 vols (London, 1859), I, 709.
[15] J.S. Barrow, 'Libraries', *VCH Ches.*, II, 293–94.
[16] Carnegie, 'The Best Fields for Philanthropy', *The Gospel of Wealth*, 25–26; J. Simkin, 'Public Libraries Act', *Spartacus Educational* (1997; 2020): <<https://spartacus-educational.com/Llibrary.htm>> accessed 29/11/21.
[17] Macclesfield Library: <<https://discovery.nationalarchives.gov.uk/details/r/bc59162b-85b1-453a-a118-5edfcc515053>> accessed 29/11/21.
[18] N. Colley, 'Remember When: A Tale of Two Northwich Libraries', *Northwich Guardian*, 22 Sept. 2016: <<https://www.northwichguardian.co.uk/news/14753958.remember-when-a-tale-of-two-northwich-libraries/>> accessed 29/11/21.
[19] Nantwich Free Library: <<https://nantwichmuseum.org.uk/permanent-exhibitions/nantwich-buildings/nantwich-free-library/>> accessed 29/11/21.
[20] G.W. Place, ed., *Neston 1840–1940* (Wirral, 1996), 115–17. 'Neston Library': <<https://carnegielegacyinengland.wordpress.com/category/cheshire/>> accessed 1/9/21.
[21] O. Prizeman, C. Jones, A. Black, C. Pezzica, M. Boughanmi and M. Parisi, 'Typical Features', Shelf-Life Project: <<https://carnegielibrariesofbritain.com/typical-features-2/>> accessed 1/9/21.
[22] F.J. Burgoyne, *Library Construction: Architecture, Fittings and Furniture* (London, 1897).
[23] A.L. Champneys, *Libraries: A Treatise on their Design, Construction, and Fittings* (London, 1907).
[24] Edwards, *Memoirs of Libraries*, II, 1,445–1,995.
[25] S. Taylor, M. Whitfield and S. Barson, *The English Public Library 1850–1939* (London, 2008): <<https://historicengland.org.uk/images-books/publications/iha-english-public-library-1850-1939/heag135-the-english-public-library-1850-1939-iha/>> accessed 29/11/21.
[26] British Listed Buildings: <<https://britishlistedbuildings.co.uk>>.
[27] Historic England: <<https://historicengland.org.uk/>>.
[28] Shelf-Life: <<https://carnegielibrariesofbritain.com/>>.
[29] The Carnegie Legacy in England and Wales: Libraries Funded by Andrew Carnegie: <<https://carnegielegacyinengland.wordpress.com/category/cheshire/>> accessed 1/9/21.

[30] N. Pevsner and E. Hubbard, *The Buildings of England: Cheshire* (London, 1971), 252. The description is repeated in C. Hartwell, M. Hyde, E. Hubbard and N. Pevsner, *The Buildings of England: Cheshire* (rev. edn, New Haven and London, 2011), 422.
[31] CALS, D 6880: Knutsford, deeds of former library, Brook Street, 1868–69.
[32] Knutsford Library, British Listed Buildings: <<https://britishlistedbuildings.co.uk/101388310-knutsford-library-knutsford#.YgJJEurP1Hw>> accessed 1/9/21.
[33] Knutsford Library: <<https://www.cheshireeast.gov.uk/libraries/nearest_library/knutsford_library.aspx>> accessed 29/11/21.
[34] Runcorn Carnegie Library, British Listed Buildings: <<https://britishlistedbuildings.co.uk/101392040-carnegie-library-mersey-ward#.Ygo0q-rP1>> accessed 19/11/21.
[35] Carnegie Library, Egerton Street: <<https://historicengland.org.uk/listing/the-list/list-entry/1392040?section=official-listing>> accessed 1/9/21.
[36] Pevsner and Hubbard, *Buildings of England: Cheshire*, 324.
[37] Hartwell et al., *Buildings of England: Cheshire* (rev. edn), 561.
[38] Halton Libraries: <<https://library.haltonbc.info/>>.
[39] Runcorn Library, The Carnegie Legacy in England and Wales: Libraries Funded by Andrew Carnegie: <<https://carnegielegacyinengland.wordpress.com/category/cheshire/>>.
[40] Carnegie Court, Runcorn: <<http://www.ssh.org.uk/carnegie-court-runcorn/2020/05>> accessed 22/3/22.
[41] Planning Applications, Halton Borough Council: <<https://webapp.halton.gov.uk/planningapps/index.asp>>.
[42] Place, *Neston 1840–1940*, 116.
[43] Vine House: <<https://britishlistedbuildings.co.uk/101387709-vine-house-neston#.YgpMAerP1Hw>> accessed 29/11/21. Vine House, 26 Parkgate Road: <<https://historicengland.org.uk/listing/the-list/list-entry/1387709>> accessed 29/11/21.
[44] Place, *Neston 1840–1940*, 116. Neston Pictorial: A Photographic History: <<http://monologues.co.uk/Neston/Parkgate-Route.htm>> accessed 1/9/21. Neston Library: <<https://carnegielegacyinengland.wordpress.com/category/cheshire/>> accessed 1/9/21.
[45] Hartwell et al., *Buildings of England: Cheshire* (rev. edn), 503.

[46] Neston Library, The Carnegie Legacy in England and Wales: <<https://carnegielegacyinengland.wordpress.com/category/cheshire/>> accessed 1/9/21.
[47] Place, *Neston 1840–1940*, 117.
[48] Neston Library: <<https://www.cheshirewestandchester.gov.uk/residents/libraries/find-a-library/neston-library.aspx>> accessed 29/1/21. Neston Library: <<https://www.neston.org.uk/useful-links/neston-library/>> accessed 29/1/21.
[49] Lea, *Birkenhead 1877–1974*: <<https://www.wikiwirral.co.uk/forums/ubbthreads.php/topics/275119/Re_Birkenhead_Central_Library_.html>>; Z. Gibson, 'Wirral Libraries': <<https://www.facebook.com/wirrallibraries/photos/fascinating-article-by-local-historian-zoe-gibson-for-local-history-wednesdayand/3381919671828040/>> accessed 1/9/21.
[50] Lea, *Birkenhead 1877–1974*.
[51] *Kelly's Directory of Cheshire* (London, 1914), 73.
[52] *Kelly's Directory of Cheshire*, 73.
[53] A. Black, S. Pepper and K. Bagshawe, *Books, Buildings and Social Engineering: Early Public Libraries in Britain* (Abingdon, 2016), 165–66; M. Lea, *Birkenhead 1877–1974* (Birkenhead, 1974).
[54] Birkenhead Central Library: <<https://www.wirral.gov.uk/libraries-and-archives/find-library/birkenhead-central-library>> accessed 24/1/22.
[55] G. Morgan, 'More than 700 back campaign to save Hoylake Library', *Wirral Globe*, 17 Jan. 2022: <<https://www.wirralglobe.co.uk/news/19854043.700-back-campaign-save-hoylake-library/>> accessed 24/1/22.
[56] Hartwell et al., *Buildings of England: Cheshire* (rev. edn), 356.
[57] Category: Cheshire <<https://carnegielegacyinengland.wordpress.com/category/cheshire/Brief description>> accessed 1/9/2021.
[58] Hartwell et al., *Buildings of England: Cheshire* (rev. edn), 356.
[59] Pevsner and Hubbard, *Buildings of England: Cheshire*, 217.
[60] Wallasey Library, Shelf-Life: <<https://carnegielibrariesofbritain.com/archetypal-buildings/wallasey-library/>> accessed 9/1/21.
[61] Pevsner and Hubbard, *Buildings of England: Cheshire*, 372.

[62] Wallasey Library: <<https://carnegielegacyinengland.wordpress.com/category/merseyside/>> accessed 1/9/21.
[63] Z. Gibson, 'Wirral Libraries': <<https://www.facebook.com/wirrallibraries/photos/fascinating-article-by-local-historian-zoe-gibson-for-local-history-wednesdayand/3381919671828040/>> accessed 1/9/21.
[64] Wallasey Library, Shelf-Life: <<https://carnegielibrariesofbritain.com/archetypal-buildings/wallasey-library/>> accessed 9/1/21.
[65] *The Building News and Engineering Journal*, XCVII (July-Dec. 1909), 195; Wallasey Library, Shelf-Life: <<https://carnegielibrariesofbritain.com/archetypal-buildings/wallasey-library/>> accessed 9/1/21.
[66] Wallasey Library, Shelf-Life: <<https://carnegielibrariesofbritain.com/archetypal-buildings/wallasey-library/>> accessed 9/1/21.
[67] For multiple photographs of the library and the Carnegie letter, see Ronnie's blog, 'Wallasey: A Tale of Two Libraries', *A Sense of Place*, 13 Sept. 2014: <<https://asenseofplace.com/2014/09/13/wallasey-a-tale-of-two-libraries/>> accessed 1/9/21.
[68] G. Morgan, 'More than 700 back campaign to save Hoylake Library', *Wirral Globe*, 17 Jan. 2022: <<https://www.wirralglobe.co.uk/news/19854043.700-back-campaign-save-hoylake-library/>> accessed 24/1/22.
[69] Wallasey Central Library: <<https://www.wirral.gov.uk/libraries-and-archives/find-library/wallasey-central-library>> accessed 24/1/22.
[70] Central Library, Stockport Historic Environment Database: <<https://interactive.stockport.gov.uk/shed/Search/ViewDetails/473%20StatutoryListed>> accessed 1/9/21.
[71] Stockport Central Library, British Listed Buildings: <<https://britishlistedbuildings.co.uk/101440524-stockport-central-library-brinnington-and-central-ward#.Yg0QT-rP1Hw>> accessed 1/9/21.
[72] Central Library, Stockport Historic Environment Database: <<https://interactive.stockport.gov.uk/shed/Search/ViewDetails/473%20StatutoryListed>> accessed 1/9/21.
[73] Stockport Central Library, British Listed Buildings: <<https://britishlistedbuildings.co.uk/101440524-stockport-central-library-brinnington-and-central-ward#.Yg0QT-rP1Hw>> accessed 1/9/21; Central Library, Stockport Historic Environment Database: <<https://interactive.stockport.gov.uk/shed/Search/ViewDetails/473%20StatutoryListed>> accessed 1/9/21.

[74] Stockport Library, The Carnegie Legacy in England and Wales: <<https://carnegielegacyinengland.wordpress.com/category/manchester/>> accessed 1/9/21.
[75] Pevsner and Hubbard, *Buildings of England: Cheshire*, 342; Hartwell et al., *Buildings of England: Cheshire* (rev. edn), 598.
[76] Central Library, Stockport Historic Environment Database: <<https://interactive.stockport.gov.uk/shed/Search/ViewDetails/473%20StatutoryListed>> accessed 1/9/21.
[77] For superb photographs of the interior, see Lydia Lighten (31 Aug. 2021) and Dave Moran (16 Dec. 2021) in 'Memories of Stockport': <<https://www.facebook.com/groups/528431680617024/search/?q=stockport%20library>> accessed 1/9/21 and 24/1/22; and Glazed Domes and Leaded Lights, Shelf-Life: <<https://carnegielibrariesofbritain.com/typical-features-2/structure/glazed-domes-and-leaded-lights/>> accessed 1/9/21.
[78] Stockport Central Library: <<https://historicengland.org.uk/listing/the-list/list-entry/1440524>> accessed 1/9/21.
[79] Central Library Stockport: <<https://libraryopeningtimes.co.uk/listing-3182.html>> accessed 21/11/21.
[80] J. Pearson, 'Save Stockport's Historic Central Library', 38 Degrees: <<https://you.38degrees.org.uk/petitions/save-stockport-s-historic-central-library?fbclid=IwAR1jPemnB1DjWgmM7qimPE_pddyEcay5OGVjAATm_6DOJqW4UrTpe47FVzI>> accessed 21/11/21; N. Statham, 'Stockport library set for controversial move', *Manchester Evening News*, 17 Nov. 2021: <<https://www.manchestereveningnews.co.uk/news/greater-manchester-news/stockport-library-set-controversial-move-22184730>> accessed 21/11/21; N. Keeling, 'Heritage group joins fight against plans to relocate Stockport Central Library from Grade II listed building', *Manchester Evening News*, 17 Jan. 2022: <<https://www.manchestereveningnews.co.uk/news/greater-manchester-news/heritage-group-joins-fight-against-22778025>> accessed 24/1/22; D. Moran, 'Bad news about the library', 14 Feb. 2022: <<https://www.facebook.com/groups/528431680617024/search/?q=stockport%20library>> accessed 16/2/22.
[81] 'Proposal to move Central Library services to Stockroom Consultation': <<https://consultation.stockport.gov.uk/policy-performance-and-reform/central-library-proposal/>> accessed 1/9/21.

[82] 'Stockport Council pledge', 16 July 2021: <<https://www.stockport.gov.uk/news/stockport-council-pledge-to-safeguard-historic-central-library-building>> accessed 24/1/22; D. Whelan, 'Stockport forges ahead with library switch', *Place North West*, 18 Aug. 2021: <<https://www.placenorthwest.co.uk/news/stockport-forges-ahead-with-library-switch/?fbclid=IwAR3-w7-R-Sd_85grx9EVpi144Iz9Ui3HQq4pVYBgtVRI_ufC1o2S4lDbcFQ>> accessed 1/9/21.

[83] M. Shoard, 'Overwhelming support, my arse', *Memories of Stockport*, 19 Aug. 2021: <<https://www.facebook.com/groups/528431680617024/search/?q=stockport%20library>> accessed 1/9/21.

[84] Public Libraries and Museums Act, 1964: <<https://www.legislation.gov.uk/ukpga/1964/75>> accessed 29/11/21.

[85] Ronnie, 'A Tale of Two Libraries': <<https://asenseofplace.com/2014/09/13/wallasey-a-tale-of-two-libraries/>> accessed 9/1/21.

[86] See, for example, the resources and activities on offer at a typical CWaC Library such as Neston: <<https://www.cheshirewestandchester.gov.uk/residents/libraries/find-a-library/neston-library.aspx>> accessed 9/1/21.

[87] Public Libraries: <<https://www.politics.co.uk/reference/public-libraries/>> accessed 21/11/21.

[88] 'Net Book Agreement (NBA)' in A. Bullock, C. Jennings and N. Timbrell, *A Dictionary of Publishing* (Oxford, 2019): <<https://www.oxfordreference.com/view/10.1093/acref/9780191863592.001.0001/acref-9780191863592-e-159>> accessed 21/11/21.

[89] Shelf-Life Project: <<https://www.cardiff.ac.uk/research/explore/find-a-project/view/ahrc-funded-project-shelf-life-re-imagining-the-future-of-carnegie-public-libraries>> accessed 1/9/21.

[90] Carnegie, *The Gospel of Wealth*, 26.

7
THE EFFECT OF PLANNING LAWS ON SETTLEMENT DEVELOPMENT IN TWENTIETH AND EARLY TWENTY-FIRST CENTURY SOUTH-WEST CHESHIRE

Polly Bird

Introduction

The landscape in south-west Cheshire had been dominated by major landowners until the early twentieth century. They aimed to keep out the poor and preserve their agricultural land by restricting building, which resulted in smaller 'closed' settlements in those townships where only a few landowners dominated. In spite of national trends the area's settlement pattern remained largely unaltered as local patterns of landownership and the importance of agriculture controlled the extent and type of development. Planning laws introduced during the twentieth century moved power over the built landscape from landowners to central and local government. Here we examine how these authorities maintained or altered existing settlement patterns until the early twenty-first century and how far the built landscape changed.

South-west Cheshire is here defined as the area bounded by the River Dee on the west, the Peckforton Hills (Mid Cheshire Ridge) to the east and south, the Wych Brook to the south and the A534 from Broxton to Farndon on the north.[1] It is a mainly agricultural area of early enclosure where 'occasional small, compact villages are to be found in a broad spread of dispersed and semi-dispersed dwellings',[2] an area typified by dispersed settlement within Roberts's 'Cheshire Plain Sub-Province'.[3] The 34 townships in south-west Cheshire became civil parishes in 1866 with virtually no change to their boundaries until 2015. After local authority changes

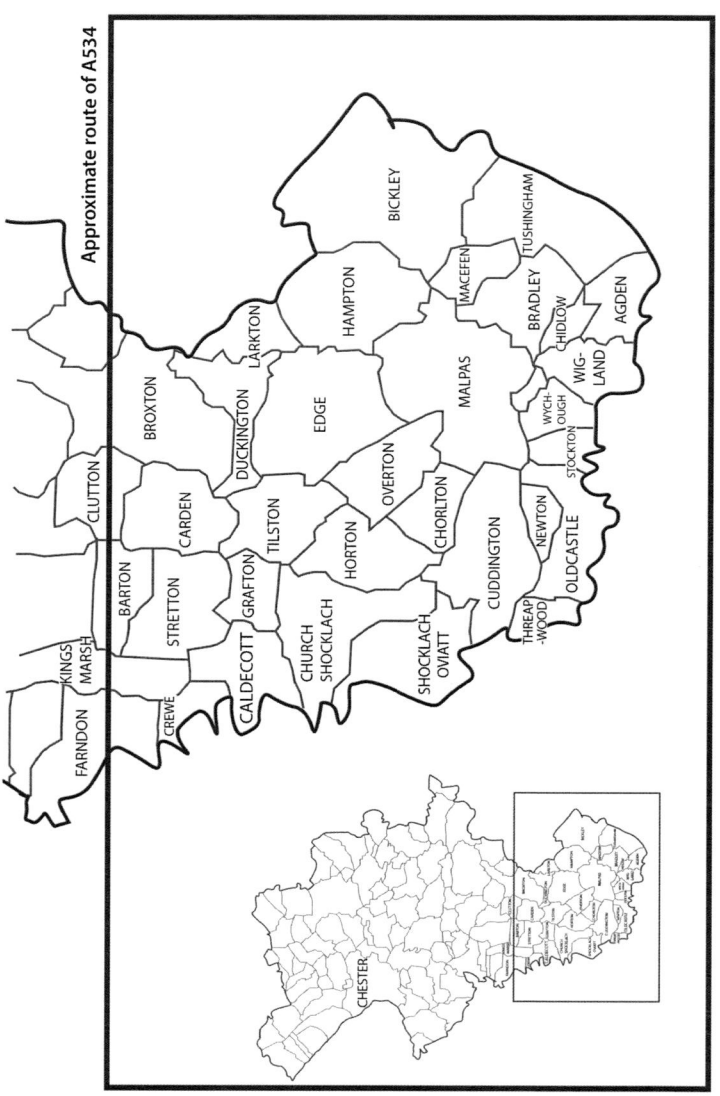

Figure 1: Southern part of Chester District showing the townships of south-west Cheshire.

The Effect of Planning Laws on Settlement Development

in 1936, 1974 and 2009 they are now part of Cheshire West and Chester (CWaC)[4] (Figure 1, opposite).

The traditional 'open' and 'closed' method of referring to the amount of landowner control in towns and villages is used where an 'open' settlement has a low concentration of landowner control – typically, a multiplicity of small landowners – and a 'closed' settlement has a high concentration of landowner control, usually dominated by one to three major figures.[5] This paper will show that 'open' townships such as Farndon, Malpas and Tilston were of a very different character to 'closed' ones like Barton and Carden and this difference was largely carried forward from the era of landowner control to that of local authority planning.

Building Before 1918

During the early twentieth century, the power of major landowners over the built landscape decreased as estates were sold to smaller landowners and there was more government control over what building took place and where. Smaller administrations such as Rural District Councils were free to adopt Part III of the 1890 Housing of the Working Classes Act which empowered slum clearance and the building of houses to a publicly acceptable standard of sanitation.[6]

Physically, however, there was very little to show in the way of development in south-west Cheshire during the early twentieth century until the end of World War One and there was apparently little need for new housing during that period. Where limited development did take place it was notably in the larger, 'open' townships of Malpas and (to a lesser extent) Hampton. For example, Malpas Parish Council agreed a building scheme in 1902 under the 1900 extension[7] of the 1890 Act for 12 three-bedroom semi-detached houses, each with an allotment, for the Moss Land nearest the town on the east side of the Malpas to Whitchurch Road.[8] A year later Malpas Rural District Council (RDC) approved a further 12 cottages on the Wrexham Road and five cottages in Well Street in Malpas town.[9] The Parish Council agreed to lease the Moss Land to the RDC on condition that it was used for the purposes of the Act.[10] Another 12 houses were built in Malpas in 1907 and six in Hampton in 1908. Following the Housing and Town Planning Act 1909, RDCs began to sell or lease land for building and Malpas RDC did so in 1910.[11] In 1919 the sanitary inspector reported on a survey of all the houses in south-west Cheshire, and stated that no houses had been built in any (civil) parish except Malpas since 1911 (although two cottages were in fact approved at Hampton).[12]

Inter-War Housing
Between the wars major landowners were under pressure to sell their land. Local authorities were buying land to provide housing for returning soldiers and, in large towns and cities, to rehouse people moved in slum clearance projects. This increased the amount of land and buildings under local authority rather than individual landowner control. The government was also tightening its planning laws. These laws moved ownership of some land from individuals to local authorities and, simultaneously, strengthened the regulations concerning what, how and whether land could be developed.

Other Acts encouraged planning and development and meant that more land was made available to speculative builders. This led to a boom in private housing during the 1930s, but the legislation was only minimally enforced.[13] An indication of the type and number of properties approved by the RDC in south-west Cheshire is shown in Table 1 (opposite), but not all buildings gaining planning permission were built. Sir Philip H.B. Grey Egerton, whose family owned 5% of the area in 1910,[14] was still building in 1927. Therefore, although the RDCs were becoming more powerful, some of the area's major landowners were still developing land.

Most building in this inter-war period took place or was intended to take place in the larger, more 'open' settlements, such as Malpas, Farndon or Tilston, which were permitted large scale development.

The Effect of Planning Laws on Settlement Development

Table 1: Dwellings approved in south-west Cheshire, 1922 to 1939.

Date	Building	Place	Builder/Buyer
16 Oct 1922	Bungalow	Mr Lowe's Field Crewe by Farndon	
16 Oct 1922	Houses (2 pairs of semis)	Farndon	Sir H. Barnston
22 Sept 1923	Bungalow (1 bed)	Farndon	Mr R. Stones
22 Sept 1923	Bungalow	Farndon	Mr G. Thomas
18 Mar 1926	Bungalow (2 beds)	Farndon	N.S. Parker
18 Mar 1926	House	Broxton	F.W. Stant
18 Mar 1926	Bungalow	Farndon, near Dee	McKee, esq.
Oct 1926	Bungalow (2 bed semi)	Farndon	J.B. Jones
5 March 1927	House (2 beds det.)	Farndon	Sir Harry Barnston, MP
2 Apr 1927	Pair cottages (3 beds)	Barnhill, Broxton On Broxton to Bickerton Road	Sir P.H.B. Grey Egerton
25 June 1927	Bungalow	Broxton, Brown Knowl	Mr Walter Stant
7 Jan 1928	House (to replace existing)	Broxton, Brown Knowl	Mr Lloyd
4 Feb 1928	Bungalow (replacing 2 cotts.)	Shocklach (Vicar's Cottages)	Thomas Pugh
3 Mar 1928	Bungalow	Farndon, below Farndon Hall in garden adjoining boathouse	Mr A.S. Evanson
18 Aug 1928	House (3 beds)	Farndon, Churton Road	
22 June 1929	New farmhouse (3+2 beds) (replacing old farmhouse)	Stretton, south of Stretton Hall	
27 Apr 1929	Bungalow	Farndon	Mr. J. Simon
25 Sept 1929	2 houses (3 beds)	Tilston, Wet Lane	Mr G.F. Ince, Mr J. Simon
1931	32 council houses	Malpas	
12 July 1932	House	Tilston	Mr Ashley

4 Mar 1933	House (3 beds det.)	Farndon	
6 May 1933	House (3 beds det.)	Farndon, on road to Cock O' Barton and Barton to Farndon Road	
2 Sept 1933	Bungalow	Farndon, on Farndon to Chester Road	Mr H.C. Nicholson
3 Mar 1934	House (3-beds)	Farndon, Old Brewery on Chester Road	Mr Lewis
2 Jan 1937	4 houses	Clutton	Messrs Tyrie
16 Apr 1938	12 houses	Farndon	J. Cresswell
2 July 1938	Additional 2 pairs of houses	Farndon	J. Cresswell
3 Sept 1938	New Public Elementary Church of England School	Malpas	Chester Diocesan Church School Association
7 Oct 1939	Pair of agricultural cottages	Malpas, 'The Bank'	
TOTALS			
Houses	26 (7 definitely detached)	(It was clear from the context that some of these are semis although not specifically stated)	
Cottages (pairs of)	4		
Farm	1		
School	1		
Bungalows	12		
Council houses	32		
Sources: CALS, RRT/394-404, RRT/14, pp. 48, 84, 184.			

This followed a national trend of the growth of former market towns or villages to accommodate counter-urbanisation.[15] In Farndon, buildings were detached houses or small groups of semis, including a few council houses, while the main building in Malpas was a large estate of 32 council houses – although a few single dwellings were built in the smaller settlements such as Crewe by Farndon (Table 1). One of the former 'closed' settlements, Clutton, was included in development plans. Four houses were built there in the late 1930s because it was one of the few townships in south-west Cheshire with a school, which had opened in 1840; buses also stopped there.[16] It therefore had the minimum of basic services that planners considered necessary for a viable community. The construction of council houses in Malpas and Farndon in the 1930s heralded the start of a slow, but significant, growth in local authority building in south-west Cheshire, following the national trend.

In south-west Cheshire there were 1,389 dwellings in 1921 but 1,478 dwellings by 1931, an increase of 6%.[17] Though there was limited inter-war development in south-west Cheshire, it started a trend of increased growth in the area. However, it came under the ever more prescriptive planning laws as they were introduced.

World War Two – Marking Time and Changing Planning

As World War Two approached, the number of house completions fell rapidly and by 1941 civil building development had virtually ceased because of strictly controlled building licences and a shortage of materials.[18] However, extra taxation and high death duties meant that land sales continued into 1941 and the value of agricultural land rose.[19]

There was no change in settlement distribution, and little change either in settlement development or the built landscape in general, in south-west Cheshire during World War Two. Land acquired for housing before the war, but not built on, was rented out on condition that it was vacated when required for housing. Most building in the area during World War Two involved 'temporary' structures, mainly garages, barns and wooden bungalows that were intended to be removed when the war ended.[20] However, occasionally these structures were declared permanent after the war, as was a Dutch Barn in Oldcastle in 1949.[21]

1940s Planning

Despite having limited impact on settlement development in the area at the time, World War Two did mark a significant turning point in the development of the built environment. From the 1940s onwards, the power of individual landowners became clearly subordinate to the power of planners, as a series of reports laid the foundations for post-war development nationally for the second half of the twentieth century. These included some recommendations specifically aimed at rural areas such as south-west Cheshire.

The Barlow Report (1940) praised decentralisation and referred to the growth of secondary or market towns that encouraged employment and became central to their regions.[22] The Scott Report (1942) understood the need to improve and maintain the rural infrastructure and allow new housing, albeit in line with the needs of rural areas, while the Uthwatt Report (1942) tackled the question of compensation because local authorities increasingly used their powers of compulsory purchase of land.[23] Other reports followed between 1942 and 1947.[24] Although advocating even more controlled planning, the emphasis was on the preservation of agricultural land. However, at the same time the reports sought to stimulate rural development by developing existing larger rural settlements rather than by encroaching into the open countryside.

Looking ahead to post-war reconstruction, the Town and Country Planning Act 1944 enabled local authorities to buy land for a limited period after the war to deal with extensive post-war regeneration, to obtain land to sell to private developers and to list individual buildings of historical importance.[25] In 1946 the Barlow, Scott and Uthwatt reports, backed by legislation, provided a planning framework for regional and local authorities. Relevant to south-west Cheshire was the appointment of rural land utilisation officers to advise on proposed housing sites so that good agricultural land was not wasted.[26] By 1946 all land was subject to planning control and any development had to conform to 'interim

The Effect of Planning Laws on Settlement Development

development control' as laid down in the Town and County Planning Act (General Interim Development) of 1946.[27] As a result of these planning regulations, local authorities were encouraged to examine planning issues in their areas. Cheshire was the first county in England and Wales to take up the challenge and in 1946 produced what was to be, locally and nationally, an influential plan which informed rural planning for at least 25 years.

Post-War Planning – A Plan for Cheshire

Post-war planning for the built landscape in rural Cheshire had its origins in the county's first major planning report *A Plan for Cheshire*[28] published in 1946 (hereafter the *Plan*). It advocated the limited development of rural settlements while maintaining agricultural land. It utilised the Scott and Barlow reports to introduce new concepts into the planning process for the area, and many of the *Plan*'s ideas were adopted later by other local authorities throughout the country.[29] The *Plan* claimed to be the first report to provide a 'reasoned pattern of village development based on the natural and economic functions of varying types of rural settlement'.[30]

The *Plan* recognised that below an optimum size (presumably of population, although this was not specifically stated) a town would be too small to provide the social and economic amenities that a modern (1946) population required and specified a set of settlement sizes. It proposed that new development should be confined to non-agricultural land or land so close to urban areas that its value had declined, which would make the loss to agriculture negligible.[31] The importance of preserving agricultural land was emphasised throughout the report. In this respect it continued a trend maintained by earlier major landowners in the area. In south-west Cheshire planning concentrated on developing a limited number of settlements in the area, while maintaining the integrity of both the historical footprint of the settlements and the agricultural land around them. Several larger settlements in south-west Cheshire were eventually singled out for development while only minor development was allowed in smaller settlements, with exceptions such as Clutton which were allowed more expansion.[32]

In 1947 the Town and Country Planning Act stated that no development could take place without planning permission, which would be enforced by central government planning control.[33] The laws enabled local authorities to increase their house-building while ensuring that they did so within guidelines. Both the *Plan* and the 1947 Act formed the basis for planning in Cheshire until the early 1970s.

How far did the *Plan* affect south-west Cheshire, particularly after the 1947 Planning Act? There was enough of an increase in population and settlement size in the area to approach the level required for minimum viable communities as envisaged in the *Plan*. The area already included settlements reflected in two of the *Plan*'s three settlement categories. The categories were Grade I small villages and hamlets (<200 inhabitants), Grade II villages (*c.* 500 inhabitants) and Grade III urban villages (*c.*1,500 inhabitants). In 1951 Grade I small villages would have included, for example, Duckington, Barton, Horton and Carden while Tilston, Broxton, Farndon and Malpas would have been Grade II villages. By 2001 Farndon was large enough to become a Grade III settlement in its own right with its own service area. Malpas with a population of 1,650 in 2001 retained its role as the area's central place[34] with its wider range of amenities while some settlements had one or more amenities, thus creating the spread of service access throughout the area as the *Plan* had envisaged, albeit on a smaller scale. This continued a trend of the expansion of larger settlements.

The *Plan* aimed to restrict most building to existing settlements and to prevent ribbon development from encroaching on agricultural land. An example is the B5069 road from Malpas towards Hampton Heath where ribbon development from the nineteenth and twentieth centuries was not continuous along the route because it was interrupted by farmland (Figure 2, opposite). There were also restrictions on building country houses, except near or within

The Effect of Planning Laws on Settlement Development

village zones. These were adhered to until planning permission was granted in 1996 for one new country house, 'Grafton Hall', on 54 acres of 'plum farmland' at Stretton with an opportunity to increase it to 113 acres. Although close to Tilston on the road to Farndon, it was not within Tilston's village zone. It remains unbuilt.[35]

The *Plan*'s main contribution to settlement development in south-west Cheshire was to preserve agricultural land, to expand larger settlements that most closely approached its idealised settlement sizes for the area as a whole, and to permit small amounts of infilling in certain smaller settlements to cater for farmers' employees.

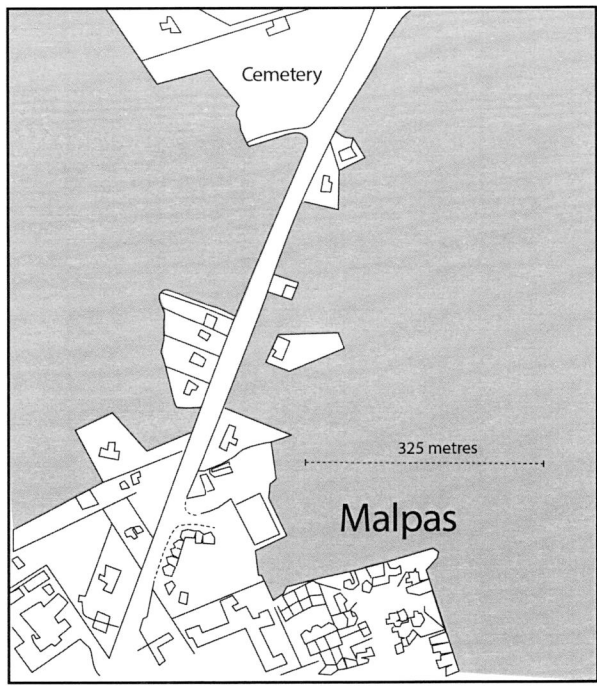

Figure 2: B5069 from Malpas towards Hampton Heath showing agricultural land bordering the road.

Table 2: Numbers of dwellings receiving interim planning permission in south-west Cheshire 1946–67.

Townships (parishes)	Cottages (agricultural)	Detached houses	Bungalows	Semis (pairs)	Unspecified dwelling or site for house or bungalow	TOTAL SINGLE BUILDINGS (including sites for intended dwellings and semis)	Housing developments
Agden	2				1	3	
Barton					3	3	
Bickley	1 (bailiff's)					1	1
Bradley		1 (farmhouse)				1	
Broxton	2	1	8	1	1	13	1
Clutton			7			7	
Cuddington		2				2	1
Duckington						0	1
Farndon		10	6+	3		19+	4
Hampton		1	1			2	
Larkton				1		1	
Macefen		1	3			4	1 (for 53 dwellings)
Malpas		3	6	3	3	15	3
No Man's Heath		3				3	1
Oldcastle		1				1	
Shocklach	1		1			1	
Tilston			3	1	4	8	2

The Effect of Planning Laws on Settlement Development

Threapwood		4	2			6	1
Tushingham						0	1
Wigland			1			1	
Wychough (Lower Wych)		1				1	
TOTALS	6	28	38	9	12	92	17
Source: CCALS, RRT/392.							

This preserved settlement distribution in the landscape. Table 2 (opposite) shows data on the number of dwellings receiving interim planning permissions in south-west Cheshire between 1946 and 1967. It is striking that the most notable building increases were approved for the area's three largest settlements. Notably, Farndon, the area's second largest settlement, showed the most increase closely followed by the central place of Malpas and Broxton. The construction of only six firmly designated agricultural cottages was agreed during the post-war period up to 1967, strongly suggesting that fewer agricultural workers were needed and few had to live close to their work. The majority of the individual buildings (built by private developers) were bungalows, a style of building that had gained popularity since the inter-war years.[36]

New housing was permitted where it encouraged a spread of amenities around the larger settlements of Malpas, Farndon and Tilston, which were the largest settlements by 2001. These were permitted the most new housing, with each approved development ranging from as few as eight houses to over 19. Exceptionally, the 'closed' settlement of Macefen was granted planning permission between 1946 and 1967 for a housing development for 53 dwellings as part of the development of No Man's Heath at the conjunction of the townships of Malpas, Hampton, Bickley and Macefen. It was close to the A41 and had a bus service. It was probably chosen for development because of its good transport links out of the area and its proximity to the area's central place, Malpas. Table 3 (overleaf)

Looking at the Landscape

Table 3: Houses receiving interim planning permission in post-war south-west Cheshire showing their relationship to the population in 1951 and 1971.

Townships (parishes)	1951 Census	1971 Census	TOTAL SINGLE BUILDINGS (including sites for intended dwellings and semis) 1946–1967	Housing developments
Malpas	1,219	1,493	15	3
Farndon	688	1162	19+	4
Broxton	471	392	13	1
Tilston	377	489	8	2
Bickley	325	328	1	1
Hampton	290	307	2	
Threapwood	290	219	6	1
Edge	267	218		
Shocklach (in Church Shocklach and Shocklach Oviatt)	252	c.180	1	
Cuddington	219	146	2	1
Tushingham	217	173	0	1
Wigland	109	85	1	
Bradley	105	78	1	
Overton	101	109		
Carden	98	87		
Barton	85	83	3	
Chorlton	82	57		
Oldcastle	71	74	1	
Clutton	67	125	7	
Macefen	62	95	4	1 (for 53 dwellings)

The Effect of Planning Laws on Settlement Development

Crewe by Farndon	61	30		
Agden	60	82	3	
Duckington	59	52	0	1
Stretton	58	49		
Kings Marsh	56	35		
Larkton	53	46	1	
Caldecott	30	25		
Wychough (Lower Wych)	13	12	1	
Stockton	12	15		
Chidlow	11	10		
Newton	9	12		
Grafton	4	6		
(No Man's Heath in Malpas, Hampton, Bickley, Macefen)	n/a	n/a	3	1
TOTALS			92	17

Sources: National census 1951, 1971; CCALS, RRT/392.

Note: The No Man's Heath nucleation contained housing developments in each of the townships it straddled.

shows the number of dwellings approved for building during the post-war years, probably the result of increasing counter-urbanisation. Between 1961 and 1971, for example, approximately 60% of the increase in Cheshire's population (which rose by 13% overall during the decade) was due to in-migration.[37] Even so, the 92 dwellings approved between 1946 and 1967 represented a virtually-identical annual rate to the 76 of 1922–39.

Thus the post-war planning strategy in south-west Cheshire continued to be based on maintaining agricultural land, favouring infilling where possible, and this not only preserved the earlier settlement patterns but also limited additional new development.

Significantly, new building often took place within the confines of nineteenth-century field boundaries. Although twentieth-century planning laws allowed for a certain amount of rural expansion they were still constrained by earlier field shapes. These earlier landscape patterns exist in the settlements in south-west Cheshire where plots were often fields sold for building. Examples at Malpas, Shocklach and Tilston show where modern estates were built within the boundaries of fields still traceable on tithe maps (Figure 3, opposite).

Typically, this planning strategy resulted in modern housing round a core of older buildings with the effect of creating settlements with development stages similar to Burgess's concentric circle ideal of urban development with modern housing built around older cores.[38] This is evident in Tilston where the remnant of the green is surrounded by the oldest houses, with newer private houses further along the roads leading out of the settlement and local authority housing beyond this (Figure 4, overleaf).

In south-west Cheshire this concentric development created some settlements that appear to be older than the majority of their housing because of where and how this was placed. The settlements in the area could be perceived as typical of Cheshire's black-and-white villages because some contain the black-and-white buildings for which the area is famous. Yet in the larger settlements, many consist of red-brick eighteenth- and nineteenth-century buildings with a large number of modern dwellings. Buildings in Malpas, for example, spread out from the older core with modern developments built downhill and hidden from view. Malpas, as planning and conservation strategy dictated, has preserved its older character while permitting limited modern development. The much older pre-eighteenth-century buildings are actually few in number (Plate 8).

From the late 1960s Cheshire planners' work also included conservation and environmental planning regulations that restricted the type and placing of new building or even forbade it.

The Effect of Planning Laws on Settlement Development

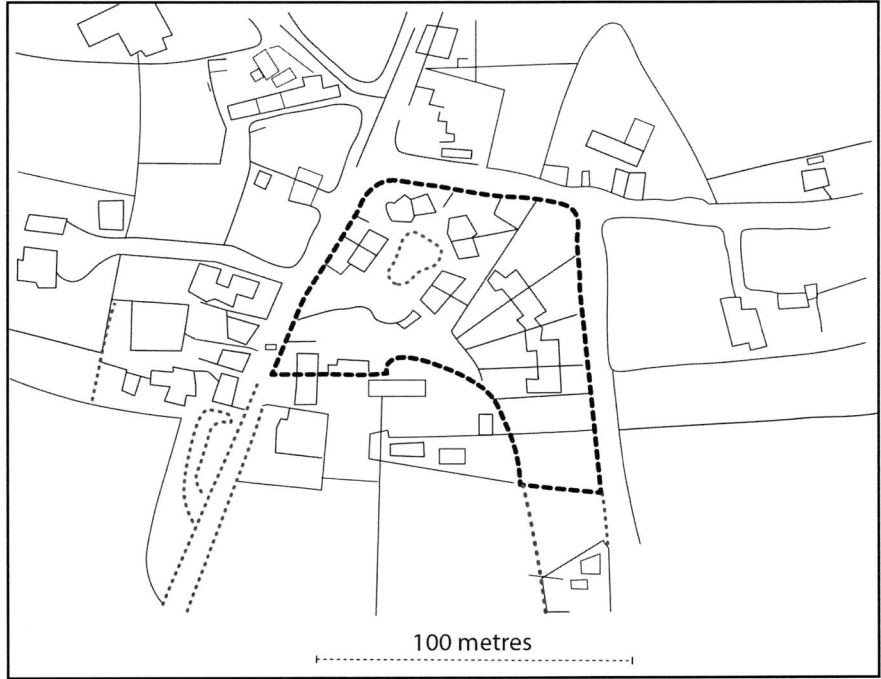

Figure 3: Modern housing in Shocklach built within the boundaries of a nineteenth-century field owned by Sir Richard Puleston (field no. 72, part of the Green, 'Greencroft'. CALS, EDT 355/1 & 3: Shocklach Tithe Map and apportionment, 1839 (reproduced by permission of CALS and the owner/depositor to whom copyright is reserved).

This introduced new factors to the planning process. In the Rural Plan area four of the 23 Conservation Areas created under the Civic Amenities Act 1967 were in south-west Cheshire,[39] each requiring a separate conservation or environment plan – Barton, Farndon, Malpas and Tilston.[40] Under the Malpas plan, only three sites for new building were permitted within the town's Conservation Area.[41]

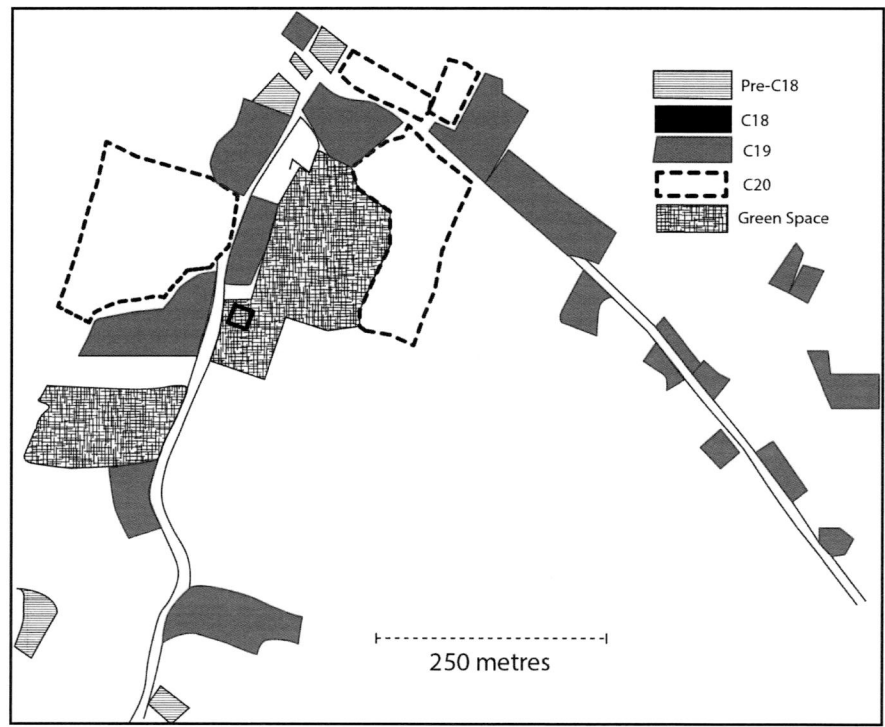

Figure 4: Building development in Tilston, pre-eighteenth to twentieth century.

Planning from 1971 to 2000

The Town and Country Planning Act 1971, consolidated from the Town and Country Planning Act 1968, introduced the concept of a Structure Plan, a development plan that identified a goal-based planning strategy for local authority areas. This continued to stress that agricultural land should be preserved, and supported the development of larger settlements. This was essentially a continuation (under a different framework) of the established pattern. Strategic (or structure) plans were supplemented by

The Effect of Planning Laws on Settlement Development

district (or local) plans and small scale basic town and village local plans.[42] Structure plans were produced at county and urban level and the majority of local plans at district level.[43] This commitment to planning at a local level remains important to this day, as does the need to ensure the 'sustainability' of communities.[44]

From the 1970s to the early twenty-first century several plans and reports were produced which affected south-west Cheshire (Table 4, overleaf). All drew upon and built upon the County's 1946 *Plan*. These documents reinforced three ideas which continued in planning regulations throughout the remaining years of the twentieth century: first, containment by restricted building in rural settlements and designated Conservation Areas; second, block expansion, where councils decided how much new building – generally housing – was necessary for an area, and so was permitted within specified limits; third, piecemeal expansion where individuals were allowed to build or convert a house if, for example, they lived or worked in the area. In south-west Cheshire the additional restriction on building on agricultural land remained and continued to be reinforced in plans for the area from the 1970s onwards.

The new planning policies again had to factor in population change. In 1971 in south-west Cheshire, 23 of the area's townships (and therefore main settlements) had populations of fewer than 100 people, nine had between 100 and 500 people and only two (Malpas and Farndon) had more than 500 people. Farndon's increase during the 1960s (from 818 people in 1961 to 1,162 in 1971) was particularly high, showing its growing importance as a commuter town for Chester and Wrexham (Table 5, on p. 186). Between 1971 and 2001 the population of England increased by 7% but the population in south-west Cheshire increased by 13%.[45] This tallies with the general observation that counter-urbanisation has been a factor in the modern development of settlements in the area.

Table 4: Plans and Reports affecting south-west Cheshire from 1966 to 2000.

Date	Name of plan or report	Date plan to last	Type of plan	Area covered	Main aims
1966	Rural Planning Policy in Cheshire: An Interim Report				Physical, social and economic remodelling
1967	Civic Amenities Act			National	
1973	Structure Plan	1986	Structure	Rural North Cheshire, Rural South Cheshire	Restriction of new houses in rural areas
1973	Policy for Rural Cheshire			Rural Cheshire	
1973	Rural Conservation Area Character Assessments			Local areas of environmental or historic character	
1977	Structure Plan		Structure		
1979	Chester Rural Area District Plan	1991	Local	Chester Rural Area	Planning guidance
1980	Rural Community Study			Includes south-west Cheshire	
1985	Rural Area Local Plan. Written Statement		Local		Planning guidance based on structure plan
1992	A Landscape Strategy for Cheshire	2001	Environmental	Cheshire	A structure for landscape policies and aims

The Effect of Planning Laws on Settlement Development

1992	Cheshire 2001 Replacement Structure Plan	2001	Structure	Cheshire	
1992	A Historic Buildings and Conservation Strategy for Cheshire	2001	Environmental	Cheshire	Strategy for the man-made environment
1994	PPG 15			National	Economic growth while protecting the natural and historic environment
1997	Chester District Local Plan	2011	Local	Chester District	A framework based on the structure plan so that planning can be carried out at a local level
1998	Chester District Landscape Assessment and Guidelines	2011	Environmental	Chester District	Guidance on management and conservation
2000	Regional Planning Guidance for the North West (RPG13)	2010		North West	
2000	Our Countryside: The Future	2010			'to sustain and enhance the distinctive environment, economy and social fabric of the English countryside' (p. 6)
Sources: Documents as named in column two.					

Looking at the Landscape

Table 5: Change in population of townships in south-west Cheshire 1961 to 1971 and 2001.

Townships (parishes)	1961 Census	1971 Census	2001 census	Percentage change between 1961 and 1971 census	Percentage change between 1971 and 2001 census	Overall percentage change 1961 to 2001
Malpas	1,310	1,493	1,650	+14	+11	+26
Farndon	818	1,162	1,540	+42	+33	+88
Broxton	444	392	390	-12	-1	-12
Tilston	426	489	600	+15	+23	+41
Bickley	311	328	450	+5	+37	+45
Hampton	258	307	370	+19	+21	+43
Threapwood	239	219	270	-8	+23	+13
Edge	243	218	160	-10	-27	-34
Church Shocklach	89	81	90	+9	+11	+1
Shocklach Oviatt	117	99	80	-15	-19	-32
Cuddington	159	146	170	-8	+16	+7
Tushingham	183	173	160	+5	-8	-13
Wigland	93	85	90	-7	+6	-3
Bradley	95	78	70	-18	-10	-26
Overton	109	91	60	-17	-34	-45
Carden	96	87	70	-9	-20	-27
Barton	72	83	70	+15	-16	-3
Chorlton	71	57	50	-20	-12	-30
Oldcastle	74	66	50	-11	-24	-32
Clutton	119	125	230	+5	+84	+93
Macefen	76	95	90	+25	-5	+18
Crewe by Farndon	43	30	20	-30	-33	-53
Agden	72	82	50	+14	-39	-31

The Effect of Planning Laws on Settlement Development

Duckington	65	52	50	-20	-4	-23
Stretton	43	49	40	+14	-18	-7
Kings Marsh	46	35	30	-10	-14	-35
Larkton	47	46	30	-2	-35	-36
Caldecott	26	20	20	-23	0	-23
Wychough	15	12	10	-20	-17	-33
Stockton	12	15	20	+25	+33	+67
Chidlow	10	10	10	0	0	0
Newton	15	12	10	-20	-17	-33
Grafton	12	6	10	-50	+67	-17
Horton	77	63	90	-18	+43	+19
TOTALS	5,885	6,306	7,100	+7	+13	+21

Sources: National census 1961, 1971, 2001.
NB: The overall percentage change does not equal the sum of two intermediate percentage changes because of compounding. The 2021 census is due to be published in 2022/3.

The 1977 Structure Plan noted that allowing the development or redevelopment of approximately 50–100 dwellings overall could improve certain areas sufficient for local needs. The 1979 Chester Rural Area District Plan (CRADP) consultation proposed to concentrate any limited future residential development in larger communities such as Farndon and Malpas and only 'allow a few houses in each settlement throughout the area'.[46] Again, it was the larger settlements that were earmarked for development.

Clutton continued to be an exception to the trend of more 'open' settlements being developed. Although it had been a 'closed' settlement in the nineteenth and early twentieth centuries it was by the later twentieth century one of the higher-populated settlements, with 119 inhabitants in 1961 increasing to 230 by 2001 (Table 5). It was on the Broxton to Farndon road and was self-contained within a minor road system that enabled infilling to take place without encroaching on agricultural land. Its school and bus service qualified it for late twentieth-century development because it had, and still has, basic services.[47]

Looking at the Landscape

Most houses built between 1961 and 1978 in rural Cheshire were in the larger villages, often as new estates, mainly three-bedroom with some smaller properties for elderly people. During the 1970s in south-west Cheshire approval was granted for approximately 400 domestic buildings, including a new farmhouse, agricultural cottages, bungalows and housing estates: clearly a quickening of the pace.[48] Thereafter, alteration to the county's Structure Plan (1977) provided for infilling, conversions and small groups of dwellings in the Rural Plan. The overriding criterion was to assess sites that could be developed without spoiling the rural character.[49]

The aim of permitting only restricted building in order to retain the character of villages was continued into the next decade. In 1980 each village in the Rural District Plan (RDP) area was examined for potential infilling and the provision of small groups of houses that would not damage a village's character.[50] In south-west Cheshire there were outstanding planning permissions in Farndon (36 units), Malpas (22 units) and Threapwood (6 units)[51] and an additional suitable site was identified in Barton (4 units).[52] The largest settlements of Farndon, Tilston and Malpas were to meet 289 units or almost a fifth of the total 1,504 proposed units for the whole CRADP area, with Malpas meeting about half of these.[53] Under Council Housing Schemes during 1979–82, five bungalows were built in Malpas, with 12 in Bickley and three in Clutton under consideration. Previously proposed sites at Shocklach and No Man's Heath (historically largely part of Macefen) had been discarded.[54] Special consideration was given both to preserving conservation areas and to permitting infill where this was feasible. Malpas, for example, was allowed limited building at three sites in its conservation area and specific infill at the site of the garage and chapel in Old Hall Street.[55]

The RDP Village Policy Areas included, among others, Barton, Clutton, Farndon, Hampton, Malpas, No Man's Heath, Shocklach and Tilston. Some settlements, including Farndon, Malpas and No Man's Heath, were given planning permission for sites with three

The Effect of Planning Laws on Settlement Development

or more dwellings, for example, Top Farm in Farndon, off Mercer Close in Malpas and Meadow Park in No Man's Heath. Barton had a site but no planning permission at that point implying scope for future development.[56] In 1910, five of these settlements had been the larger, more 'open' settlements of Malpas, Hampton, Shocklach, Farndon and Tilston while Barton, Clutton and No Man's Heath were 'closed'. Clearly, the original larger settlements continued to be singled out for development but a few smaller settlements were also permitted limited expansion. When selecting settlements for Village Policy Areas, importance was attached to the presence of a range of community facilities and the availability of suitable sites.[57] Few settlements fitted all these criteria for amenities so the presence of one or more of these features was important for promoting a settlement's development.

Further policies protected some villages. For example, the new buildings on land at the east of Top Farm, Farndon were to be built close to the road to fit in with other buildings. Barton was to have no new housing except on the allocated site and this had to be built in 'soft local brick' and slate. Hampton's existing industrial estate was to be extended to include five hectares of land on the opposite side of the new service road. In Tilston there was to be a presumption against infill in Church Lane and retention of its walls and hedges.[58]

In the 1990s the RDC's planners were taking a more landscape-orientated approach than in previous years and explicitly identified objectives for Cheshire's landscape: to ensure that new development did not harm important landscape areas, to conserve and enhance the rural landscape, to improve the urban fringe, to get maximum landscape development when reclaiming derelict land and to understand further the Cheshire landscape.[59] But planners could also not ignore the problems caused by rural decline nationally. Even settlements in south-west Cheshire that had attracted urban incomers and could still support a school could not always attract other services such as shops (Table 6, overleaf). Even today in an expanding settlement like Tilston, the residents, while able to drink in two local pubs, must rely on one small post office cum store for other services.⁶⁰

Table 6 shows that although most settlements in south-west Cheshire were eventually on a bus route, at the beginning of the twenty-first century only three settlements had the basic minimum deemed necessary for community survival of a post office/shop, primary school and bus service (Farndon, Malpas, Tilston). All three settlements were larger 'open' settlements that had grown during the nineteenth century,⁶¹ but only one, Malpas, the area's central place, had a wide range of facilities.

Table 6: Basic amenities in settlements in south-west Cheshire, 2001.

Settlements in townships (parishes)	Post Office/shop	Secondary School	Primary School	Chemist	Bank	Bus service	Pub	Church	Chapel
Agden									
Barton						☐	☐		
Bickley								☐	
Bradley									
Broxton						☐	☐		
Caldecott									
Carden									
Chidlow									
Chorlton									
Clutton			☐			☐			
Crewe by Farndon						☐			
Cuddington						☐			

The Effect of Planning Laws on Settlement Development

Settlement									
Duckington									
Edge						☐			
Farndon	☐		☐	☐		☐	☐	☐	
Grafton						☐			
Hampton	☐						☐		☐
Horton									
Kings Marsh									
Larkton									
Macefen						☐			
Malpas	☐	☐	☐	☐	☐	☐	☐	☐	
Newton									
No Man's Heath						☐			
Oldcastle									
Overton									
Shocklach (Church and Oviatt)			☐			☐	☐	☐	☐
Stockton									
Stretton						☐			
Threapwood						☐			
Tilston	☐		☐			☐	☐	☐	☐
Tushingham			☐				☐	☐	☐
Wigland									
Wychough									

Sources: <<http://www.chester.gov.uk>>; <<http://www.pubinnguide.com/pubs.asp>>; <<http://www2.cheshire.gov.uk/scripts/webtriplanner.dll>>

Planning in the Early Twenty-First Century

During the first 20 years of the twenty-first century the landscape of south-west Cheshire has been potentially affected by several Local Plans and Neighbourhood Plans. The main Local Plan affecting the Area is the Cheshire West and Chester Local Plan (CWCLP) which includes the Chester District Local Plan.[62] The CWCLP looks towards 2030 and aims to produce 'vibrant towns and rural villages'[63] by enabling enough development in what it regarded as 'key service centres' to support the rural communities they serve. It encourages the use of existing buildings and previously built-on land and tries to keep development within and on the edge of existing main urban developments in any area.[64] The key to areas such as south-west Cheshire is that development should continue to take place mostly in the larger central settlements such as Farndon and Malpas. However, the CWCLP states that local communities are best placed to decide about development in their areas.[65] Although its aims are to maintain the existing landscape by restricting development to existing towns and villages, it permits development where there is agricultural need or where replacing buildings is necessary. This includes small-scale farm diversification and the re-using or expansion of existing buildings.[66]

Several Neighbourhood Plans for south-west Cheshire have been completed in the period since 2016, including those for Malpas and Overton, No Man's Heath and District, Farndon, and Broxton and District.[67] These aim to maintain the local character of the landscape and ensure that any development integrates sympathetically. However, increased housing is a necessity to cater for a growing population.

The Malpas and Overton Plan points out that between 1919 and 1945 there were three developments of six or more houses with an average 20.7 units per development. Between 1945 and 1980 there were also three such developments but the average number of units per development had increased to 58.7. Since 1980 the number of such developments increased to 14 but the average number of units

The Effect of Planning Laws on Settlement Development

per development fell back to 20.1. Over the period the average number of units per hectare increased from 23.7 between 1919–45 to 35.7 post 1980. So an increased number of smaller developments of higher density have been built since 1980.[68] The plan aims to restrict new development to a maximum of 30 houses per scheme and aims for development which will integrate with the town and maintain its character and historic environment.[69]

The No Man's Heath and District Plan includes the surrounding areas of Edge, Bickley, Hampton and Larkton and peripheral properties. Like its larger neighbours, the plan recommends small scale infill development and renovations. Since about 1980 most development has been in the form of new buildings or the conversion of farm buildings with some housing development. Most of the housing growth has occurred in No Man's Heath itself, historically within Macefen. The preferred development scale is up to five houses a year.[70]

Farndon's Plan respects the distinctive character of its landscape and is against major new developments in the village, aiming to restrict development to seven new houses a year. Ideally, development will be restricted to previously developed land within the settlement boundary with small developments allowed on previously developed land in open countryside. It aims to preserve its built heritage.[71]

The Broxton and District Plan, while wanting to improve infrastructure and facilities, places particular emphasis on maintaining important landscape views. It stresses the need for development to respect the scale and position of existing buildings and to reflect their particular local styles.[72]

The consensus is clearly to keep necessary development to a minimum and to preserve the heritage of both natural and built local landscape. However, in August 2020 the consultation White Paper *Planning for the Future: Planning Policy Changes in England in 2020 and Future Reforms* was published and in July 2021 the National Planning Policy Framework was updated.[73] These are likely to increase building but could lead to a lowering of housing standards, with less local oversight.

Conclusion

Modern planning laws have continued the trend established by major landowners in south-west Cheshire of conserving agricultural land by restricting building on it. Post-war planning policies stressed the importance of adequate rural housing within carefully defined limits, while at the same time preserving the agricultural land on which the area's prosperity depended. This was achieved by allowing most building to take place in the larger, formerly 'open' settlements and in a few smaller 'closed' settlements with good transport links. In all settlements building was intended to take place close to the existing settlement, thus maintaining the existing settlement distribution pattern. Building within existing field boundaries close to settlements means that eighteenth-century landownership still influences development. Mid-twentieth-century laws, alongside the various plans which succeeded them, stress the importance of maintaining the heritage aspect and restrict the type and placing of new buildings.

In south-west Cheshire planning laws have therefore not greatly changed the built landscape. Settlement distribution has remained broadly the same since the mid-eighteenth century – a landscape of dispersed settlements, with relatively small nucleations. Where limited building has taken place outside these constraints it has not encroached much on to agricultural land. Modern buildings lie outside the older settlement cores and do not detract from the heritage aspect of the buildings.

It remains to be seen whether proposed twenty-first century changes to national planning laws will change the built landscape of south-west Cheshire. It is clear that local communities recognise the importance of limiting building development and maintaining agricultural land. Possibly the pace of building might slow with a shift back to urban centres. The future will show whether the tendency for larger settlements to grow even more will continue or whether new developments will be allowed at the expense of farmland in many of the smaller settlements, so breaking with the traditions of the past.

Endnotes

[1] P. Bird, 'Landownership and Settlement Change in South-West Cheshire from 1750 to 2000' (Univ. of Liverpool PhD thesis, 2007), 22.

[2] D. Sylvester, 'Rural settlement in Cheshire: some problems of origin and classification', *THSLC*, CI (1949), 1–38, at 1: <<https://www.hslc.org.uk/wp-content/uploads/2017/06/102-2-Sylvester.pdf>> accessed 31/1/22.

[3] B.K. Roberts and S. Wrathmall, *An Atlas of Rural Settlement in England* (London, 2000), 54.

[4] In 1894 most civil parishes in south-west Cheshire became part of Malpas Rural District (RD) with a few remaining in Tarvin and Wrexham RDs which had been formed in 1872. In 1936 all the parishes in south-west Cheshire became part of Tarvin RD. In 1974 Tarvin RD became part of the new non-metropolitan district of Chester. This was absorbed into Cheshire West and Chester in 2009. Major changes were made to parish boundaries in 2015 (GB Historical GIS/University of Portsmouth, Malpas RD through time; Census tables with data for the Local Government District, *A Vision of Britain through Time*: <<http://www.visionofbritain.org.uk/unit/10003374#tab02>> accessed 28/2/22; *VCH Ches.*, II, 196, 198–99; TNA: <<https://discovery.nationalarchives.gov.uk/details/r/681d1b9c-8fa0-4f3e-a0ae-67aba419359c>> accessed 28/2/22; UKBMD Cheshire West & Chester Registration District: <<https://www.ukbmd.org.uk/reg/districts/cheshire%20west%20and%20chester.html>> accessed 27/2/22).

[5] The Herfindhal-Hirschman Index (HHI) can be used as an alternative to the traditional 'open' and 'closed' terms to determine the amount of landowner control in towns and villages. High HHI (>3,000) denotes a high concentration of landowner control and a low HHI (<3,000) denotes low concentration of landowner control. By these criteria, according to the 1831 land tax returns, Farndon, Church Shocklach, Hampton, Tilston, Malpas and Broxton were among the 'open' settlements. Shocklach Oviatt, Macefen, Clutton, Barton, Stretton and Carden were among the 'closed' (Bird, 'Landownership', 67–83, 96; P. Bird, '"Open" and "Closed" in South-West Cheshire: A New Methodology for Assessing Landownership

Concentration', *Ches. Hist.*, LIII (2013-14), 151-76, esp. 164-65; P. Bird, '"Open" and "Closed" villages: A New Methodology for Assessing Landownership Concentration', *The Local Historian*, XLIV:1 (2014), 35-50).

[6] *Houses of the Working Classes Acts Amendment Bill* (1906).

[7] *Housing of the Working Classes Act*, 1900, c.59.

[8] CALS, ZRP10/1/2-17: Malpas Parish Council Minute Books [hereafter MPCMB], 1894-1919, insert facing 163, between 164 and 165, 7 Jan. 1902.

[9] CALS, ZRRM/3: Malpas Rural District Council Minute Book [hereafter MRDCMB], 1903-09, 34, 9 Sept. 1903; 72, 9 Mar. 1904.

[10] CALS, ZRP10/1/2-17: MPCMB, 1894-1919, 219, 18 Aug. 1905.

[11] CALS, ZRRM/3: MRDCMB, 1903-09, 388, 13 Feb. 1907; 282, 11 Sept. 1908; ZRRM/4: MRDCMB, 1909-1916, 44-45, 8 June 1910.

[12] CALS, ZRRM/4: MRDCMB, 1909-16, 44-45, 11 Nov. 1914; ZRRM/5: MRDCMB, 1916-26, 131, 12 Nov. 1919; D. Hayns, 'Almshouse to Housing Trust: Philanthropic, Affordable and Social Housing in Malpas, *c.*1500 to the Present', *Ches. Hist.*, LII (2012-13), 107-27, at 117.

[13] E.g. *Housing Act (Chamberlain Act)*, 1923, 13 & 14 Geo. V c.24; *Town and Country Planning Act*, 1925, 15 & 16 Geo. V c.16; *Agricultural Land (Utilisation) Act (Geddes Act)*, 1931, 21 & 22 Geo. V c.41; *Housing (Rural Workers) Act*, 1926, 16 & 17 Geo. c.56; *Housing (Rural Workers) Amendment Act*, 1931, 21 & 22 Geo. V c.22; *Housing (Financial Provisions) Act (Wheatley Act)*, 1924, 14 & 15 Geo. V c.35; *Town and Country Planning Act*, 1932, 22 & 23 Geo. V c.48; *Housing (Financial Provisions)*, 1933, 23 & 24 Geo. V c.15; *Housing Act*, 1935, 25 & 26 Geo. V c.40; *Agriculture Act*, 1937, 1 Edw. VIII & 1 Geo. VI c.70; S. Merrett and F. Gray, *Owner Occupation in Britain* (London, 1982), 5, 23; C. Greed, *Introducing Planning* (London, 2000), 100.

[14] Bird, 'Landownership', 90, Table 4.3.

[15] A. Howkins, *Reshaping Rural England: A Social History 1850-1925* (London, 1991), 290.

[16] Council of the City of Chester, *Chester Rural Area Local Plan. Written Statement* (Chester, 1985), 21: Clutton CE (Controlled) Primary School.

[17] GHS Historical GIS/University of Portsmouth: <<https://www.visionof Britain.org.uk>> accessed 18/2/22.

[18] D. Cannadine, *The Decline and Fall of the British Aristocracy* (New Haven and London, 1990), 629.

[19] Cannadine, *The Decline and Fall*, 630.

[20] CALS, ZRRT/391: Register of Temporary Buildings, 1937-67.

[21] CALS, ZRRT/391. This was an agricultural building and not, therefore, on housing land.
[22] CALS, 016590: W.D. Chapman, *County Palatine: A Plan for Cheshire* (Chester, 1946) [hereafter Chapman, *Plan*], 3, 4.
[23] Chapman, *Plan*, 5, 6.
[24] E.g. *Design of Dwellings: Report of the Design of Dwellings Subcommittee of the Central Housing Advisory Committee Appointed by the Minister of Health and Report of a Study Group of the Ministry of Town and Country Planning on Site Planning and Layout in Relation to Housing* (London, 1944); *The Control of Land Use*, White Paper, 1944; J. Dower, *National Parks in England and Wales (Dower Report)*, 1945: <<https://landscapesforlife.org.uk/application/files/4015/8928/8652/The_Dower_Report_1945.pdf>> accessed 13/9/21; Interim Report of the New Towns Committee, (Reith Report), 1946; Chapman, *Plan*; Report of the National Parks Committee (England and Wales), (Hobhouse Report), 1947: <<https:www.friendsofthedales.org.uk>> PDF download accessed 13/9/21; P. Hall, *Urban and Regional Planning* (4th edn, London, 2002), 61. 13/9/21; *Interim Report of the New Towns Committee, (Reith Report)*, 1946; Chapman, *Plan; Report of the National Parks Committee (England and Wales), (Hobhouse Report)*, 1947: <<https:www.friendsofthedales.org.uk>> PDF download accessed 13/9/21; Hall, *Urban and Regional Planning*, 61.
[25] Chapman, *Plan*, 7.
[26] L.F. Scott, *Report of the Committee on Land Utilisation in Rural Areas* (*Scott Report*) (London, 1942), 90.
[27] Chapman, *Plan*, 6. Chapman maintained that planning still relied on the 1932 Act.
[28] Chapman, *Plan*. The *Plan* provided guidance for at least 20 years from its publication (i.e. to about 1966).
[29] Lord Justice Scott's Committee, *Land Utilisation in Rural Area (Scott Report)*, cmd 6378 (London, 1942); *Royal Commission on the Distribution of the Industrial Population* (Barlow Commission).
[30] Chapman, *Plan*, x.
[31] Chapman, *Plan*, 87.
[32] Chapman, *Plan*, 89, 110.
[33] Greed, *Introducing Planning*, 103–4.
[34] A central place is a settlement of primary importance to its surrounding area and serving subordinate places around it. The *Plan* clearly based its designation of different rural settlement grades on Christaller's Central

Place Theory of 1933. Cheshire must have been one of the first English planning authorities to envisage putting Central Place Theory into practice. Chapman, *Plan,* 115; I. Carruthers, 'A classification of service centres in England and Wales', *Geographical Journal,* CXXIII (1957), 371-85; Pragya Agarwal, *Walter Christaller: Hierarchical Patterns of Urbanisation,* 11 Nov. 2005: <<https://escholarship.org/content/qt6188p69v/qt6188p69v.pdf?t=o0wtud>> accessed 29/7/22; R.J. Johnson, *Spatial Strutures* (London, 1973), 18, 27.

[35] *Chester Chronicle,* 3 Nov. 2000, 12: <<https://www.cheshire-live.co.uk/homes-and-property/revealed-majestic-cheshire-country-home-12027794>> accessed 28/10/21. The seventeenth-century Grafton Hall was demolished in 1963.

[36] T. Wild, *Village England: A Social History of the Countryside* (London, 2004), 134.

[37] Cheshire Planning, *County Structure Plan: Report of Survey/Housing* (Chester, 1977), 18.

[38] F.S. Hudson, *Geography of Settlements* (2nd edn, Plymouth, 1976), 235.

[39] Chester City Council Planning Office, *Rural Conservation Area Character Assessments* (Chester, 1973).

[40] Modern planning requires separate plans for Conservation Areas.

[41] Chester City Council Planning Office, *Chester District Local Plan* (Chester, 1977), 55.

[42] A draft structure plan must go out to public consultation, then the plan is amended, a Public Enquiry is held and the plan is finally approved by the government Inspector.

[43] M. Bruton and D. Nicholson, *Local Planning in Practice* (London, 1987), 86, 96-97.

[44] E.g. Bruton and Nicholson, *Planning,* 4-6, 19.

[45] J. Gardiner and N. Wenborn, *Companion to British History* (London, 1995), 611: <<https://www.statistica.com/statistics/975956/population-of-england/>> accessed 24/2/22; Office for National Statistics: <<https://www.ons.gov.uk/peoplepopulationandcommunity/populationandmigration/populationestimates/adhocs/004359englandpopulationestimates1971to2014>> accessed 28/2/22.

[46] C.M. Morris, *Chester Rural District Plan. Consultation on Key Issues* (Chester, 1979), 16.

⁴⁷ CALS, EDT 119/2, Clutton tithe map *c*.1840: Cheshire Tithe Maps Online: <<https://maps.cheshireeast.gov.uk/tithemaps>> accessed 24/2/22.
⁴⁸ CALS, CPL 2/2/20 (ZRRT): Tarvin RDC Record [Planning] Applications 1972-74.
⁴⁹ Chester City Area Planning Office, *Chester Rural Area Local Plan. Written Statement* (Chester, 1985) [hereafter Chester Planning, *Local*], 3-5, 8-9.
⁵⁰ Chester Planning, *Local*, 10, 3.15.
⁵¹ Chester City Council, *Chester District Local Plan* (Chester, 1997); Chester Planning, *Local*, 11, Fig. 3a.
⁵² Chester Planning, *Local*, 12, Fig. 3b.
⁵³ Chester Planning, *Local*, 14, Fig. 3d.
⁵⁴ The settlement of No Man's Heath was historically largely within the boundaries of Macefen civil parish until the boundary changes in 2015 created the civil parish of No Man's Heath and District.
⁵⁵ Chester Planning, *Local*, 55.
⁵⁶ Chester Planning, *Local*, 21, 22.
⁵⁷ Chester Planning, *Local,* 18, 21-22.
⁵⁸ Chester Planning, *Local,* 30-31, 49-50, 53-59.
⁵⁹ *A Landscape Strategy for Cheshire*, Cheshire Environmental Planning (Chester, 1992), 9.
⁶⁰ Morris, *District*, 11.
⁶¹ In 2003 an improved bus service was introduced between Chester and Whitchurch including stops at Clutton, Barton, Tilston, Edge, Hampton Heath, Malpas, No Man's Heath and Macefen thus putting some smaller settlements on the route (Cheshire County Council, *News*, 13 Mar. 2003): <<http://www.cheshire.gov.uk/NR/rdonlyres/1095BCF7-ABD9-4462-953D-5B404C65E49C/0/Improved_Bus_Service_Between_Chester_and_Whitchurch.doc>> accessed 14/11/05.
⁶² Cheshire West and Chester Local Plan (Part One) Strategic Policies (2019) [hereafter CWCLP(1)]: <<https://consult.cheshirewestandchester.gov.uk/kse/event/24907/section/3252243>> accessed 2/9/21.
⁶³ CWCLP(1), 2 Vision, 2.1.
⁶⁴ CWCLP(1), 3 Strategic objectives, SO3, SO9.
⁶⁵ CWCLP(1), 5 Spatial strategy, Strat 8, 5.67.
⁶⁶ CWCLP(1), 5 Spatial strategy, Strat 9.

[67] *Malpas and Overton Neighbourhood Plan 2010 to 2030*, made 8 July 2015; *Farndon Neighbourhood Development Plan 2010 to 2030*, made 6 Mar. 2018; *No Man's Heath and District Neighbourhood Plan, The Way Forward – 2010 to 2030,* made 28 June 2018; *Broxton and District Neighbourhood Plan 2015 to 2030,* made 30 Nov. 2016: <<http://consult.cheshirewestandchester.gov.uk/portal/cwc_ldf/np/>> accessed 22/7/21.
[68] *Consultation. Malpas and Overton Neighbourhood Plan*, 9.
[69] *Malpas and Overton Neighbourhood Plan*, 20, 25, 27, 30.
[70] *Consultation, No Man's Heath and District Neighbourhood Plan*, 3, 6, 8, 19.
[71] *Consultation, Farndon Neighbourhood Development Plan*, 10, 27, 28, 30, 36.
[72] *Consultation. Broxton and District Neighbourhood Plan*, 9–12.
[73] *Planning for the Future: planning policy changes in England in 2020 and future reforms*: <<https://commonslibrary.parliament.uk/research-briefings/cbp-8981/>> accessed 2/9/21; National Planning Policy Framework: <<https://www.gov.uk/guidance/national-planning-policy-framework>> accessed 28/10/21.

INDEX OF PLACES

Locations are in the historic county of Cheshire unless otherwise stated. All numbers indicate pages. References to illustrations are shown in italics, references to tables are in bold.

Aldford 4, 33, 34, 35–40, *36, 39*
Ambleside (Cumbria) 65, 67, 71, 72, 77, 78, 81

Bagley (Baggy) Moor (Shrops.) 106
Barmston (E. Yorks.) 23
Barton *166*, 167, **170**, 174, **176**, **178**, 181, **186**, 188–89, **190**, 195, 199
Bickley *166*, **176**, 177, **178–79**, **186**, 188, **190**, 193
Bidston *12*, 19, 23, *23*
Birkenhead 140–41, 143, 149–51, *150*, **150**
Bromborough *12*, 19, 21, 25
Brompton (N. Yorks.) 23
Broxton 165, *166*, **169**, 174, **176**, 177, **178**, **186**, 187, **190**, 192, 193, 195
Brunanburh 25

Carden *166*, 167, 174, **178**, **186**, **190**, 195
Castle Bolton (N. Yorks.) 40, *41*
Chester:
    canal: see canals
    castle 33
    early Christian landscape 5, 10–15, *12, 13, 14*, 20, 24–26
    industry 124, 126
    library 141
    principality 42
    newspapers 81, 126
    port 84, 85, 104, 123
    railway 6, 7, *58, 59*, 116–23, **118**, 123, 125–27, 132–33
    roads/routes 35, 37, 38, 40, 43, 85, 87, 92, 97, 103–4, 123
    other refs 31, 47, 48, 49, 183, 195

201

Clutton *166*, **170**, 171, 174, **176**, **178**, **186**, 187–89, **190**, 195, 199
Cringlemire 2–3, *56*, 63–81

Dee: see Rivers
Dudleston (Shrops.) 97
Duckington *166*, 174, **176**, **178–79**, **186–87**, **190–91**
Dunfermline (Fife, Scotland) 137–38, 139

Edge *166*, **178**, **186**, **190–91**, 193, 199
Edstaston (Shrops.) 89–90, 97–98, *98*, 104, 105, 106
Ellesmere (Shrops.):
    agriculture 105, 109
    canal: see canals
    settlement 6, *57*, 84, 90, 93–94, *95*, *96*, 97
    trade 99–105, *99*, *101*, *103*, 110–11
    other refs 112, 113
Ellesmere Port 87, 105, 141, 143, 151–52, *152*
Ely (Cambs.) 24

Farndon:
    inter-war housing 168–71, **169–70**
    'open' settlement 167, 168, 188, 195
    post-war development/planning 174, **176**, 177–79, **178–79**, 181
    post-1971 development/planning 183, **186**, 187–89
    roads/routes *46*, 165, 175
    township *166*
    twenty-first century development/planning **190**, 190–93
    other refs 35, 40, 46
Flint (Flints.) 43, 45, 48
Flookersbrook 119

Grafton: *166*, **179**, **187**, **191**
    Hall 175, 198
Grindley Brook (Shrops.) 93, 94

Index of Places

Hampton:
    Heath 174, *175*
    'open' settlement 167, 189, 195
    post-war development/planning **176**, **178–79**
    post-1971 development/planning **186**, 188–89
    pre-1918 development/planning 167–68
    roads/routes 199
    township *166*, 177
    twenty-first century development/planning **190–91**, 193
Hampton Bank (Shrops.) 94, *96*
Handbridge 11, 35, 119, 124
Hilbre 10, *12*, 15, 16, 17, *17*, 19–20, 21
Holt 4, 33, 35, 40–46, *44*, *46*
Hoole xiii, 6, 119, 123, 129–32
Horningsea (Cambs.) 24
Horton *166*, 174, **186–87**, **190–91**

Kendal (Cumbria) 64, 65, 67, 68, 70, 71
Kirby (in Walley) *12*, 17, 19
Knutsford 140, 141, 144–46, *145*

Landican *12*, 15, 17
Larkton *166*, **176**, **178–79**, **186–87**, **190–91**, 193
Llanymynech (Shrops./Montgomerys./Powys border) 87
Lymm 64
Lythe (N. Yorks.) 23

Macefen *166*, **176**, 177, **178–79**, **186**, 188, **190–91**, 193, 195, 199
    (see also No Man's Heath)
Malpas:
    inter-war housing 168–71, **169–70**
    'open' settlement 167–68, 189, 195
    post-war development/planning 174, **176**, 177–81, **178–79**
    post-1971 development/planning 183, **186**, 187–89
    pre-1918 development/planning 167–68

roads/routes 174, *175*
   township *166*
   twenty-first century development/planning 190, **190–91**, 192, 199
   other refs *62*
Meols 10, 11, *12*, 24
Maelor Saesneg (English Maelor) 34, 47, 49
Mersey: see Rivers

Nantwich 85, *86*, 90, 109–10, 111, 117, 142
Neston 19, 21, *22*, *60*, 140, 142, 148–49
Newcastle-under-Lyme (Staffs.) 31
No Man's Heath (see also Macefen) **176**, 177, **178–79**, 188–89, **190–91**, 192, 193, 199
Northwich 142

Oldcastle *166*, 171, **176**, **178**, **186**, **190–91**
Overchurch 15, *16*, 19, 21
Overton *166*, 178, **186**, **190–91**, 192

Pontcysyllte (Denbighs.) 4, 87–89, *88*
Prees (Shrops.) 87, *88*, 89, 97, 103

Quina Brook (Shrops.) *88*, 89, 94, 98

Redcliff 20
Runcorn 85, *86*, 140, 146–48, *146*

Saltney (Ches./Flints.) 6, 119, 123–29, *128*, 131, 133
Severn: see Rivers
Shocklach 40, *166*, **169**, **176**, **178**, 180, *181*, **186**, 188–89, **190–91**, 195
Shrewsbury (Shrops.) 86, 87, 89–90, 97, 102, 104, 112, 125, 126
Skelghyll (Low/High) *66*, 67, 73, 75
St Ives (Cambs., formerly Hunts.) 45–46, *47*
Stockport *61*, 141, 143, 154–56
Stretton *166*, **169**, 175, **178–79**, **186–87**, **190–91**, 195

Index of Places

Thelwall 3, 6, 63–65, 74, 80, 81
Threapwood 4, 33, 35, 46–49, *50*, *55*, *166*, **176–77**, **178**, **186**, 188, **190–91**
Tilston:
    development *182*
    inter-war housing 168, **169**
    'open' settlement 167, 168, 189, 195
    post-war development/planning 174–75, **176**, 177, **178**, 180, 181
    post-1971 development/planning **186**, 188–89
    roads/routes 175, 199
    township *166*
    twenty-first century planning 190, **190–91**, 199
Trent: see Rivers

Upton (Wirral) 15

Wallasey *12*, 15, 25, 141, 143, 153–54, *153*
Warrington 3, 63, 64, 74, 81
Welshampton (Shrops.) 94, 102
Wem (Shrops.):
    agriculture 105–6, 109
    settlement 6, 84, *88*, 90, 97–98, 110
    trade 84, 89–90, 98, 99–105, *99*, *101*, *103*, 109, 110–11
    other refs 87, 94, 107, 112, 113
West Kirby 17, 19–20, 21, 23, *23*
Weston/Weston Lullingfields (Shrops.) 87, *88*, 106
Weston Wharf (Shrops.) 89, 94
Whitchurch (Shrops.):
    agriculture 105–6, 109
    canal 87–90, *88*
    settlement 6, *57*, 84, *88*, 90, 92–93, 94, 97, 98,
    trade 84, 99–105, *99*, *101*, *103*, 110–11
    other refs 112, 113
Whixall (Shrops.) 94, 106
Windermere 2, 63, 64–67, *66*, 69–71, 75, 76, 77–78, 80

Wirral peninsula 5, 9–12, *12*, 15–26, 86, 87, 141
Woodchurch *12*, 15, 19, 21

References to other regions/counties and countries:
Birmingham 7, 85, 90, 104, 129
Gwynedd 34, 39
Ireland 10, 20, 73, 104, 109, 125, **140**, 142
Lake District 2–3, 6, 64–65, 67, 74, 76, 77
Liverpool 7, 85, 87, 89–90, 92, 104, 117, 125, 142
London 7, 85, 92, 102, 103–4
Manchester 7, 85, 89–90, 92, 104, 117, 144, 153, 155
Powys 34
Scandinavia 5, 7, 11, 20–21, 67
Wales:
    general 4, 121, 144, 156, 173
    North 3–4, 7, 23, 31, 33–34, 39, 40, 42, 43, 64, 87, 116, 117–18, 123
Yorkshire 23–24, 40, *41*, 102, 117

INDEX OF SUBJECTS

All numbers indicate pages. References to illustrations are shown in italics, references to tables are in bold.

Acts of Parliament:
    Enclosure 106, 123
    Housing and Town Planning (1909) 168
    Housing of the Working Classes (1890) 167
    Public Libraries (1850, 1919) 140, 141, 149, 156, 157
    Public Libraries and Museums (1964)   156
    Railways (enabling) 125, 127
    Town and Country Planning (1925-71) 172, 173, 174, 182, 196
    Union with Wales (1536, 1543) 34
    Welsh Church (1914) 49
aqueducts 5, 87, 89

boats 81, 87, 90, 93, 118
boathouses 11, *95*, **169**
boundaries:
    county 7, 31, 34, 47, 49, 124
    field 70, 73-75, 131, 180, *181*, 194
    national 3, *32*, 34-35, 40, 47, 124
    other local authority 125, 150, 165, 195, 199
    other refs 25, 128, 193
brickmaking 92-93, 97-98, 99
brickwork *57*, *60*, 64, 75, 92, 132, 144, *145*, 146-49, 151-53, *152*, *153*, 155, 180, 189
bridges:
    in or about Chester 120, 121-22, 123, 124, 126, 132
    other refs 33, 35, *36*, 40-41, 43-46, *44*, *46*, 47, 52
Bridgewater family and estate 85, 93-94, 100, 111

builders 67, 78, 99, 126, 129, 143, 168, **169-70**
building stone:
    as principal material 38, 40, 46, 70, 73-77, 80, 146-47, *146*
    other refs 42, 63, 139, 144, 151, 152, *152*, *153*, 154, 155
burials 11, 14-15

canals:
    Chester 85, *86*, 87, 89, 90, 92, 109, 117, 121
    Ellesmere 5-7, 84-111, *86*, *88*, *95*, *96*, *98*, 112
    other refs 5-6, 84-85, *86*, 90, 110, 123
Carnegie, Andrew 137-40, 143-44, 157
castles:
    Aldford 4, 33, 35-39, *36*
    Chester 33, 123
    Holt 33, 40-45, *44*
    other refs 35, 40, *41*, 51, 81
cathedral (Chester) 11, 13, 118, 141
census 72, 82, 91, 99, **99**, 105-6, 113, 117, **118**, 131, 135, **178-79**
central place 174, 177, 190, 197-8
Cheshire Magna Carta 31
Christianity 5, 9-26
churches:
    minsters and mother-churches 10, 11, 35
    pre-Conquest 10, 11, 13-14, 15, 17-21, 25
    post-Conquest 35-37, *36*, 40, 43-46, *44*, 51
    nineteenth/twentieth century 35-37, *36*, 48-49, *55*, 63-64,
        121, 131, 136, 152
    various **190-91**
churchyard (graveyard) *36*, 38, *39*
city walls (of Chester) 14, 118, 119, 122, 133, 141
clergy 9, 14, 15-16, 20-21, 24, 25-26, 35, 38, 64, 141, 148
coal 84-87, 89-91, 93, 94, 97-98, 102, 105, 108-9, 110, 116, 124, 129, 135
crosses 11, 14, *14*, 17, *17*, 20-21, *22*, 23-24

Index of Subjects

Domesday Book (Inquest) 14, 27, 31, 34, 35, 37, 50

Edwardian conquest 33, 34, 39, 40, 43, *44*
enclosure 15, 38, 47-49, 106-7, 110, 123, 165
engineering 5, 6, 67, 87, *95*

fairs 38-39, 43, 45-46, 92
farming, farmland:
    in place-names 17-19, 25, 29, 30
    nineteenth century 72, 91, 93, 102, 103, 105-9, 111, 124
    twentieth century 174-75, *175*, 188-89, 192-93, 195
    see also: housing
field-names 11, 18, 67, 71
frontier 3-4, 31-50, *32*

gardens 3, *56*, 63, 65, 72-73, 74-75, 79-81, 82, 121, 128, 130
gas 93-94
graveyard: see churchyard
greens *36*, 37-40, *39*, *41*, 180, *181*
Grier, John, of Ambleside 72-75, 77-80, 82

Harrying of the North 35
hermitage 15, 20
hogbacks 20, 22-23, *23*
hotels *59*, 67-68, 70, 120-22, 133, 134
housing:
    council 167-68, **169-70**, 170-71, 188
    farm 102, **169-70**, **176**, 188
    grand 2-3, *56*, 63-81, 175, 198
    large urban 57, 92-93, 98, 109, 119, 124, 130, 143, 146-47, 148, 153-54
    malt 94, 102-3, 113, 114
    public: see inns
    small urban 124, 127-28, 129, *130*, 131, 137

other refs 48–49, 167–72, **169–70**, **176–77**, 177, **178–79**, 180, *181*, 183, 187–89, 192–94

inns (public houses) 67, 92–93, 97, 100, 105, 120, *128*, 128–29, 132, 134, **190–91**
iron 35, 87, 89, 93, 94, 126, 128–29, 139, 147

lairage 72, 82
landownership 4, 69, 111, 119, 124, 130, 142, 165, 167–68, 172–73, 194, 195
libraries 3, *60*, *61*, 137–58
liming 89, 92–94, *96*, 97–98, 107–10
local authorities:
    borough council 140–42, 147, 149, 153–54, 155–56
    city council 128, 132
    county council 140, 146, 149, 152
    Justices of the Peace 48
    parish council 167
    rural district council 167–68, 189

malting 84, 89, 92–94, 97–98, 100–3, *101*, *103*, 105, 108–11, 113, 114
markets 38–39, 42–45, *44*, 72, 82, 89, 91–94, 102, 105, 108, 110, 122, 155
market towns 5–6, 42, *62*, 84–111, 170, 172
mills 92, 93, 105

Napoleonic Wars 84, 104, 106, 108, 109
newspapers *68*, 81, 121, 126, 134, 136, 143, 163
Nicholson family, of Thelwall Hall 2–3, 63–65, 69–71, 73–74, 76–81
nonconformism 48, 121, 131, 152, **190–91**

place-names:
    Old English 11, 15, 16–18, 19, 28, 37, 40, 46
    Old Norse 11, 15, 17–19, 67
    other refs 15, 31
planning 4, 40, 49, 147, 165–95, **169–70**, **176–77**, **178–79**, **184–85**, 197, 198

Index of Subjects

Planning Reports 49, 172-73, 183, **184-85**
    see also: Acts of Parliament
Plans:
    Local 183, **184-85**, 192
    Neighbourhood 192
    Structure 182-83, **184-85**, 187-88, 198
    see also: settlements, planned
population:
    growth (within Cheshire) 117, **118,** 129-30, 174, **178-79**, 179, 183, **186-87**, 192
    growth (within Shropshire) 91, 92, 94, 98-99, *99*, 110
    growth (elsewhere) 91, 109-10, 116, 117, 183
    other refs 31, 35, 42, 91, 97, 113, 124, 135, 173
ports 10-11, 84, 85, 87, 89, 104-5, 117, 123, 126, 133

railways 6-7, *58*, *59*, 64-65, 70, 116-33, 134, 138-39, 148
religious communities 5, 9-11, 13-20, 31, 45
Rivers:
    Dee 10, 11, 14, 20, 26, *32*, 42, 85-87, *86*, *88*, 90, 117, 118, 123-24, 126-29, 165
        crossings 4, 23, 33-35, 37, 40, 42, *44*, 45, *46*, 87, 123
    Mersey 63, 84-87, *86*, *150*, 151
    Severn 85-86, 90, 105
    Trent 85
    other refs 34, 39, 45-46, *47*, 87, 106
Romans:
    roads 10, 35, 37, 51, 65-67, *66*
    other refs 4, 13-14, 40, 117-18

schools *36*, 48-49, 64, 130, 131, 132, 134, 138, 148, **170**, 171, 187, 189-90, **190-91**
settlements:
    dispersed 49, *50*, *55*, 141, 165, 194
    frontier 3-4, 31-50, *32*
    Norse 5, 10-11, *12*, 15-26, 67

    open and closed 97, 165, 167-68, 171, 177, 187, 189, 190, 191,
        194, 195
    planned 31, 33-34, *36*, 37-40, *41*, 42-43, *44*, 45-46, *47*
    squatter 34, 47, 49, *50*, 97
    subsidiary 18-20
shipbuilding 117, 129, 133
stagecoaches 90, 97, 103-5
Statute of Rhuddlan (1284) 34
stone sculpture 11, 13-17, *13*, *14*, *16*, *17*, 19-24, *22*, *23*
suburbs (of Chester) 6, 119, 123, 126, 129, *130*, 131-33

tithe (awards, maps, returns) 107, 124, 130, 180, *181*
town halls 122, 146, 148, 155
trade directories 6, 84, 89, 90, 91-94, 99, 103, 108, 109, 112, 130, 134
traders/trading:
    pre-Conquest 10-11, 20, 22-24, 26
    post-Conquest 40, 42, 45-46
    eighteenth/nineteenth-century 6, 65, 67, 84-85, 89-105, *99*, *101*,
        103, 108-10, 117, 129
tunnels 6, 87, 119, 127, *150*, 151
turnpikes 67, 85, 94, 126, 127

vernacular architecture 76
viaduct 119, back cover

Warenne family, lords of Holt 34, 40, 42, 45
wasteland 4, 47, 106, 108, 128
weather 74-81
Westminster, 1st and 2nd marquis of 122-23, 124, 127
wharves 89-90, 93-98, *95*, *96*, *98*, 124, 128
workmen 78-79